BRANDO

BRANDO

RICHARD SCHICKEL

THUNDER'S
MOUTH
PRESS

Published in the United States by
Thunder's Mouth Press
841 Broadway, Fourth Floor
New York, NY 10003

First published in Great Britain in 1999 by
PAVILION BOOKS LIMITED
London House, Great Eastern Wharf
Parkgate Road, London SW11 4NQ

Designed by Bernard Higton

Library of Congress Card Number: 00-104000

ISBN 1-56025-291-X

Set in Bodoni Book
Printed in Spain by Bookprint
Colour origination by Anglia Graphics in England

10 9 8 7 6 5 4 3 2 1

Distributed by Publishers Group West

CONTENTS

INTRODUCTION

When you talk to him on the phone these days, Marlon Brando speaks in the elaborately polite and patient tones of a man who has spent his life trying to explain himself to puzzled strangers. He's conscious of your feelings, careful not to offend, even occasionally flattering. His conversation is informed by his premature political correctness and by anecdotes from his distant past. When we spoke some months ago, the fact that Elia Kazan had sowed distrust between him and Anthony Quinn on *Viva Zapata*, forty-seven years earlier, was much on his mind. It was only recently, he said, that he and Quinn had made up their differences, and he was cranky that Kazan, whose motive, he admitted, had simply been to edge their performances in that film with distrust, had never apologized for this affront.

Right: Brando in his Oscar-winning comeback role as the Godfather, Don Corleone.

Opposite: The Hollywood newcomer photographed for *Life* magazine in 1950.

As he rambled on (the conversation consumed nearly an hour) I became aware of a slight shift in tone when I demurred from some of his opinions. The impatient edge of a man who was used to being deferred to, crept into his voice. He was intermittently amusing – his lifelong gift for wacky metaphors was still functioning – but he knew what he knew and that was all that he cared to know about the topic at hand, which was the honorary Oscar the motion picture academy was preparing to bestow on Kazan, and which he deplored, despite owing his career as much to the director as to any other man.

He was, in short, an old man – the fires of youth banked, but full of live embers. That surprised me, although of course, it should not have. Brando is, after all, 75 years old now, authentically aged, and all pretense of being 'middle-aged' abandoned – embarked on life's last irresistible decline. It had been over two years since his last disastrous movie appearance (in *The Island of Dr Moreau*) and when he worked now it was doing voice-overs for commercials – his Godfather voice for Pizza Hut, something else for Japanese television – picking up celebrity's (relatively) small change in a venue where appearance doesn't count.

It somewhat shocked me to think of this man in this slightly enfeebled condition. I had been writing about him off and on for years, sympathetically so. I find it difficult to abandon the hopes I have always retained for him, hopes that conditioned the tone of the first somewhat longer version of this book when it appeared, in a different format, in 1991 and which cannot – perhaps should not – be excised from its text. Like so many in the generation that came of age in the 1950s, a decade after he did, I felt that he spoke for us – for our impatience with the older crowd, those bland masters of that long-gone universe dominated by suburban hypocrisies and cultural caution. On the broader cultural fronts he had not always fought his war terribly well – too many Sasheen Littlefeathers – but there had been rude wit in it sometimes, and (most important to me) always the hope of some singular performance, something that redeemed heroism for ambivalence. Indeed, you could say that within his art he had won his war. For as Dustin Hoffman,

one of his inheritors, recently said, he 'altered acting. He changed me, an entire generation.' That is to say, all acting now comes from a place deeper inside the actor and is aware of that mixture of motives – yearning, hesitant, hell-for-leather – that must be sorted through (often at lightning speed) before any sort of decisive action can be undertaken in life or on screen or stage.

What one thinks now, sadly, is that Brando is no longer a 'contender' in this realm. He's too old for it, and like many old men unable to focus and sustain his attention on the issue – especially since he was never in any case profoundly interested in leading the revolution in performance. It was a role pressed upon him by the Stanislavskians who had, for a couple of decades, been looking for such a figure, someone both gifted and drop-dead gorgeous, to carry their revolution – which included among its goals a wholesale reformation of the entire corrupt showbiz world of well-made plays and movies, the primary goal of which was entertainment, not behavioral 'truth'.

But, although Brando had taken on that responsibility in the 1950s (and for a few years played the role with a certain passion), the casting was wrong, mostly because he remained – remains today, I think – at the heart an adolescent – lazy, infinitely distractible, unable to distinguish between the causes that are worth fighting for and the ones that are of merely momentary concern. Then, too, in any large sense, show business remained fundamentally un-reformable. Yes, it could make room for a new manner of acting, but it has long since abandoned the kind of movie-making he was born for – intense, small-scale, black-and-white movies about small-scale issues or morality and behavior, grown more obsessed with wide screens, empty spectacle and (lately) special effects, blockbusters and would-be blockbusters, where it makes no difference how anyone acts – or, indeed, if he or she acts at all in any sense that a Brando might recognize. His response to this new order of things – never mind that it has actually been going on for at least a couple of decades – has largely been disgust and cynicism of, yes, a perpetually adolescent kind – a sort of sulky attempt to throw his weight around, which has usually got him nowhere and often enough ended in apologies – for like many adolescents, he retains his sweet, ingratiating quality, a need to be accepted and liked. On his own terms, of course.

Those terms now include, alas, tragedy. The son convicted of manslaughter, the daughter who committed suicide. A man does not easily transcend such devastations. They are bound to afflict him, and his capacity to take seriously something as trivial as mere acting. Then, too, there is the question of his appearance. How do you cast a man of his enormous girth? It is, like that other youthful 'genius', Orson Welles, something more than an accident. It is an assertion of contempt for the values that prevail in the public arts, which include an attempt to hold the aging process at bay. It may also be a test of our feelings as well; for the shock of recognition is registered now by a horrified gasp. It asks whether or not we can penetrate this grotesque disguise and rekindle our feelings for the dangerous beauty, the heedless revolutionary – or was he merely an anarchist? – that once so thrillingly was.

About such matters no one can speak definitively. What we know about Marlon Brando is that he lurks at the fringe of the celebrity circus that our public life has become. People now make cruel jokes about him: First Guy: 'What do Elvis Presley and Marlon Brando have in common? Second Guy: 'Many people believe they're both still alive.' Yet somehow one does not feel like laughing.

Yes, there was a time when we – his generational audience, trying to get our parents over their fear of his image ('What are you rebelling against?' 'What have you got?'), make them see the suffering sensibility, the sheer vulnerability, beneath his poses, trying to make them understand that he mumbled only when it suited his character – thought he would be Olivier, thought he might explore the full range of his seemingly immeasurable gift, and give us both his interpretations of the classic roles as well as the unimagined new things by writers following in the line of Tennessee Williams. That was not to be, and we found it hard to hide our disappointment, and equally hard to convey our enthusiasm for the work that actually existed, often enough in contexts that were not entirely

worthy of him. There are those among us who still wish he could simply have ridden out his disappointments (and ours), kept going, kept trying. We understood, even when he did not, that that was show business, that it was bound to offer more failures than triumphs to anyone, that true bravery in this context consists of knowing that it's not over until it's over. Look – for only slightly ludicrous example – at Don Ameche, who went from has-been to Oscar winner in his eighth decade.

That kind of patience and perhaps cunning Brando did not have. Or maybe, after the authentic comeback he did make (*The Godfather*, *Last Tango in Paris*) he just did not have the energy or the focus to pursue it further. Anyway, he was careless, if not feckless, in what he did undertake. Surely the choices available to him were better than what we – fleetingly – saw on the screen. Or, perhaps, he really did all that he was capable of doing. The 'maybes' and 'perhapses' start to pile up now, obscuring the man.

We are possibly better off to rest content with what we have – a half dozen definitive performances in movies worthy of them, an equal number of good jobs in variously disappointing contexts. Come to think of it, only a very few movie actors achieve more than that, no matter how many movies they make. The difference between them and Brando is only one of promise, which conceivably was too great for anyone to completely fulfil. If so, he is entitled to his crotchets, his defences, his final irrelevancy. We will all, after all, come to that point. And – most of us – finally with less to show for our efforts than he has. Let's put the point simply: it's time to stop hectoring the old guy. To count the blessings he has bestowed upon us, which are not inconsiderable, and forget the promises that must now remain forever unfulfilled.

CHAPTER ONE

AGE OF INNOCENCE

The two-year-old Bud Brando, wrapped up for the Nebraska winter.

This is a book almost as much about audiences as it is about an actor so let it begin with Marlon Brando's first fully appreciative audience, an audience of one named Stella Adler. There had been, of course, small audiences before – parents, teachers, schoolmates – but Adler was the first to see in Brando's rough, unrehearsed act something treasurable. To her, as opposed to virtually everyone who had been exposed to it before, the self-portrait he had worked up by late adolescence seemed utterly unique and, in most important respects, admirable – well worth polishing, finishing, exhibiting.

There would be huge audiences later. But Adler was the last to see the actor's potential in its pure form, unsullied by artifice and adulation. And she was the last to have a large and helpfully shaping influence on his gift. After her, that gift would mostly be shaped, for better or worse, solipsistically.

It was not a role, according to her, that at first she was eager to accept. Adler's first glance at the young man – eighteen going on nineteen – who turned up in her acting classes at the New School in Greenwich Village in the wartime winter of 1942–43, revealed two aspects of his nature. On the one hand, there was originality and vitality. On the other, there seemed to be something hurt and hidden about him. His air of bravado did not quite succeed in covering a vulnerability that was, to her, equally apparent.

It was possible, she thought, that the self-explorations and revelations demanded by the study of acting might unhinge a spirit rather more delicately balanced than most. Here, perhaps, was someone who was not merely entitled to his privacy, but more needful of its healing balm than most of his contemporaries.

Moreover, Adler could not help but contrast him with the other young people who came to her. Most of them were already firmly dedicated to the theater, willing to let a strong-minded, strong-willed teacher take them over and remold them in the shape of her desires. Brando's presence in her classes seemed to Adler not to represent an act of commitment of that order, but rather an experiment in self-definition.

In sum: 'I thought there was something terribly sensitive, the kind of thing you don't want to touch. This puppy thing – I didn't know if I should.' And so, decently, she hesitated. But not for long.

For Brando was irresistible to her, just as she was irresistible to Brando. It may be too much to suggest that their encounter was fated, but the timing certainly could not have been improved upon. If Brando was at that time a character in search of a defining author, Adler was an author in search of actors who could embody her theories of performance in major roles. Since these theories had been gestating for close to a decade, there was a certain urgency in her search for instruments by which she could assert herself against what she conceived to be enemies within the theatrical community and, perhaps, impose her beliefs on its future history.

Admittedly, passion of that kind – even from the never dispassionate Stella Adler – seems improbable to us now, when the American theater is bereft of serious artistic or intellectual dispute, when Broadway is mostly a haven for imports, and when even the sometimes promising regional theater movement often resembles opera, dependent on subsidies and a cult following for survival. But in those days many people cared greatly about the outcome of the struggle in which Adler was engaged, believing that the very future of the theater as a relevant social institution might depend on how issues agitating its most committed people were resolved.

When she met Brando, Stella Adler was forty-two or forty-three, not quite the *grande dame* she would soon become, but with her legend nonetheless on the way to solid establishment. Beneath her flamboyance, however, there was shrewdness, a belief in the theater as a morally and intellectually serious enterprise, and an authentic, if relatively new-formed, passion for teaching.

She was the daughter of legendary Yiddish actor Jacob Adler, and she began her career in his company, before moving on to Broadway. Wooed by the idealistic rhetoric of director-theorist-critic Harold Clurman (she would later marry him), she joined The Group Theater at the time of its foundation by Clurman, Lee Strasberg, and Cheryl Crawford. She gave what is generally thought to be her greatest performance in The Group's production of Clifford Odets's *Awake and Sing*, but she never took to the communitarian life of the organization. That shared life was one leg of the intellectual tripod on which The Group suspended its large hopes for theatrical reform. Another was its ideological commitment, which was to an idealistic radicalism and to new plays that were (mainly) realistic in manner, often about lower-middle-class life, generally didactic in intent. The last, but most lasting in influence, of The Group's underpinnings was its commitment to Stanislavskian technique in acting – 'The Method', as Strasberg, the self-appointed American disciple of the Russian director-theoretician, started calling it as he began to build *his* legend.

This relatively new, psychologically oriented manner of performance, introduced to the US when the Moscow Art Theater visited in 1923, was an integral part of The Group's reformist efforts. It would give actors a tool enabling them to play a grittier kind of drama than was then prevalent in the commercial theater, and it would help them maintain their air of veracity when these works made their inevitable swerve toward the unveraciously rhetorical. But the most important thing about the Method was that it was in itself a kind of moral statement. It proposed a codifiable discipline, a teachable tradition, for acting, and a standard toward which performers could work through intensive study. Though no one seems to have put it in precisely these words, Strasberg and his disciples implicitly believed that with Stanislavskian theory as a base, acting could become a true profession. And if it did, that might well have a profound effect on a theater dominated by the star system and drowning in (as they saw it) commercial trivia.

From the start, however, Adler was dubious about Strasberg's 'Method'. He placed particular emphasis on 'affective memory', insisting that the actor draw on his own psyche for emotions analogous to those of the character he was playing. As Adler would put it later, she felt this led to 'hysteria' on the part of the actor. Moreover, she believed that the plunge into subjectivity might very often subvert the playwright's text and intentions. Finally, it seemed to her, as it did to others (notably Bobby Lewis, another Group member, and an actor-director who would also become an influential teacher), that the Method was the enemy of styles other than the realistic – not much use in Restoration comedy, for instance.

Adler's opposition to Strasberg, however, did not crystallize until, by chance, she encountered Constantin Stanislavski himself in Paris in 1934, and accused him of ruining her life as an actress with his theories. Her charges puzzled and intrigued the Russian, who informed her that he had substantially modified his views. He no longer held with affective memory, and was now placing his emphasis on observation and imagination rather than self-examination.

This was a revelation to Adler, and she spent six weeks at the master's side, returning home with a diary in which she recorded his revised thoughts. When she confronted Strasberg with it, he was outraged, according to her. He

insisted that Stanislavski had fallen into error and that he, Strasberg, was now the one true keeper of the flame. Their contention did not break up The Group, which continued to produce plays, though in increasingly straitened circumstances, through 1940. But like many of its most gifted actors and playwrights, Adler began working elsewhere, even doing a couple of movies – the source of all corruption for hard-core Group members – her brief appearance in *Shadow of the Thin Man* powerfully and memorably interrupting its slick banter. She made one last film in 1947, and continued to take occasional parts in the commercial theater while she established herself as a teacher. She did not entirely abandon performance until after she founded her own acting school in 1949.

What Adler was primarily looking for among the young actors who presented themselves to her for instruction were observers, sympathetic students of human behavior. On an excellent television documentary about her life and work, first broadcast in 1989, she by no means discounted the uses of memory as a fuel for performance: 'The actor has in him the meaning of everything he has ever tasted or touched or eaten. And he is by nature gifted with memory. He can go very far back, and he does go very far back. . . .'

That, in a sense, brings her to Brando. A puppy he may have been, but he was her kind of puppy, and perhaps one she had not imagined finding at the New School. Its Dramatic Workshop was the creation of Erwin Piscator, disciple of Max Reinhardt, refugee from Hitler's Germany, and a formidable *avant-gardist*, with a taste for theater on an epic scale. Piscator was not a Stanislavskian, and realism was not at the center of his aesthetic. He tended to see actors as extensions of the director's will and the director as the servant of the playwright, interpreting his work. He was, nonetheless, tolerant of Stanislavskians on his faculty (Lee Strasberg also taught there), and Cheryl Crawford would later say that Piscator's workshop formed the most important link between The Group Theater and The Actor's Studio in the seven years between the former's demise and the latter's founding.

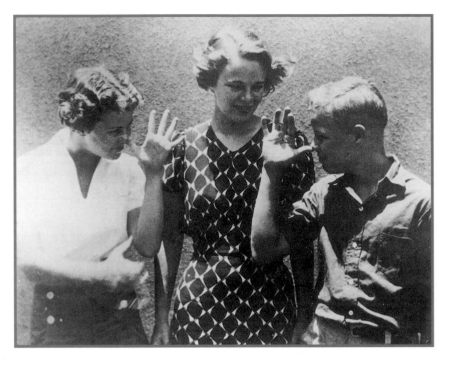

Bud, aged thirteen, with his sisters Frances (left) and Jocelyn. In the early years he and Fran used to run away from home almost every weekend.

Be that as it may, almost immediately after Brando enrolled in her classes Adler began predicting that he would soon be acknowledged as the best young actor in America. A few years later, when that prediction had emphatically come true, she was still saying, 'He's the most keenly aware, the most empathetical human being alive . . . He just knows. If you have a scar, physical or mental, he goes right to it. He doesn't want to, but he doesn't avoid it . . . He cannot be cheated or fooled. If you left the room he could be you.'

Of course, young Bud Brando (as everyone called him in those days) could not have had ideas as firm as hers about what he was looking for at that time. But she had enough for both of them, and they matched his best instincts. 'Actors have to observe, and I enjoy that part of it,' Brando was to say some years later, after stardom had seriously interfered with what was perhaps his most precious artistic freedom, the freedom to observe unobserved.

But Brando had more than a canny watchfulness to offer. He had imagination and daring, too. A story Elaine Stritch, the actress, recently told catches what one imagines to be his truest self in those days. She was in one of Adler's classes with Brando when the teacher set this exercise: a coop of chickens has just learned that an atomic bomb is about to be set off near them; show us their reactions. Naturally most of the students leaped to their feet and started running about, cackling madly. Brando alone kept still on his perch, miming the laying of an egg. But, of course! What does a chicken know about the destructive potential of nuclear fission? Come hell or high water, she will do what she must do – no more, no less. To imagine lack of imagination – and to dare stillness – may be the highest achievement available to a young actor.

One other quality completes the youthful profile of Marlon Brando: consistent autobiographical refusals. And this, finally, made him the perfect challenge for his teacher. If Adler could make an actor out of someone as reticent, as hidden as this young man was, wouldn't that show Strasberg a thing or two? One searches the anecdotal record of Brando's early years in vain for evidence of subjectivity in his work, or for that matter in conversations with friends, and almost nothing comes to hand. Stunts and pranks and general goofiness we hear about, and a ready sympathy for the pains and problems of others, and girl-chasing, naturally; but of personal history, recalled emotions, virtually nothing.

I don't think Brando ever wanted to plunge down into the abyss of himself. I don't think he knew, when he wandered into Adler's class, that such an effort was now beginning to be regarded as a requisite for serious acting. For that matter, it seems unlikely that he knew, definitely, that he wanted to try to make a living as an actor. Yes, his mother had been an amateur actress of some local repute at one time in her life, and, yes, his sister Jocelyn was pursuing a theatrical career, and, yes, the thing he had liked best about prep school had been acting in plays, but in everyone's reminiscences Bud Brando has the air of someone taking a few courses because he couldn't think of anything better to do with his time.

Adler felt his commitment to acting was 'touch and go', and she would characterize him in those days as a young man basically 'against things', adding that when she first met him there was no place where he 'functioned with continuity and discipline'. Adler would confide to an interviewer that, after he began to find himself as an actor, his mother came to her and said: 'Thank you, you've saved Marlon. He had no direction; now he has direction.'

Perhaps Mrs Brando and Ms Adler spoke too soon. Looking back now, one feels that Brando's pleasure in the young actor's life and his relatively quick ascent to stardom disguised his growing doubts about his choice of a profession. Indeed, by the early Fifties friends and relatives were predicting early retirement for Brando, a prediction in which he frequently joined.

It made sense. For it was obvious, even then, that Brando would never gratefully, gracefully settle into his success, which, for practical purposes in post-war America, was starting to mean what it now most assuredly means: more or less accepting other people's definition of you and living to fulfil the peculiar needs of others, among them – once celebrity is attained – perfect strangers.

That, as it happens, was the basic issue with Brando *before* he was famous. Naturally, no one outside his immediate family much cared what was going to become of him. But *they* cared a lot. Couldn't help it, being middle-class, Middle-western WASPs they were born fussers after respectability, which always includes an overwhelming drive to see their children placed firmly in the paths of predictability.

Perhaps that anxiety was more vivid for the Brandos of Omaha, Nebraska, and, latterly, of Evanston and Libertyville, Illinois, than it was for others. The surface impression they created was an archetype of bourgeois

solidity in its time and place: Marlon Sr, a stern, taciturn man in a dark suit, implacably, prosperously purveying useful, glamorless products – cattle feed, chicken feed, limestone – to businessmen reassuringly like himself; his wife, Dorothy, known to all as Dodie, in manner rather like the characters Billie Burke used to play – pretty, high-spirited, distracted, always in a bit of a dither, but warm and sweet and 'cultured'; three children – Jocelyn, born in 1920, Frances, two and a half years younger, and, finally, Marlon Jr, born April 3, 1924. All the Brando children were intelligent and talented – paternally encouraged to accept discipline and responsibility, maternally encouraged to express themselves in whatever manner suited them. This was a classic 'nice' family according to the standards of its time and place. Their life seems to have been perpetually elm-shaded. Even during the Depression there appears to have been no hint of economic instability.

But emotional instability? Yes. Of course. This was Sinclair Lewis country, after all. One expects to find something not quite right hidden behind the comfortable, provincial façade. One would be disappointed not to find it.

An irony now arises. Privacy – no, secrecy – was, and is, a major value for people like the Brandos. And, gossipy, neighborly speculations aside, they can usually count on maintaining it. Except when their fractious, fretted over, difficult child, that dagger in the heart when he is growing up, becomes a consequential figure in the great world. Think of it: you worry for twenty years that your child will not make something of himself, then he goes and does so, and your life suddenly becomes an open book. If the boy had fulfilled your worst expectation, at least you would have remained anonymous and ultimately untraceable.

One almost feels like apologizing for saying it . . . but . . . well . . . Dodie drank . . . and Marlon Sr was an unyielding moralist who was also, typical of his breed, a hypocrite, since he too drank, albeit more secretively. And womanized as well. Of the two, she is the more sympathetic figure, the more tragic figure.

Dorothy Pennebaker Brando was the kind of alcoholic who could remain sober – and in her case charming and spirited – for long periods, only to disappear on binges, often to be discovered in degrading and even dangerous situations. In the early years of marriage her problem was apparently disguisable, for she had in those days an ideal outlet for her talents and energies. She was one of the founders of the Omaha Community Playhouse, which would ultimately become one of the most solidly established amateur theatrical companies in the country. It was she who recruited a handsome young man named Henry Fonda to play juveniles in the company, and over the years she would play leads in everything from O'Neill to *Lilliom* to *Ten Nights in a Barroom*, becoming something of a local celebrity in the process. Everybody said that she might have had a professional career if she had not married.

Doubtless her drinking was, in part, a response to simple disappointment at ambitions unfulfilled. Doubtless it increased after 1930, when Marlon Sr found a larger business opportunity in Chicago and the family moved to Evanston, a much more straight-laced community. It offered nothing comparable to the Playhouse to deflect and absorb Dodie's troubled spirit.

We are dealing here with something more than a frustrated actress; Dodie had come to see her marriage as a sham. Eventually, it seems she confronted Marlon Sr with evidence of his philanderings. There are also unverifiable claims that he may have beaten her. And more than once she absented herself from their home for an extended period – trial separations in fact, if not in name.

And little Bud? What did he make of all this? In Jocelyn's nice description he was, in the Omaha years, 'a blond, fat-bellied little boy, quite serious, very determined'. As the oldest sibling she was often pressed into service as something more than a baby-sitter, almost a surrogate mother, while Dodie devoted herself to the Playhouse.

The middle sibling, Fran – closer in age, and as it happened closer emotionally to her little brother – would remember that he loved to win the card games he played with her, and that he was inventive at making up rules as

they went along in order to assure that end. Gamesmanship is, in fact, a feature of everyone's early memories of Bud Brando: word games, and made-up games (who can dance faster, balance a match, or stand on one foot longer). The family and Middle-western friends would also remember Bud and Fran running away from home on a fairly regular basis, almost every Sunday for a time. They didn't get far, but these attempts at escape, more symbolic than real, established a lifetime pattern for Bud: dodging away, disappearing into clouds of his own creation.

Another salient characteristic also manifested itself early. It began with Bud's concern for the animal kingdom. The household population of pets, always extensive, was constantly added to as he brought home lost and injured creatures to care for. But there was more to this interest than simple sentiment. Animals seemed straightforward, trustworthy, unduplicitous in a way that human beings seemed incapable of – at least within Bud's limited experience of them.

Similar feelings were extended to people who presented themselves as emotionally lost or unusually put-upon. Wherever the Brandos lived, Bud was always at the center of the neighborhood gang, even then attempting to use his star power to extend protection to the unfortunate. Fran would recall a little girl with a habit, in games, of getting lost in her own thoughts, coming close to a trance-like state. Bud always chose her to be on his side.

His friendship with funny little Wally Cox, not at all a typical boy's boy, which began in Evanston when they were about ten, had the same sweet protective air about it. And it continued beyond the grave. 'It wasn't an unlikely friendship,' Brando told a reporter in 1976, three years after Cox died, 'because Wally didn't resemble in the remotest his Mr Peepers character.' He had, rather, 'the mentality of an axe murderer'. Brando claimed he had kept his friend's ashes in his house and talked to him all the time. 'I can't tell you how I miss and love that man.'

He was entirely capable of extending his elaborate kindness to strangers as well. A significant moment in family mythology has Bud coming upon a woman who had

Jocelyn, the eldest sibling, who became a talented actress. Often, in the Omaha years, while their mother was occupied with amateur theater, Jocelyn was almost a surrogate mother to Fran and Bud.

people even more troubled, more in need of sympathetic attention than the errant father and/or mother, and direct one's concern toward them, it serves the youngster's hidden agenda.

Jocelyn: 'He was drawn to people shyer than he, more in trouble with their families, who were not able to cope with life as well. I don't like to use the word "underdog", but anyone he felt was insecure he wanted to help. Perhaps he was drawn to them . . . because they reflected something in himself . . . He was defending them, but I also think he was identifying with something in them.'

swooned on the street and insisting that she accompany him home, where she was made comfortable and a doctor was called.

In a way, all of this is something of a relief. It implies that Brando's subsequent and more famous devotion to such causes as civil rights and the plight of the American Indian was not merely a star trip, that it was the logical extension of something deeply rooted in his nature.

We must bear something else in mind. Bud Brando was the child of alcoholics. And one of the things recent research into the psychology of such children teaches us is that they do whatever they can to deflect attention away from the source of their shame. If, therefore, one can find

Yes. Unquestionably. Though by local middle-class standards it is hard to see how anyone could be in more trouble – this side of outright juvenile delinquency – than Marlon Jr habitually was with Marlon Sr. All the more reason to continue fulfilling the most basic requirement of a successful Middle-western boyhood: attending to one's popularity with one's peers. This, of course, has its practical benefits. It gives one a way of escaping tensions at home. But another element begins to creep into the portrait of Bud Brando as he headed toward adolescence: reserve, watchfulness, 'shyness'. Shyness! Such a perfect Middle-westernism, that word. Little kindnesses of the kind we have been discussing are an almost perfect expression of a shy soul's feelings, because they can be modestly shrugged off. Shyness is also a way of muffling the effects of sudden and quite unpredictable emotional earthquakes of the kind that periodically shook the Brando household – a mother's sudden loss to alcohol, a father's sudden rage. It is a way of preserving an illusion of untouchability.

The conflict in which Bud was caught was utterly basic. It was a conflict between loyalty owed on the one hand to his mother – sweet, indulgent, ineffectual, and increasingly pitiable – and on the other to his father – strict, unyielding, uncomprehending. Jocelyn would later put it well: 'Father thought when we were growing up we should have responsibilities, and mother thought we were still growing up and should be let alone. In many ways he [Bud] got along better with mother because the pressures she put on him were of a different kind. Pressures of living, getting along with people, understanding life . . . She was much more patient during those years than father. Father was not very articulate, and wasn't able to give of himself too well, and his attitudes were much stricter. With him, performance was the thing, not the intention. The opposite with mother. She was a very encouraging person. She had plenty of foibles herself and acknowledged them, so was more tolerant.'

There speaks, in carefully measured words, a daughter dutiful to her family, to the discreet traditions of her time and place, but also to the truth. Foibles! Well, all right, foibles. But as Bud Brando grew older he was obviously responding to something more potent than 'foibles' in the family drama. We speak now, I think, of endless and terrible parental tensions, and of the corrosive damage being done to Dodie by them. At a certain point her alcoholism became obvious to perfect strangers, possibly even a subject of suburban scandal. It was impossible, needless to say, for the son to intervene between his parents, or to express himself openly on the central issue of his family's life.

So . . . withdrawal. Recalcitrance. Indifference. Drumming. (Yes, drumming, a wonderful way to shut out the world while at the same time driving it crazy.) Jocelyn would expand somewhat on her characterization of

Marlon Sr and Bud's relationship with him. An 'intense, scared, inarticulate man,' she would call him. 'He thought it best to push Bud. . . . Father wanted a lot from him and for him in a practical sense. . . . Bud was many times not so practical.'

Bud was many times beside himself. Though it is almost impossible to find among the memories of those who knew him as a young man recollections of him speaking about his past, there is one that is particularly vivid. Offered by a young actor who aspired beside Brando in summer stock, it is a paraphrase of Bud's description of his father: 'A tall, looming figure who stares down hard at him, but never touches him or makes contact with him in any way.'

Eventually, in mid-adolescence, Bud did find his tongue. Witnesses have testified to overheard battles, conducted at the top of their voices by the two Marlons. There is no record of conventional juvenile delinquency – smashed cars, petty crime, girls 'in trouble'. There is, however, an insistence on serious attention being paid to the quiet young man. Here, again, his parents' problem with drink cannot be ignored. As mentioned earlier, it is fairly typical of children of alcoholics to deflect attention toward themselves and away from errant parents. This is something to bear in mind when considering Marlon Brando's seemingly curious behavior half a century later, when his son was charged with murder, notably his sudden loquaciousness with the press after decades of avoiding it. He was drawing attention to himself, away from his son, just as, long ago, he had attempted to draw it away from his parents.

Back then, military school was a threat that hovered over the head of almost every middle-class adolescent male in America. Parents would contemplate its salutary effects in voices just loud enough to be overheard by their sulking sons who would sometimes be very good for a day or two, until the current storm blew over. The obvious trouble in Brando's case was that his father was himself the product of a military school. Dear old Shattuck, in Fairbault, Minnesota. Up at 5.45. Inspection. Callisthenics in the cold Minnesota mornings. Drills. Hikes. Compulsory sports. Study Hall after dinner. Lights

Following his early departure
from Shattuck, which
disappointed his father, Bud
joined his sisters in New York
and was soon training as an
actor at the Piscator workshop.

out at 9.30. It must have seemed the perfect solution for his problem son to the elder Brando. And there the lad was sent in the fall of 1942.

Still, true to the Brando heritage of politesse, Bud was at least for a while an obliging student. He went out for football and did well until sometime in his second season a knee injury put him in the hospital (it required an operation, but it probably saved him from the draft). He made the 'Crack Squad', which was a precision drill team in which the school (and his father, who had been a member of it in his day) took inordinate pride. He did well in dramatics – at least three shows, one of which his mother saw. 'That boy can act,' she reported at home.

In other words, Bud Brando did rather well, all things considered. Oh, there were reports of more than usual class-cutting. And there was the matter of the flaming Vitalis, a hair tonic you could write a dirty word with on a wall and it would remain invisible – until you touched a

match to it and the obscenity came to fiery life. Bud caused another minor (but perhaps more biographically instructive) scandal at his first communion, when he held the wafer on his tongue and, on returning to his pew, took it out and examined it. The school saw it as irreverence. Jocelyn saw it as Bud being Bud. 'He just wanted to see what this stuff was that was so important – see it, feel it, and taste it.'

None of these constituted expulsion offenses, especially considering how nicely Bud Brando seemed to be fitting in at Shattuck. But in the fall of his second year, after the football injury, things started to deteriorate. He worked his wound for all it was worth, continuing to drag about long after his knee had healed. Malingering was suspected, and disgust was registered by school officials. Concentration had never been one of Bud's strengths, of course. But the more distant observer has to suspect something else was at work here, something that would recur subsequently in his career. Bud Brando had proved a point: he could be his father's son if he wanted to. But now he had played this role, had pleased his audience, had got out of it whatever good there was to be had from it. Now he was perhaps bored. Why go on repeating himself?

Be that as it may, it seems he was not asked to leave Shattuck because of any spectacular infraction of the rules; fizzling out, he was pushed out. There was patriarchal disgust at home, naturally, and matriarchal patience. New York, where both his sisters were then living, was mentioned – and perhaps the possibility of studying acting. Jocelyn would remember simply that Bud was 'shaky' and didn't know what to do with life when he finally decamped for Fran's apartment, cluttered with her work and her art student's paraphernalia, on West 10th Street in Greenwich Village.

CHAPTER TWO

AGE OF CONSENT

It was a good time to be in New York. As it had been for something like a half-century, the city was, to quote an early metropolitan observer, 'teeming with life, humming with trade, muttering with the thunder of passage' – especially the latter in these war years. It thronged with servicemen on leave, horny, wondering, feverish, many of them, at their impending confrontation with premature mortality. It thronged too, with refugees from Hitler's Europe – artists, musicians, men of letters, performers of all kinds – and they lent a new edge of sophistication to the city's cultural life, an edge that cut away much of its remaining provincialism.

Within five years of his arrival in New York, Brando was a Broadway star, but after his immediate success in Hollywood in the early Fifties he never returned to the theater.

Right A short-lived but significant Broadway role was in Maxwell Anderson's *Truckline Cafe* (1946), as a psychopathic war veteran who murders his unfaithful wife, played by Ann Shepherd.

Nine English-language newspapers were then published daily in Manhattan, and magazines thrived. Network radio was also an animating, glamorizing force, and a means of employment for actors. And though, then as now, everyone lamented Broadway's decline, it still mounted upward of eighty productions every season. These industries fueled a legendary night-life, of course, but also helped feed an intoxicating mixture of gossip and ideas.

There was a playfulness in New York life at this time that is perhaps the most regrettable of all its losses in recent decades. Above all, this congeries of forces fueled the hopes of a bright, ambitious, upwardly striving population of young adults, drawn from all over the United States in hopes of finding an escape into fame. Or an escape into anonymity – either one, as long as the stage on which their personal dramas were played out pulsed with wayward life.

That was the way of it in New York then. Young men and women beginning careers in the arts or some less grand form of communication could feel that they were in some real sense sharing the world of people who had made, were still making, the tradition they would inherit, perhaps expand upon. In the Forties, for example, George Balanchine's New York City Ballet was beginning to establish itself as a great new creative power in dance, while all around Greenwich Village painters were beginning to form the school that would soon be known the world over as Abstract Impressionism. Uptown, on West 52nd Street, jazz was being renovated by the likes of Dizzy Gillespie and Charlie Parker, and on Broadway *Oklahoma!*, which would revitalize the American musical, was about to open. These were powerful assertions that an indigenous American culture was coming of age, and the force this culture would exert in the post-war world was unimaginable. It was not quite as unimaginable, though, as the fact that by the time the decade turned Marlon Brando would exemplify the new, and equally potent, American style of theatrical self-presentation to the world audience.

'Young actor' – that's a good alias, and, at the time, a new one. For it was only with the beginning of organizations like Piscator's workshop that aspiring

performers began to form a community, a recognizable identity as a group. This, indeed, may have been the most important thing that these new, and by no means stable, institutions gave them: a feeling that they were apprentices to an honorable profession, absorbing a body of lore and legend they could rely on for strength, to help build a self that could stand up to the buffetings of what is, God knows, one of the most difficult and psychologically dangerous occupations on earth.

It has been claimed that Brando may actually have been the first to make blue jeans a standard element in this crowd's dress code, though there is no proof on that point. But we do know that their life consisted of living in lofts, eating in cafeterias, second-acting shows (that is, sneaking into an empty seat at the intermission), nursing a cup of espresso for hours in one of the Italian cafés on Bleecker or MacDougall Street, while an impassioned discussion of a new production or a new acting phenomenon, or just a good performance in yesterday's class, rolled on through the evening. How harshly bad 'work' was condemned; what a sense of awe good 'work' engendered. But what a relief – to be eighteen and in New York, to be judged on what you did, not who you were, to be free of parental anxiety and disapproval, to be broody and gorgeous among people to whom both qualities were a source of attraction rather than a cause for alarm, to be part of a new family that loved easily and forgave readily.

Fran put it mildly: 'They were very intense about their school. They were terribly absorbed in their dancing and their movement and their make-up' [all subjects taught at the Piscator workshop]. The group, she recalled, was 'very closely-knit . . . At last there were lots of people he could talk to.' Adler, predictably, put it less mildly: 'Young actors as a group are just screwballs. They have nothing to do with ideas. They are a separate group, apart from all. And they cannot be with anyone else – they are not happy.' Commenting almost a decade later she observed: 'Marlon only has to do with them.'

Ultimately, as she implied, that may have been limiting. But for the moment it was a blessing. And it was accompanied by quite startling success. By the fall of

1943 Bud Brando was working in the little scenes that another Dramatic Workshop teacher, John Gassner, used to illustrate his lectures on theatrical history. By January 1944 he was cast in Piscator's production of Gerhardt Hauptman's dream play, *Hannele's Way to Heaven*. It was a dual role: that of the eponymous heroine's beloved schoolteacher and that of a dark angel who haunts the long slumber into which she sinks after a suicide attempt. Such was the power of Piscator's reputation that critics from the major papers often reviewed these plays, and Brando got his first good notices in this, and in *Twelfth Night*, which was staged the same week. Though it was *Hannele* that his friends would remember more powerfully, it was *Twelfth Night* that most interested the first agent to sign him, Maynard Morris, of the Leland Hayward office.

The following summer Piscator included Brando in the company, drawn from the Dramatic Workshop student body, that did a fairly serious summer of stock in Sayville, Long Island. The season opened with the *Twelfth Night* of the previous winter. But Piscator had turned rehearsals over to associates while he finished up some work in New York, and deplored the chaos he found when he joined his troupe just prior to the first night. There were two or three more shows, and then another expulsion.

The company had been having the usual swell time associated with summer stock: all-night sessions drinking and talking, plenty of goofing off, plenty of romances. Brando had perhaps the best time of all, for he and his best friend Carlo Fiore had the ideal bunk – in the hayloft of a barn on the theater grounds, away from the house where most of the company lived, and with a glorious ocean view. It was, obviously, a great place to entertain young ladies. Piscator was not amused. Too much of that sort of thing had been going on throughout the company, in his stern view. For the director was a theater saint, all dedication and self-denial in pursuit of high ideals; in a business rife with corruptive influences, his type is not unfamiliar, and not without value, either.

Piscator had noted Brando's frequent absences from class all spring, and he suspected a lack of proper sobriety about theater art. Sure enough, one afternoon he

found Bud Brando in what was by all accounts quite innocent congress with one of the girls in the company when he might have been studying lines. Studying Boleslawski's *Six Lessons*, doing something usefully self-improving. Both miscreants were asked to leave, though Brando was in this instance somewhat in the condition of a typical Hitchcock hero: on the specific charge blameless, but of a general lack of moral-aesthetic seriousness (at least by Piscator's standards) guilty as charged.

Many of Brando's elders looked upon him in this way at this time. And if they looked to him like potential father figures, in either the forbidding or the distant manner, then he was likely to react rebelliously. For example: an audition for Alfred Lunt; the usual worklight dimly illuminating the stage; the house, also as usual, dark. From it, the bored, disembodied voice of the great man. 'Say something, just anything.' Panic. Anger. Both piled on top of the normal tensions and anxieties of a reading. Most actors, even today, would swallow those feelings and announce that they had worked up a little something. Not Marlon Brando. 'Hickory-dickory dock,' he declaimed, 'The mouse ran up the clock.' Whether he got to the end of the nursery rhyme before stalking out is not entirely clear.

Around the same time he had had his first screen test, for Twentieth Century-Fox. As these things go, it was quite simple: they perched Brando on a stool and asked him to turn this way and that, so they could see how he photographed from various angles. At some point the man conducting the test engaged his discomfited victim in conversation. 'What do you want to be?' the director asked. Disgusted reply: 'A yo-yo player.' Or, in the improved version of the story, he pulls out a yo-yo and starts playing with it.

No matter which is correct. The point of both stories is that he did what every actor has always wanted to do: raise a protest against the degrading, demeaning process of auditioning, the whole dreadful business by which (if you're lucky) you are granted five minutes to state your essence, show your skills, strut your stuff. The occasion is meaningless for the grandees lurking in the theater, behind the camera, but it is everything to the actor. He is often confronting a question of immediate survival – next month's rent, last month's unpaid phone bill – and he is always confronting career pressure: keeping it moving, keeping himself visible, viable.

Jocelyn, a fine actress who never attained such security as stardom has to offer, knew exactly what her brother was feeling and what he was trying to say to his auditioners. 'Someone out there in the dark, whom you can't see, will judge you. Your life begins or ends at this moment . . . Bud simply felt the whole ridiculousness and awesomeness of it . . . the whole futility of the thing. And then they say, "Oh, that weird boy."'

But not for long. He was scarcely back from Sayville when he got his first Broadway show: *I Remember Mama*. Of all things. Produced by Rodgers and Hammerstein, it was an adaptation by the smooth, commercially-knowing John van Druten of *Mama's Bank Account*, Kathryn Forbes's memoir of growing up poor, but with excellent values, in a family of Norwegian immigrants in turn-of-the-century San Francisco. They were, of course, warm, loving, mildly fractious, sweetly eccentric – in short, appealing and utterly untaxing folks with whom to spend

an evening. Moreover, this family had obvious commercial potential, for they and the vehicle in which they were presented were not far in spirit from the Day family of the comfortably nostalgic *Life With Father*, then about half-way toward setting the record it still holds as the longest running non-musical play in Broadway history.

It is obvious why Brando hesitated when offered the role of Nils, the family's youngest son, in a cast headed by Mady Christians and Oscar Homolka, both popular character leads of the time. For *Mama* was just the kind of thing Brando and his peers viewed scornfully, if not with revolutionary outrage – bourgeois theater of the most blatant sort.

But Adler read the script and urged him to take it. She knew as well as anyone what it was, but she was no Strasbergian purist. She saw that Nils aged a few years over the course of the play, which is always a nice, noticeable trick for an actor to achieve. More importantly, she observed that the role consisted very largely of watchful silences. In other words, the casting was perfect.

When *Mama* opened, the critics were dismissive ('pleasantly undisturbing'), but in a way that signalled to

Brando's first Broadway show was *I Remember Mama* (1944), a comfortable piece about a Norwegian immigrant family, written and directed by John van Druten.

1944

His portrayal of Nils, the young son who grows up in the course of the play, made a forceful impression on Edith Van Cleve, of the MCA agency, whose client he would soon become.

the middle class that they would have a very nice time at The Music Box theater. Though it did not challenge the success of *Life With Father*, the play would run almost two years and became, in its subsequent versions (movie, TV show, musical), an inescapable, seemingly unstoppable presence in American popular culture.

In 1944, the reviewers were so preoccupied with van Druten (whose recent record included *The Voice of the Turtle*, another great wartime success) and the bullet-proof Christians and Homolka that they didn't pay much attention to Marlon Brando. But truly knowledgeable theater-goers, the professionals, did. 'I went to see *I Remember Mama*,' Bobby Lewis would recall a few years later, 'and I noticed this kid on stage. I checked with my program and it said "Marlon Brando". I turned to a friend of mine sitting beside me and said: "This is probably a mistake. This Marlon Brando is probably sick and somebody else is in the part." You know, like they have to put a stage-hand in the role . . . in an emergency. I mean everybody else on the stage was acting or not acting, but this boy was a note of reality. He was so real. He really lived in that house there.'

Edith Van Cleve, the MCA agent whose client Brando would shortly become, had a similar revelation. 'Everybody was watching Oscar Homolka, Mady Christians, Joan Tetzel, and so on. And afterwards everyone was saying, "Wasn't Homolka wonderful?" And I'd say, "Yes, but wasn't the boy good?" "Wasn't Christians wonderful?" "Yes, but wasn't the boy good?" And finally someone said, "What boy? Oh, the one in knee pants who grew up." The way he listened. He stood on that stage for twenty minutes without a line, and when he did speak it was if he had been speaking all the time. You didn't jerk your head around because of a new voice. How extraordinarily he played the scene. He made it seem like he had a long part.'

Van Cleve, who specialized in the movies, sent for Brando, who told her he had representation and wasn't interested in movies in any case. She replied that he wasn't ready for them anyway, but that she'd be glad to turn down offers on his behalf. And that was that for something like six months. Then in the midst of a blizzard, Brando

appeared at her office and announced he had fulfilled all obligations to Maynard Morris and was ready to sign.

The problem now was getting Brando to leave *Mama*. The pay was steady, the work light. Adler, in particular, felt obliged to pry him loose from the play she had talked him into, for it was beginning to feed his natural laziness, she felt. What came of the withdrawal from *Mama* was almost a year without theatrical employment. But, again, Adler to the rescue – or so she would recall.

In 1945–46 her husband, Harold Clurman, had formed a producing partnership with Elia Kazan, and their first presentation was to be Maxwell Anderson's *Truckline Cafe*, with Clurman directing. She recommended her student for a role as a psychopathically troubled war veteran, and despite doubts, they hired Brando. It was, for all concerned, a moment more significant than it seemed at the time. For *Truckline Cafe* would turn out to be a true theatrical rarity: a consequential flop, a play of no great merit that would, nevertheless, have several unintended effects on the course of future history.

Setting aside Tennessee Williams's *The Glass Menagerie*, which had opened just before the end of the war, and which was, in any case, a less blatant assault on the status quo, *Truckline* can be seen as the first post-war challenge to Broadway's pre-war mentality. For it represented a coming together of two important strands in the recent history of the American theater. Clurman's involvement in the production obviously signals the influence of The Group Theater on everyone's calculations. So does the presence of Kazan, who had been an actor and director in the company. The two would become perhaps the most significant figures in shaping American theatrical history in the post-war era. Between them they would direct a majority of the most

Elia Kazan, the pioneering Broadway director turned film director, who in both capacities did much to shape Brando's early career.

Although *Truckline Cafe* closed after only a week in 1946, it challenged the Broadway status quo and brought Brando to Elia Kazan's attention.

1946

important plays of the era, introducing significant new American voices to the theater and, in the case of Clurman, many of the more interesting European modernists. Kazan's work as a movie director would, of course, be as important as his Broadway career, and Clurman would soon take up duties as a drama critic (for *The Nation*) of uncommon knowledgeability and influence – especially on theater people.

Given their backgrounds and convictions, it is significant that at this moment they chose to do a play by Maxwell Anderson. With Robert E. Sherwood and Sidney Kingsley, he had been for almost two decades one of the most highly regarded of Broadway's serious playwrights. Anderson was drawn alternately to high-flown historical pageantry (*Elizabeth the Queen*, *Mary of Scotland*) and contemporary socio-political issues (*High Tor*, *Key Largo*). His plays have not worn well, but at the time he was taken very seriously as a 'playwright of ideas'. It was no small thing for this establishment writer to link his fortunes with Group alumni, and there was high interest in what they would bring forth.

As it happens, *Truckline Cafe* found Anderson going among the lowlifes, a group by chance gathered one evening at a roadside diner perched on the Californian coastline. Brando's role – a supporting one – was that of Sage McRae, a psychopathic war veteran returning home and discovering, in the course of the drama, that his wife, played by Ann Shepherd, has been unfaithful. Sage murders her and swims out to sea to dispose of her body, but then returns to the stage, dripping wet, teeth chattering, and, almost beatifically, awaits the arrival of the police and eventual doom.

Brando dieted down to almost wraithlike proportions, the better to suggest his character's tormented nature. But rehearsals were troubled. Karl Malden, whose career would for some time be intertwined with Brando's, was in the cast and remembered him as 'a terribly shy, sensitive boy', who had trouble projecting. To say the least. Anderson couldn't hear his precious lines, and Clurman fretted anxiously over a performance that refused to take shape. People did not yet know that this was one of those actors whose rehearsals are terrible to behold. Clurman guessed correctly that he was unable to voice his deepest emotions because 'it hurt too much'. Malden was wiser. 'I guess actors are formless,' he would say later. 'Nine-tenths of the people who become actors are that way.' The point was, he suggested, that his young colleague needed to lose himself, and his shyness, in a role – and that loss happened not when he was thinking about the part, and talking about it in rehearsal, but when he was doing it under performance pressure. Or, as Malden put it to a reporter, 'Once on stage, he became a character so much he wasn't Marlon any more.'

I suspect we come close, here, to one of the prime reasons Brando abandoned the stage. A play in the making is a cave of the winds, everyone talking actor-talk about motives and emotional recall and what-have-you. Movies are different: the production schedule sets the pace: get up and do the scene – bang – then move on to the next set-up and the next. There's no time for self-examination. On set or location the actor is just supposed to hit his mark and say his lines. In other words, and despite all the contemptuous words he has lavished on the medium, Brando's psychological priorities suit the exigencies of the movies better than they do those of the stage.

Yet a performance – and by all accounts an astonishing one – did at last emerge in *Truckline Cafe*. Pauline Kael, the movie critic to be, happened to catch Brando in it. Arriving late for a performance, she settled into a second row seat 'and saw what I thought was an actor having a seizure on-stage. Embarrassed for him, I lowered my eyes, and it wasn't until the young man who'd brought me grabbed my arm and said, "Watch this guy!" that I realized he was *acting*.' The reviewers in their variously dim ways agreed for the most part. But everybody hated the play. It would close after a week's run.

But not before the producers who could not bear to see their work buried made a fight for it. Clurman and Kazan took out an ad in the *Times*, attacking the critics. 'There is a black-out of all taste, except the taste of these men,' they wrote, urging the public to come and see the play and make up its own mind. '*Truckline Cafe* has faults,' they conceded, 'but it is the kind of play that, in our opinion, every theater lover should see. That is why we

did it . . .' Anderson, 'a great, shy bear of a man, rich in humility and conscience,' as John Mason Brown, the drama critic, described him, chimed in with a far more intemperate, and quite out-of-character attack on the critics. 'A sort of Jukes family of journalism,' he called them in a Sunday newspaper letter. 'It is an insult to our theater that there should be so many incompetents and irresponsibles among them.'

This particular show was beyond saving, but these unprecedented diatribes against a breed that – Walter Kerr excepted – has not notably improved over the years did send a message: that the non-commercial (indeed, anti-commercial) radical fringe of Thirties theater was starting to move on the center, and that it would find there surprising allies like Anderson. Add to this its importance in Brando's personal history, and *Truckline Cafe* was rescued from the dustbin of history.

It performed two other significant functions as well. It brought Brando to the attention of Kazan, and that had, as we all know, a major effect on both careers, as well as on the larger history of American theater and film. More immediately, according to Kazan, it precipitated renewed thoughts about creating some kind of theatrical institution that would perform some of the functions that The Group had once performed. For one thing, he would remember saying to Clurman, 'We needed our kind of actors to play the leading roles in our productions.' Besides Brando, he had liked Malden and some of the others in *Truckline*, but many roles he had thought 'inadequately performed'. He also harbored hopes of restoring some of the communal spirit of The Group at its best. Clurman agreed, and said he'd mention it to Stella. No thanks, Kazan thought, having had his difficulties with her in the past. So he took the idea to Bobby Lewis, and in the course of an afternoon's walk in Central Park, The Actor's Studio was born – for good, ill, or some combination of the two.

No matter to Marlon Brando, all these plans. He had a job. Guthrie McClintic, Katharine Cornell's husband, manager, and director, had seen him in *Truckline*, and conceived the odd, daring notion that he was right to play Marchbanks, the palely loitering poet, opposite Cornell in a revival of *Candida*, with Sir Cedric

Hardwicke cast as her pastor husband. And so our young rebel was again thrust back into the well-spoken mainstream, with one of theater's designated Great Ladies, who, as it happened, counted Shaw's play one of her great triumphs of a decade ago.

Curiously, nothing bad came of this involvement. Actors in the company would recall Brando being extremely reserved and polite to his elders, though Cornell's theatrical manner and McClintic's directorial style were clearly antithetical to him. But the show opened to respectable, if not wildly enthusiastic, notices. Some reviewers even liked Brando in it, thinking he caught the skittish inwardness, the tormented shyness, of unformed youth. Others thought he somewhat flattened out the character. The play had a short Broadway run and moved on to Chicago for a few weeks (Cornell remained a great draw on the road), where Brando's performance is reported to have deteriorated.

In the fall of 1946, more work, more theatrical legends: Ben Hecht, Luther Adler, Paul Muni. Hecht, one of Hollywood's most brilliantly facile screenwriters (and a renowned script doctor), had written *A Flag is Born*, a sort of propaganda pageant for Zionism masquerading as a play, with music by Kurt Weill. Luther Adler, Stella's brother, and a man of immense ego, was engaged to direct it. Muni, who had also begun his career in the Yiddish theater, and was held in general awe as an actor, agreed to star.

There was no question about Brando's participation when asked. These were certainly more his kind of people than Cornell and her crowd had been. And surely there was a timeliness, and a controversialism, to the subject-matter that was absent from yet another Shaw revival. Indeed, the establishment of a Jewish state, welcoming the homeless survivors of the holocaust, was a cause that naturally enlisted Brando's sympathies. This would be the first time, but hardly the last, that he insisted upon placing the demands of his conscience ahead of professional calculation. But it must be admitted that the role, that of a heroic young freedom fighter who has the play's concluding inspirational harangue, after the Muni character has sacrificed his life, was not without its obvious appeals.

Finally, the opportunity to work with Muni was irresistible. He had been the original *Counsellor at Law* on Broadway, and *Scarface* in the movies, and had worked marvelously in another touchstone film of the 1930s, *I Was a Fugitive from a Chain Gang*. But he had gained his greatest fame in a succession of movie biographies of great historical figures, hiding behind heavy accents and make-ups. He had great technique, and had found a way to hide in plain sight while the 'real' Paul Muni – if there was one – eluded detection. And that intrigued Brando.

Not that rehearsals went smoothly. Muni had trouble getting hold of his part and his lines. Adler, and occasionally Muni, entered the usual complaints about Brando's rehearsal habits. Finally, in performance, there was an incident that passed into showbiz lore and legend. When Muni finally expired on stage Brando was supposed to drape him in the flag of Israel and then launch into the ringing peroration that was supposed to bring down the house. Muni, though, was not entirely content that his face be hidden from view, and on this occasion he tugged the flag down, bit by careful bit, while his young colleague was in the middle of his speech, until the famous face was once again revealed. Titters, of course, ensued.

Yet the reviews, especially of Brando, were good; *A Flag is Born* achieved a respectable run (127 performances); and of all the actors Brando worked with he has remained most voluble in his admiration for Muni. Thirty years later he would tell a reporter: 'Night after night that man gave me goosebumps. Most plays you go mad with the boredom of repetition. But Muni was electrifying, the best I've ever seen . . .' We may be hearing about a role model here, a demonstration of a way to make a living as an actor without indulging in prodigies of self-exposure.

Of course, not every encounter with a legend works out so well. Consider Tallulah Bankhead and *The Eagle Has Two Heads*, Jean Cocteau's dour Graustarkian fable, in which a queen's mourning for a mate done in fifteen years earlier is interrupted by the intrusion in the bedchamber of a revolutionary. He has come for murder, but he stays for love. At the end, both queen and commoner die for their sins.

The question is why Brando was invited to participate in the first place. Edith Van Cleve and John C. Wilson, Bankhead's tame, socialite director, thought he was her kind of hunk. But first impressions should have told all concerned that he was not ideally cast in this situation, if only because of Bankhead's notorious alcohol problem. Still, a job was a job, and an interview was arranged. Bankhead had a home in Westchester, and she, predictably, was well along in drink when Brando arrived. When she offered him something he asked, 'Are you an alcoholic?' 'No, Darling,' she replied, 'just a heavy drinker.' She also had certain sexual expectations of young men associated with her in theatrical enterprises, and she was soon trying to grope Brando through his jeans. It would not be her last pass.

But, strangely enough, she engaged him. It was a truly monumental – even risible – mistake. As everyone discovered at the beginning of an endless pre-Broadway tour in Wilmington. Up to now, the gap between the new generation of actors and the previous ones had been papered over. Ultimately, mutual respect had been formed between Brando and Cornell, Brando and Muni. But Tallulah was not just a star. She was a star turn. And she was surrounded by people who catered to her iron whims, even found in them moral imperatives.

As Richard Maney, Bankhead's press agent and drinking companion for a quarter of a century, would tell it in his autobiography, Brando passed rehearsals in his customary state, described as 'trancelike', arrived surly in Wilmington, and then proceeded to upstage Bankhead's treasured first-act 'aria', said by some historians to be the longest soliloquy in theatrical history. 'He squirmed. He picked his nose. He adjusted his fly. He leered at the audience. He cased the furniture. He fixed his gaze on an off-stage property man instead of on his opponent.' Maybe it was pure wickedness. On the other hand, it may well have been acting. Brando's character was supposed to be a loutish peasant, after all.

Brando was not fired on the spot, but in Boston he achieved that highly desirable end. The temptation, of course, is to see all this symbolically – the old Broadway versus the new, or, if you prefer, the new mannerism versus the old. Old-fashioned star acting on the stage, as opposed to the movies, where it was quite different and infinitely more refined, had by this time become a bore: aging ladies and gentlemen receiving heedlessly respectable New York notices, then trotting their tired turns around to wow the provincials.

Maybe Brando was cruel to Tallulah; maybe it was just acting up, sheer youthful devilry. Maybe something deeper was at work as he played opposite an alcoholic woman who was roughly his mother's age. But with the critics supinely indulgent of the names they had built up in the past, and the public glamorized by press agentry, let's see Brando's behavior on this occasion as what it surely was in some measure – a small gesture of disgust with the status quo, a sign that maybe times were beginning to change.

Perhaps faster than he might have guessed. For by the time *Eagle* finally crash-landed on Broadway, with Helmut Dantine in the Brando part, for a run of twenty-nine performances in March 1947, Kazan's production of Arthur Miller's *All My Sons* had opened. Its success, combined with the earlier triumph of *The Glass Menagerie*, suggested that the Broadway theater might finally be entering upon its long predicted new era.

There is, of course, a certain irony in the linkage of Miller and Tennessee Williams as the leading figures of this period in the American theater, for it is hard to think of two more antithetical sensibilities. Except for this: at their early best both of them wished to explore the torments of that most basic of institutions, the family. Miller was, self-consciously, a playwright of ideas, Williams, equally self-consciously, a poet of the theater. But *Menagerie* explored the relationship between a mother and a daughter, *All My Sons* that between a father and a son, and both of them did so in near-tragic terms.

In any event, the success of *All My Sons* emboldened Williams to get in touch with Kazan to direct his next play, even though, as he said, 'Gadge [the director's nickname] likes a thesis and I haven't made up my mind what the thesis of this play is.' *A Streetcar Named Desire* was to be produced by a newcomer, Irene Mayer Selznick, daughter of Louis B. Mayer, estranged wife of

David O. Selznick: in Broadway's mind, a picture person, to be looked at somewhat askance; in her own mind a novice, needing to tread cautiously.

Her first choice as director was Joshua Logan, who was then, arguably, the theater's most reputable director, though not perhaps an ideal choice for a Williams work. Her first choice for the role of Stanley Kowalski was John Garfield – another dubious idea. He was a good actor, but he was a slight man, who though he had played tough city types, had tended to play them in a rather romantic and boyish vein. There was nothing of Stanley's animalism – or menace – about him. And, at thirty-three, he was perhaps a shade too old for the role.

In any case, a stage wait ensued. Kazan went off to Hollywood to direct *Gentlemen's Agreement* (in which Garfield co-starred), continuing to campaign subtly for the assignment to *Streetcar*, as did Williams, who came to the coast to work on script revisions with the director. There, also, they found their Blanche du Bois, or perhaps, as Kazan came to suspect, had her subtly thrust upon them. Hume Cronyn, knowing Williams was in town, and also knowing the one-act play that was the sketch for *Streetcar*, staged it at an LA actors' workshop with his wife, Jessica Tandy, in the leading role. Williams and Kazan came – and were conquered.

When he wrapped his picture, Kazan returned to New York, and at last was officially awarded the play by Mrs Selznick. He also professed himself content with the casting of Garfield. Kazan, in addition to his several other virtues, was a shrewd man of the theater, and thus not averse to a little star insurance, especially if it was in the form of an old Group Theater colleague who apparently shared his theatrical values.

The problem was that 'Julie' Garfield (as he was known to his old pals) was now more movie star than theater idealist. He would only commit to a four-month run in the play, and he wanted first refusal of his role if a film was made of *Streetcar*. He was also casting longing eyes at another play, Jan de Hartog's *Skipper Next to God*, which contained a part more comfortably within his range, and which he did, in fact, do – though with no great success.

The *Streetcar* people began looking elsewhere, and

Kazan, recalling Brando from *Truckline*, and perhaps receiving a helpful hint from Bobby Lewis, began looking for Brando. Not an easy task, for this was a period when he had no fixed address. It is Kazan's recollection that he gave Brando twenty dollars for his fare and sent him to Cape Cod to read for Williams, himself a wanderer, who had briefly settled there. Kazan thinks Brando spent the money on food and then hitched his way to the Cape. Or maybe he just decided to proceed at his own pace. In any event, he was three days late, arriving when the house was in chaos – electricity out, the toilet overflowing, Williams in a tizzy. Brando fixed the fuses and the plumbing, then transfixed Williams with his reading. The part was his – forever, as it has turned out, since every actor who has attempted it since has had to compete against everyone else's memory of Marlon Brando in, if not the play, then the movie adaptation.

The rehearsals were in some ways like all his rehearsals. Mrs Selznick, for example, couldn't hear Brando in the back of the house. And Ms Tandy found him erratic. 'If he felt bored or tired, he acted bored or tired. If he felt gay it would go gay. I remember Karl Malden [playing Mitch, Blanche's would-be boyfriend] smashing his fist against the wall because it was so frustrating.' In short, 'I can say I enjoyed acting with him sometimes, and other times, God knows, I could have wrung his little neck.'

In some ways, however, the rehearsals were different from any that preceded them in this brief theatrical career. Brando seemed to get hold of the basics of the part sooner and more firmly than he had any earlier one. There was some natural affinity with this character that he had not found before. Looking back on Brando in *Streetcar* in the spring of 1990, Kazan would say: 'He is exactly the thing I like in actors. There's a hell of a lot of turmoil there. There's ambivalence there. He's uncertain of himself and he's passionate, both at the same time.' But there was in Kazan's view yet more to the mixture of motives with which Brando invested the part, something the director would describe as 'ambivalence . . . between a soft, yearning, girlish side to him and a dissatisfaction that can be dangerous.' This was perhaps more than

Williams consciously knew was inherent in the role as he wrote it, but he delightedly recognized it when Brando summoned it forth. In Kazan's words, the writer developed a 'crush' on the actor, not sexual but full of gratitude for the subtextual ironies and the driving force he was bringing to the play. Williams proved to be enormously supportive at times when Kazan began worrying that Brando might be unhinging the delicate balance of the play. Brando was so strong, and Tandy was so tentative in the beginning, that the sympathy was flowing toward Stanley Kowalski instead of toward Blanche Du Bois, which was not Williams's intention – at least as Kazan saw it. The author, however, remained serene. He kept saying that his play wasn't so finely poised that its moral weight could shift, depending on casting and performance. In some sense, of course, the point was academic. For as Kazan would later ask: 'What would I say to Brando? Be less good.'

And good he was, in a way that was different from the ways he had been good before. Later, the actor would attribute his success to hard work of a conscious kind. 'I made a study of guys like Stanley Kowalski. You know, guys who work hard and have lots of flesh, having nothing supple about them. They never open their fists, really . . . They grip a cup of coffee like an animal would wrap a paw around it. They're heavily muscled in body and manner of speech. You see, Stanley Kowalski wasn't interested in how he said anything. He didn't give a damn how he said it. His purpose was to convey his idea. He had no awareness of himself at all . . .'

Well, yes. All that was certainly there – if we may judge a stage performance by its film record, made some three years later. But something more was operating, and it too was something that the role drew out of the actor's essential nature. 'He challenges not only the woman,' Kazan would later say, 'he challenges the whole system of politeness and good nature and good ethics and everything else . . . He did that in life. He never knew where the hell he was going to sleep, you didn't know who he was with, you didn't know who he was running away from or who he was angry about. You never knew. Every day there was a drama that he brought on the set with him.'

All of that appealed to Kazan, the tough, charming, very smart immigrant lad who had scuffled and scrapped to the top of his profession. And he recalls that he didn't have to do much to encourage this other migrant, a migrant not from foreign climes, but from cautious respectability, to rip away at genteel convention in whatever ways his spirit moved him. In his director's notes for the play, Kazan referred to Stanley as a 'hoodlum aristocrat', and his task, he remembers, consisted of doing nothing to discourage him from acting out all the impulses contained in that nice phrase.

One is obliged to report that Brando has for years denied the possibility that he found anything in his own nature that was analagous to Stanley's. 'Why, he's the antithesis of me . . . a man without any sensitivity, without any kind of morality except his own mewling, whimpering insistence on his own way,' he would tell an interviewer. There was fear as well as loathing in the performance, he would say. 'Kowalski was always right, and never afraid. He never wondered, he never doubted. . . . And he had the kind of brutal aggressiveness I hate. I'm afraid of it. I detest the character.'

Intellectually, that's doubtless true. But as Kazan has recently asked: 'What is a person to detest but his own faults? – I wish I weren't like that.' There is, of course, something else he may detest: the forces in his past that shaped – bent – that self. The most obvious element in this characterization, the stuff that was to become the basic source of Brando imitations for years to come, was the almost satanic satirical spirit he loosed on the fine literary-romantic pretensions of his visiting sister-in-law. His rooting sexuality had already knocked that nonsense out of Stella, and now, quite literally cocksure of himself, Stanley was glad to perform the same service for Blanche – resorting, of course, to rape after his verbal assaults had failed. Before that, however, his manic anger at Blanche's genteel airs, his paranoid suspicions of her past and of her future intentions, his sheer disgust at her lack of reality, becomes, in effect, an assault on the manners and morals of an entire class.

We cannot help thinking of the Brandos, with their guilty secrets and their striving for respectability, as

1947

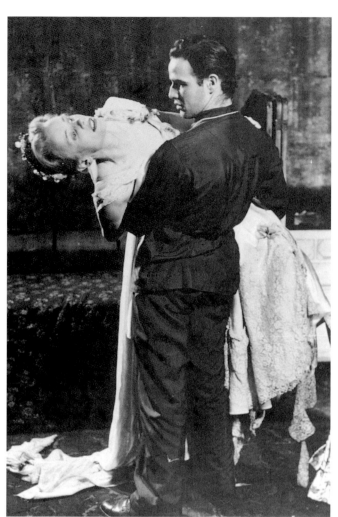

Marlon Brando and Jessica Tandy in Elia Kazan's Broadway production of Tennessee Williams's *A Streetcar Named Desire* (1947).

deeper dissatisfactions, the deeper hopelessness and cynicism. There was certainly nothing elegant about his sensualism, and there was nothing elegant about Brando's as he pursued his young actor's life. But they were similar in their quick and greedy grabs for the sweetness of the moment, their need to avoid thinking of the past or the future. As he thought about Stanley, Kazan also began to see him as a man ferociously defending what we have since learned to call a 'lifestyle', believing it a fortress that, if violated, would lead to his downfall. In the course of the play, as Kazan read it, he moves from rough, amiable acceptance of Blanche to outright hostility as he begins to see that her airs and pretensions threaten the defense-work he has constructed.

Thus were great riches brought to bear on this performance. But if, in it, Marlon Brando could not avoid himself or his past, it is also true that the elevated language of the piece, its setting, with its odor of the exotic, the melodramatic imperatives of its powerful structure, lent it just the right metaphorical distance for him, and helped to relieve the psychological pressures of its themes and subtexts. There is nearly always an element of luck in stardom, and *Streetcar* was this actor's luck – the right play at the right moment in his life, something he could handle, and live with, and yet also use to draw out of himself what needed now to come forth.

being at least cousins to Blanche, cousins, indeed, to almost all of us who came out of the same anxious provincial milieu. Let us imagine that Brando also found in *A Streetcar Named Desire* a symbolic representation of the basic family drama that was crucial in forming him. Was there not much of Dodie in Blanche – the drinking, the sexual teasing, the lost hopes that somehow must be kept alive in fantasy? And was there not something of his father in Stanley – the impatience with the impractical, the endless demands for a stern, realistic accounting of 'poetic' behavior, the threat, perhaps, of physical violence to enforce his version of reality on others?

Finally, was there not something of Brando's present self in his Stanley? In his notes, Kazan stressed Stanley's hedonism, his need to preoccupy himself with immediate physical pleasures in order to avoid confronting his

Who knew, who could even guess at the time, all the factors that had gone into the making of this production, this performance? What everyone could see was that something extraordinary was taking place on this stage. Even out of town, in New Haven and in Boston, *Streetcar* was a hit. Kim Hunter, that perfect Stella, would say later that 'we had to work hard against overconfidence,' that the company's chief anxiety was that we couldn't live up to the reputation the play had before it opened.' But they could, and did. Even the daily reviewers could not mistake the play's originality and power – and Brando's. It must have been – let's put it mildly – terribly fulfilling, a justification of all that he had been, and, more important, all that he had refused to be, across the first decades of his life.

CHAPTER THREE

AGE OF REASON

'**W**e who saw him in his first, shocking days believed in him not only as an actor, but also as an artistic, spiritual, and specifically American leader.'

Thus William Redfield, sometime colleague and close friend, looking back in sorrow, anger (and smugness) at Marlon Brando's career in his *Letters from an Actor* in 1967. That 'we' is not hyperbolic: Redfield accurately summarized what many of his theatrical generation expected of Brando. And the actor, with his preternatural sensitivity to other people's unspoken agendas, was not unaware of these entirely unrealistic yearnings.

They were a cruel burden to place on anyone, but most especially on a young man who would not turn twenty-five until after he had disembarked from *Streetcar*, a young man who had not, and never would, show the slightest inclination to lead anything, particularly a 'spiritual' revolution. His response was, or should have been, quite predictable.

Above A quiet moment with Vivien Leigh on the set of the film version of *A Streetcar Named Desire*. *Right* The serious young actor, who initially received the offers from Hollywood with scorn.

The young professional: Brando always looked for meaningful roles to explore, but on Broadway they were scarce.

In the theater he was – surprisingly – the responsible, dedicated acting professional. He did not miss performances, he worked hard and inventively to keep his work fresh, stayed on in his role longer than some people imagined he might. He also kept up with his acting classes. This kind of leadership – by example – was within his range in those days. In the rest of his life he clung desperately hard to that young actor's way of life he had embraced on his arrival in New York, and which had proved so congenial, so liberating, ever since. Again, one feels, he was setting an example. No one was going to catch him striking star poses, living big, talking big, throwing his weight around.

To his professionalism there is much testimony. Here is his co-star, Kim Hunter, as recorded by Lillian and Helen Ross in their book, *The Player*. 'It is a tremendous experience to play in relationship with him; he yanks you into his own sense of reality. For example . . . the way Marlon played the scene where Stanley goes through Blanche's trunk. Stanley had found out a little bit about her at that point in the play, and is starting to question her, and he begins to go through the things in her trunk, while Stella tries to protect her sister's belongings. Marlon never, never did that scene the same way twice during the entire run. He had a different sort of attitude toward each of the belongings every night; sometimes he would lead me into quite a fight with him, and other times I'd be seeing him as a silly little boy. I got worn out after many months in the play, but I never got bored . . .'

As he sought out Blanche's mystery, night after night, Brando, as we've seen, seems to have been seeking out the answers to some of the mysteries in his own life. It's the most reasonable explanation for his ferocious and lengthy engagement with the role. The fact that, aside from a larky summer stock tour in *Arms and the Man* in 1953, he never returned to the stage supports this view. Perhaps he did not look very hard, but clearly he never found another role that he felt could absorb (or divert) him sufficiently to balance the boredom (and terrors) of a long run.

That motivation probably extended to some of his other activities. The high school drop-out was, as he has remained, a devoted autodidact. Karl Malden shared a dressing room with him and remembered Brando immersing himself in heavy tomes about anthropology and psychology, rarely bothering with fiction less weighty than Dostoevsky.

This sobriety extended to what we might risk calling his world view. It was essentially an extension of his childhood and adolescent sympathy for the tormented and the damned. Stella Adler recalled going with him to see a film about bull fighting and casually remarking afterward that she was more sympathetic to the man than the beast. He did not speak to her for a year thereafter, she claimed, perhaps exaggerating. Brando himself would recall a yet more thought-provoking encounter with filmed images from this period. It was footage taken when the Nazi concentration camps were liberated by American troops. 'It was,' he said some thirty years later, 'the greatest trauma of my life. The film poured sulphuric acid on my hopes for the future of the human race. I was – and still am – shattered by the experience.'

For the moment at least, neither success nor despair interfered with his obligations to Stanislavski, though he left Stella Adler's tutelage – amicably – to join The Actor's Studio, which opened just two months before *Streetcar* did. There he was for a while a conscientious, and occasionally brilliant, student. Bobby Lewis dined out for years on his story of Brando's work in a scene from *Reunion in Vienna*. In an early version of the tale we find Lewis insisting on the actor doing something far out of his natural range, something, say, from Alfred Lunt's repertory: 'Where you have to be elegant, speak beautifully, play the prince with a monocle . . . I badgered him and badgered him, told him he could do it and had to do that kind of thing, even if he played Kowalskis all his life.' In a telling aside to his interviewer, Lewis observed: 'You know, Marlon and all those kids think if they speak well and move well they are compromising their manliness, that if they sweat and grunt they're manly.'

Brando and his scene partner, an actress named Joan Chandler, worked dutifully on their roles, but

procrastinated over performing in front of the class. Finally Lewis told them either to bring in their scene or to quit class. They rented appropriate period costumes, and Brando not only wore a monocle, but added a sword and a tiny mustache to his get-up. The results were not the comic fiasco many had expected. He and Chandler were, in fact, electrifying. The class burst into applause at the end of their turn. 'Well,' Lewis remembered, 'it was then that we knew Marlon was bigger than Kowalski. We knew he could do anything.'

We must not, of course, discount another explanation for his dedication to *Streetcar* and the perfection of his craft. We must suppose that even Marlon Brando was not, in those days, immune to the infinitely pleasurable possibilities opened up for him by the greatest personal triumph enjoyed by any actor in Broadway's immediate post-war era. We must imagine that the sheer fun of being the hottest ticket in town sustained him as much as his nightly exertions at the Ethel Barrymore Theater.

For public life doesn't get much better than it was for Brando in this first year of his fame. His achievement was handsomely recognized, by a knowledgeable, small, and therefore unthreatening public, and the word on him was slowly but comfortably spreading beyond the relatively narrow confines of Broadway. He was making what seemed to him good money ($550 a week), and there seems to be no question that his new prominence did him no harm in his romantic adventurings. Though he would later claim that after running for a couple of months in *Streetcar*, 'one night – dimly, dimly – I began to hear this roar,' he was not yet an international or even a full-scale national celebrity. He was still able to live as he chose and, more importantly, to move about as he chose, that is to say, freely and anonymously.

He remained devoted to his mother and his sisters. Dodie, on one of her absences from home, moved in with her son for a time, sharing vicariously in his success. And when his sisters had children he was often a doting baby-sitter for their offspring. He even achieved a curious rapprochement with his father. Because he was always broke (mainly because he was a soft touch for out-of-work colleagues) he began turning his weekly pay-checks over to Marlon Sr and living off an allowance the old man doled out. This was in one way astonishing, since their relationship was unimproved, but in another way it was not. Adolescents are used to living on allowances, and what Brando was clinging to, despite his grown-up success, was at best a post-adolescent lifestyle.

About the only things he was not eager to sample in those days were the life, luxuries, and nervous respectability of the upwardly mobile. On $150, which is

With Josanne Mariani-Berenger, the nineteen-year-old French model whom he nearly married in 1954. Although Brando shunned the press, his spectacular love life made good copy.

what Dad permitted him, Brando lived not as a star, not even as a working actor, but as one still aspiring. His dress remained a scandal, he lived in walk-ups in slovenly chaos, and his eating habits were strictly take-out. He was rarely alone, however. Rumors of homosexual behavior were rife during his early fame, but there is every evidence that they were started by his sometime room-mate in this period, wicked Wally Cox. There is also some evidence that Brando rather enjoyed these rumors. In any case, he remained devoted to Cox, no matter what gossip Wally started behind his back.

According to eye-witnesses his romantic life mostly involved young actresses, and it was by all accounts rich and varied, sometimes involving sweet serenades with the recorder he had taken to playing. It was also conducted in a communal context, for he continued to cling to the company of young actors, who generally tend to travel in packs. His door was nearly always open, and people constantly floated in and out, for he still loved to be the center of a group, just as he had in adolescence.

There was an element of manipulation – apparently benign – in his command of this crowd. He told Truman Capote that he made friends very warily, circling around and around a potential candidate for intimacy, touching then pulling back, then coming nearer again. In his infamous *New Yorker* profile of Brando, Capote quoted him thus: 'They don't know what's happening. Before they realize it, they're all entangled, involved. I have them. And suddenly, sometimes, I'm all *they* have. A lot of them, you see, are people who don't fit anywhere; they're not accepted, they've been hurt, crippled one way or another. But I want to help them, and they can focus on me.' At this point Brando used the curious phrase that gave Capote the title for his article. 'I'm the duke. Sort of the duke in my domain.'

In other words he had a star's retinue even before he was a star in the full sense of the word, though there is no evidence that he exercised the kind of sadistic control of his train that is not uncommon among the hugely celebrated. Yet there can be no doubt, either, that his needs were in certain respects as powerful as those to whom he extended his protection. Capote also quoted an anonymous 'past tenant on the ducal preserve' who observed that Brando never talked to more than one person at a time as he moved through his court. 'Makes you feel that you're under his protection and that your troubles and moods concern him deeply.' He added: 'You have to believe it; more than anyone I've known, he radiates *sincerity*.'

Capote's informant wondered what was in it for Brando? Then he shrewdly answered his own question. It was affection Brando was after. 'Affection that lends him authority over you. I sometimes think Marlon is like an orphan who later on in life tries to compensate by becoming the kindly head of a huge orphanage. But even outside this institution he wants everybody to love him.'

Not that Brando's young manhood was entirely devoted to compensatory behavior. Many of his pleasures were simply and perhaps predictably *jejeune*. He had, for example, a period of some twenty minutes in the middle of *Streetcar* when he was off-stage, and these he usually passed in the alley outside the theater, hanging out with

Something of a
physical culturist
in his stage
acting days,
Brando used to
organize
impromptu
boxing matches.
It was his
Streetcar
understudy Jack
Palance who
gave him his
broken nose.

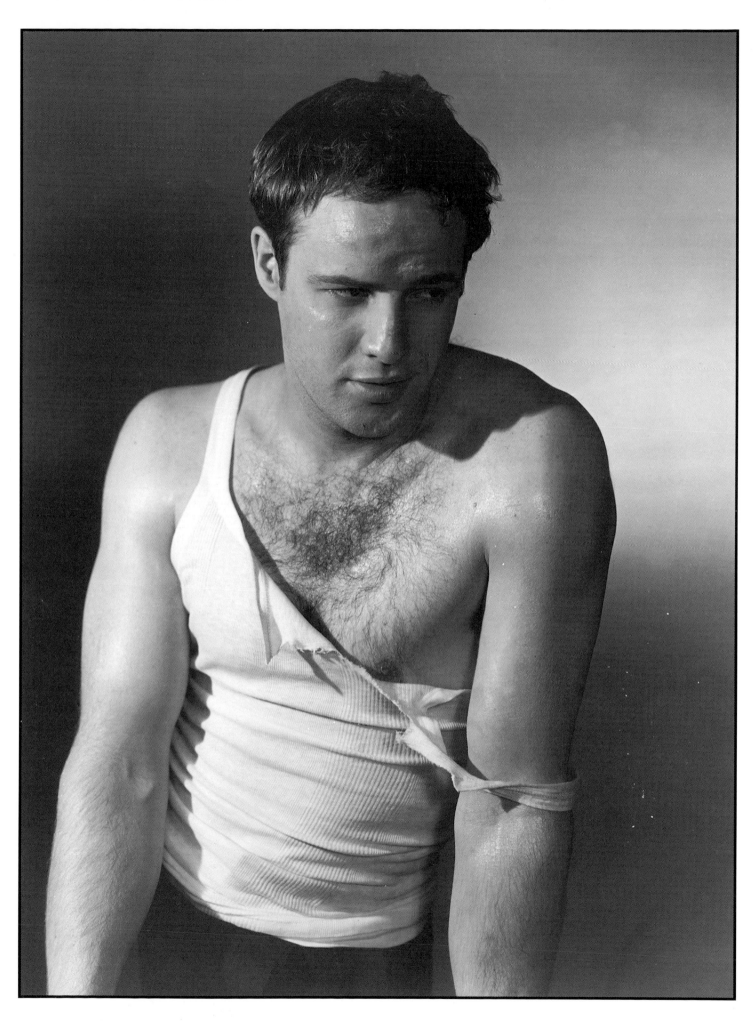

other idle members of the cast and crew. He was also something of a physical culturist in those days – as the old torn T-shirt stills attest – and he organized boxing matches among members of the company in the theater basement. In fact, he owes his nobly broken nose to Jack Palance, his understudy in *Streetcar*, who landed a solid punch in the course of one of these encounters.

His one indulgence was a motorcycle – a Harley, every boy's dream straddle. He was a familiar sight vrooming around the theater district aboard it. Jessica Tandy was once appalled to discover that his kindly offer of a lift home entailed hopping on the back of his bike. The responsible adults in his life, people like Irene Selznick and Edith Van Cleve, worried about accidents, since Brando had poor eyesight and refused to wear glasses. Younger colleagues were generally less pernickity, and he was arrested on one occasion for piling too many of them on the machine with him.

Looking back at all this from a time in which the excesses available to the suddenly celebrated include obscenely conspicuous consumption, one cannot supress a certain amount of amusement at the titillation, even scandalization, that was stirred up by this innocently Bohemian life, these trivial poses of rebellion. Indeed, Brando's desire to cling to what he knew and trusted, even though he surely saw that his success foredoomed the effort, can be read as a sign of integrity.

There may be no imperative to glide about in limousines or to lease a penthouse, but there is some small imperative for a man of twenty-five to start growing up, to accept the inevitability of adulthood, however reluctantly. That's particularly true in cases like Brando's. For his fear and loathing of 'phoniness' were, in ways Brando surely did not perceive, limiting. Acting, almost by definition, involves an embrace of phoniness. But if we perceive on Brando's behalf an obligation, owed primarily to himself, to try to transcend this attitude, we must also admit that at the time the American theater lacked the large numbers of institutions, performers, and other theatrical professionals, that were needed to help him break free of cultural constraints. The wiser

Left It was not the glamour of Hollywood which finally lured Brando away – temporarily, he believed – from Broadway, but the promise of greater artistic freedom.

heads among those who were close to Brando in those days (Adler, Bobby Lewis, Kazan) all seconded this point. Adler, for example, pointed out that Gerard Phillipe, in France, and Olivier, in England, had endless opportunities to challenge themselves and to grow by playing classics that remained part of a living tradition, thanks to their national theaters, and, indeed, to a commercial theater that still found it economically viable to mount new productions of these sustaining works.

Kazan would also observe, a few years later, 'It's not a natural thing for a man to be an actor now, as it was, say, in the nineteenth century.' Without the plays, playwrights, and directors to provide truly meaningful work, he said, 'there is something trivial about it.' He thought Brando's great predecessor, John Barrymore, had fallen into 'self-mockery', and Brando's potentially great contemporary, Richard Burton, into the idle pursuit of money in 'foolish' enterprises, precisely because there was so little grown-up work to do.

Unfortunately, the Stanislavsky tradition, at least as it was developing in New York at the time, with its stress on self-exploration and its emphasis on a rather limited and realistic repertory of plays, was of small help to Brando in dealing with this issue. It tended to keep his attention focused inward, and it did not often propose theatrical ventures that might catch his attention or stir his imagination. To put the point simply, the school of acting that had unquestionably helped him 'find himself', and to which he owed at least some part of his success, was no longer helpful in that regard.

None of which is, *per se*, an argument for going into the movies, though they certainly must have had an escapist appeal that Brando dared not speak aloud. In any case, the first offers from Hollywood began arriving immediately after *Streetcar* opened, and as he was expected to do, Brando received them scornfully.

Hollywood's prosperity, having achieved its height during the war years, and having enjoyed the greatest single year in its history between 1946 and 1948 (when ninety million movie tickets were sold every week), began to weaken visibly in the late Forties. In peacetime, even before television became the overwhelming medium, other diversions were drawing customers away from the movies; pre-war stars and the pre-war generic formulae were losing their hold on the mass audience; and the aging moguls who had managed the studios with conspicuous success for over two decades no longer seemed adaptable and energetic enough to cope with these changes. Moreover, in 1948, the studios signed a consent decree in a long-pending anti-trust action that obliged them, over the next few years, to sell off their economically stabilizing theater chains. This was a devastating blow to the industry's confidence.

The situation in Hollywood was suddenly analagous to that of Broadway. Both were institutions confronting a shrinkage in their audiences, and both appeared open to reform, possibly radical reform, as a result. Since the idealism of the Group Theater tradition had never been confined merely to a theory of acting, or to socially committed drama, some among its adherents certainly sensed the possibility that the long-awaited moment for full-scale revolution might be at hand.

Ultimately history would betray that hope. Adjustment, not revolution, would preoccupy Hollywood in subsequent decades. And Marlon Brando would be a particular victim of the large, false promises of freedom it offered, a particular victim of that curious blend of indulgence and oppressiveness with which it treats people whose talent simultaneously tempts and terrifies it. Still, it was obviously becoming possible for actors like him to avoid some of the traps in which their predecessors had been caught. It was not necessary any more to live in Los Angeles in order to work in the movies, and it was not necessary to contract oneself to a single studio for a seven-year term. You could accept and reject projects freely, return to the stage whenever you liked, do or say what you pleased without a studio hierarchy monitoring your every move. It was now also possible, at least in theory, to work full time in movies that aspired to make serious social, political, moral, and cultural statements.

It was not that Hollywood had failed to make such pictures before. It was not that all of the movies it was now beginning to make on 'adult' themes were actually preferable, by any standards, to, say, a Preston Sturges comedy or, for that matter, *Double Indemnity*. What was happening was a relatively slight mood shift; a modest trend that, as it worked itself out in the mid and late Fifties, did not fulfill its promises in ways that could sustain a career like the one Brando wanted to pursue, or, for that matter, fully engage the most sophisticated segment of the audience.

Whether we are discussing *The Lost Weekend* or *The Best Years of Our Lives*, *Crossfire* or *Gentleman's Agreement*, *The Snake Pit* or *Pinky*, the movies were beginning to take up, in an appropriately sober manner, issues that, not incorrectly, serious people believed needed to be addressed by a mass art. That, taken together with the economic evidence suggesting the motion picture industry had to make new kinds of arrangements with creative people and find new ways of appealing to its audience, was encouraging to the new theatrical generation. Maybe, just maybe, it would be possible to work in the movies without 'selling out'.

Not that Brando leaped at the chance. A screen test he made in this period still exists. In it he plays, rather warily, a young criminal urging his girlfriend to join him in fleeing the law. His 'soft, girlish' side is very much in evidence here, and so is a desire to show that he can enunciate as clearly as the next guy. But the work is extremely tentative, not at all that of a young actor determined to take Hollywood by storm. An interview, included on the same reel, finds him in a dark, neat suit and tie, and in a nervously affable mood, also quite unprepossessing.

In fact, and perhaps predictably, Brando's first serious flirtation with the movies was not directed toward Hollywood. It occurred in 1949, after he finally left *Streetcar*. It was free-spirited, ambitious, and, in its particulars, quite marvelously hare-brained. The French director, Claude Autant-Lara, who specialized in historical drama and adaptations of classic fiction, was contemplating a production of Stendhal's *The Red and the Black*, and he invited Brando to visit locations in France. Hoping to lure him into the lead, the director offered the actor expenses and a small salary for three weeks to

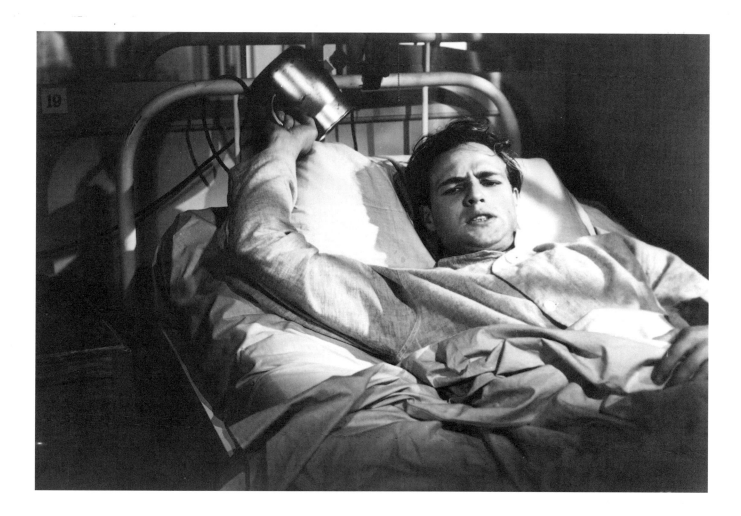

Brando's first screen role was a suitably serious one, as a paraplegic war veteran in *The Men* (1950), a liberal-minded film directed by Fred Zinnemann.

familiarize himself with the people and places of the planned production. Autant-Lara was the kind of formalist the New Wave would shortly invent itself to oppose, and Brando soon drifted out of his orbit.

The project in which he at last agreed to make his film debut carried a solid promise and, when all was said and done, a decent measure of fulfillment. *The Men* represented a reasonably good early example of the new Hollywood independence, the new Hollywood 'seriousness'. Set largely in the paraplegic ward of a veterans' hospital, it soberly took up a sobering subject: the attempt by grievously wounded soldiers of the late war to reintegrate with society and, perhaps more importantly, to reintegrate their permanently damaged

bodies with minds and spirits whose wounds, the film tried to show, need not be permanent.

This, obviously, was a story to appeal to a heart ever sensitive to the outcast and the downcast, and it was also a project in which a serious young actor could easily justify taking part. It must have been with a sense of relief at ending his own, and everyone's, anxiety about his next move, that Brando committed to *The Men* on the basis of an outline – and the offer of a $40,000 salary, which seemed huge to him in those innocent, relatively non-inflationary times. Indeed, Brando joked about it. 'I don't have the character to turn down such big money,' he said.

As he left for Hollywood he reassured an anxious theater community that his relocation was only temporary: 'I may do a picture now and again, but mostly I intend to work on the stage.' As if to make certain he would avoid

1950

Brando's character in *The Men* is an embittered man who, with the help of his girlfriend, played by Teresa Wright, gradually overcomes his anger and humiliation. To prepare for the role he lived for weeks in a veterans' hospital.

all temptation, his entire wardrobe for the trip consisted of white T-shirts and blue jeans, plus one suit with holes in the knees and a rip in the seat of the pants. His accommodation was the couch in an aunt's living-room in Eagle Rock, distinctly unfashionable suburbia. Even the trim young agent, Jay Kantor, assigned to this difficult case by MCA, turned out to be, beneath the dark suit the agency insisted all its representatives wear, a soulmate – a shrewd and protective friend who, even after he became a production executive, remained a trusted adviser. To put it simply, Brando had gone to Hollywood, but he did not 'go Hollywood'.

The atmosphere surrounding the production to which he reported was austere by traditional industry standards. The producer was Stanley Kramer, a sometime film editor and post-production supervisor who, after Signal Corps service in the war, formed a company committed to low-budget films about serious matters. His earlier releases, *The Champion* – about the spiritual corruption of a boxer – and *Home of the Brave* – about racial prejudice in the army – were very much in Hollywood's new spirit and had achieved quite respectful critical attention and reasonable box office returns. *The Men* was written, after much first-hand research in a hospital, by the literate and liberal-minded Carl Foreman, and it was directed, mainly on location in a VA hospital, by Fred Zinnemann, one of the most meticulous film craftsmen to emerge in the

Fifties. The cast mixed professional actors with actual paraplegics, whose brave and often touching presence lent the movie a high degree of realism. In all obvious respects, then, this was a more than usually conscientious film, socially useful in its plea for the humanity of the handicapped and melodramatically powerful in its narrative.

Brando joined in the spirit of the production. He prepared carefully for his role, spending some weeks living on the paraplegic ward of the Van Nuys veterans' hospital, learning to manipulate a wheelchair and, more importantly, learning what it felt like to be unable to move about unaided. On set there was some initial concern over his throw-away rehearsal style, some tension between him and the other professional actors in the company. And one has the feeling that the austere Zinnemann, though respecting Brando's gift, never warmed to him personally. Still, when the camera turned, Brando was there, with all his power mobilized and focused, and his work won over even those doubters who never took to him personally.

Our first ever glimpse of Brando on the screen presents him, in fact, as a young infantry lieutenant, named Ken Wilocek, leading his platoon into a European village that appears to have been deserted by the Germans. His uniform is Hollywood-neat and the angles on him are conventionally heroic, very much those of the standard World War Two combat film. The idea, of course, is to set up a contrast between our recent fantasies of war and the realities of its aftermath, with which the rest of the film is concerned. Equally important is the contrast that is set up between Ken's confident vigor and the near-helpless condition in which he will spend the rest of the movie. The sequence ends on a broadly ironic note, for it is as Ken turns to gesture his soldiers forward that he is shot by an unseen sniper.

Blackness. And then a voice – Brando's: 'That's funny, that's very funny. I was afraid I was going to die. Now I'm afraid I'm going to live. . . .' The accent is Stanley Kowalski's, only a trifle diluted. But it is also entirely appropriate. For Ken is also a 'Polack', also of working-class origins. There, however, the resemblance between

the two characters ends. For Ken is an orphan, whose lack of family ties may have had a liberating effect on him, permitting him to try to work his way up through society. Before the war he attended college (possibly on an athletic scholarship), and it is also possible that his army commission originally seemed to represent another lucky break for him, something he could trade on in a post-war civilian career. Finally, it is obvious that his extremely respectable girlfriend, Ellen (Teresa Wright), represented, for him, a step upward as well.

In other words, a class tragedy provides a subtext for physical tragedy. The sniper's bullet has put Ken back where he started. Only now there is no way to escape: no learned behavior that can cover the humiliation of being handicapped. His only defenses seem to be anger, cynicism, withdrawal.

The movie is, in fact, entirely about getting Ken to overcome these attitudes, to achieve what so many 1950s movie heroes had to achieve: psychological 'adjustment' – no matter what the situation. Early in the film Ken is moved out of his private hospital room on to a ward, where socialization begins with ragging and ribbing by fellow paraplegics. Soon Ellen is visiting, applying the poultice of sweet patience to his problems. He keeps sending her away – and not politely either. She does not take the hint.

At one point in the film someone tells Ken, 'Before you can change the world, you have to accept the world as it is,' which is one way of stating this film's theme. After a few setbacks – the death of one of the most popular men on the ward, a humiliating wedding night (paraplegics, we learn, cannot handle alcohol), a drunken driving charge – Ken Wilocek does indeed achieve this peculiar state of grace. At the end of the film, as he faces an obstacle he cannot navigate in his wheelchair, Ellen asks simply, 'Do you want me to help you up the step?' and he replies, even more simply, 'Please.'

Here we begin to confront the movie's major flaw, which is caution. Or, to put it another way, there is no wildness about it: very little of the black humor that we might logically expect to find in young men whom chance has singled out for a dreadful punishment; and, even worse, not much of the still blacker despair with which one also imagines them grappling. The ideal to which everyone is encouraged is pep, good cheer, normality in the face of abnormality. It seems, indeed, that once a man reacquires his get-up-and-go, despite the fact that he cannot get up and go anywhere unaided, he is, so far as the institution is concerned, cured, ready for a return to 'normal' (i.e. middle-class) society.

Vocally, Brando does his best to play that line. It has not generally been remarked that his famous mumble becomes less and less pronounced as the film proceeds, that by the end of the film his tone is firm, even 'normal'. Far from being carelessly mannered, his verbal style in *The Men* is carefully calculated. What Brando is doing is called acting, and it is acting of an order one still sees only rarely in the movies, in that it conveys something about the spiritual state of his character in quite a delicate way. But in other respects Brando's performance keeps subverting the smooth, straight-ahead progress to which the narrative aspires. One just does not quite believe that Ken Wilocek, as Brando plays him, all rage and self-pity, could be reached, and turned around, as quickly, and by such simple therapeutic devices as the

film employs – the hearty camaraderie of his buddies, the patient love of his sweetheart, a little psycho-babble.

It is Brando's preparation that is largely responsible for the way he unbalances the film. One of the most famous Brando anecdotes dates from this period. As the story is told, he joined some of his new friends in a wheelchair excursion to a nearby bar, where they were approached by a drunken woman who urged upon them the healing powers of evangelical religion. God, she insisted, could often cure what medicine considered hopeless conditions. Brando encouraged her, before pretending, finally, an on-the-spot conversion. At which point he struggled to his feet, faking a miraculous restoration of his ability to walk. He then (and here various accounts diverge) tap-danced through the bar, or leaped capering on to one of its tables – something hilariously dramatic, anyway – much to the delight of his actually crippled companions.

Across the years *The Men* retains its largest interest as Brando's screen debut. In retrospect, considered in relation to what had preceded it, and what has followed it, Brando's work is utterly original: a redefinition, an expansion of the issues a star performance might embrace.

1951

On the set of *A Streetcar Named Desire* with Elia Kazan, his director in the 1951 Hollywood film as he had been in the Broadway production.

As Stanley Kowalski in *Streetcar*, brutally stripping away the pretensions of Vivien Leigh's Blanche Dubois. Although the censors lowered the film's sexual heat, the play's power survived.

For anything comparable one needs to reach back to quite a different piece of work, that of James Cagney in *The Public Enemy* (which was not a debut), to see a movie actor exploring, and implying, the unwritten deeps and darks of a screen character, extending the boundaries of the acceptable a perceptible degree.

Of such achievements, Brando did not speak. It was known at the time that he was unhappy with the film's ending, apparently made more hopeful than it was in the original script. But in a later interview he was content to call *The Men* 'worth doing' for the attention it brought to

an ignored minority. It remains one of the rare films Brando has not subsequently decried for failing to live up to what it initially seemed to promise either to its subject-matter or to him as an actor. *The Men* did not make Brando a movie star in the same sense that *Streetcar* made him a Broadway star. It was a liberal-minded movie that did not entirely stifle the actor's radical spirit, but did manage to contain it. We reserved judgement.

But not for long. For Brando almost immediately went into the movie version of *Streetcar*. Just as there had been nothing like this performance on the stage before, there had been nothing like it on the screen, either – no comparable blend of menace and black comedy and near-parodistical maleness. It is hard to believe that any nuance of Tennessee Williams's writing was lost in the extraordinarily faithful screen adaptation. Indeed, the sweaty intimacy of the hot, over-crowded French Quarter apartment may have been heightened by the intimacy with which the camera viewed it, though Kazan thought audiences experienced a greater sense of entrapment with these tormented souls in live performance. He also conceded, however, that in one of the play's crucial moments, when Stanley forces a naked light bulb close to Blanche's face, to reveal its lines, her psychological nakedness (and her terror) was powerfully enhanced by the close-up camera. One believes, as well, that it must have revealed nuances in Brando's performance that were lost on the stage. This debate is, however, pointless – we innocents were charged up by the screen *Streetcar* in the same way that the stage version had electrified 'sophisticated' Broadway.

But, for all its importance, there is, curiously, little anecdotal material about the filming of *Streetcar*. Jessica Tandy was the only performer not asked to repeat her stage performance, for independent producer Charles Feldman yielded to studio pressure for a more widely known name, and everyone, for box office insurance, settled on Vivien Leigh (who had played the role in London). Kazan expressed regrets about hurting Tandy's feelings (and career), but she was, in those days, virtually unknown to movie audiences. Moreover, Kazan, not particularly wanting to re-do the piece, thought maybe a newcomer in the company would stir his imagination.

In the end, a multi-story set that successfully replicated, in movie terms, Jo Mielziner's famous Broadway setting, was built on a Warner Bros sound stage. It proved felicitous in ways that may not have been predicted; the look of the film has a nice dislocating quality. Not quite a photographed stage play, it is not quite a film, in the usual sense of the term, either.

Vivien Leigh also proved a felicitous choice. She gave Kazan a few problems during the first week or two of production, when she refused to abandon what he regarded as bad habits she had acquired doing Blanche

on-stage, but he soon settled her down. 'She had,' he later wrote, 'a small talent, but the greatest determination to excel of any actress I've known. She'd have crawled over broken glass if she thought it would help her performance.' And that, in effect, she did.

On the whole, production proceeded smoothly, though Brando twice suffered minor injuries – once in the bowling alley sequence, when he couldn't extricate his thumb from a ball as he let it fly; a bit more seriously when he suffered a dislocated shoulder in the fight scene, where his poker partners have to wrestle the drunken Stanley into a cold shower.

The more significant troubles that afflicted the film took place either away from the set or after shooting was completed. It was while working on it that Kazan got the first hint of the political problems that would soon engulf him and permanently mar his reputation. For it was while he was in Hollywood that the radical right, led by Cecil B. De Mille, made an assault on the Directors Guild, seeking to recall its president, Joseph L. Mankiewicz, and impose a loyalty oath on its members. Kazan, a sometime Communist, was one of their chief targets, and he ducked a confrontation. But he also understood that a time would come when he would be unable to avoid a confrontation with his political past, could not avoid a painful public break with the Stalinists and, eventually, the opprobrium they furiously orchestrated against him and the others who testified about their past political affiliations (and affiliates).

Before his reputation was damaged, however, his picture itself was, in his view, damaged. He and the studio had maneuvered the *Streetcar* script past the Breen office, enforcers of the industry's increasingly odious self-censorship code. Explicit references to the homosexual lover and the nymphomania that were part of Blanche's past were excised (though clear implications of both remained), and the rape scene – which Breen had wanted eliminated – was staged less brutally than it had been on Broadway. Now that the picture was finished, however, the final cut ran afoul of the enforcer's enforcers, the Catholic Legion of Decency. The motion picture code,

Right Brando on Kowalski: 'He never wondered, he never doubted ... and he had the kind of brutal aggressiveness I hate.'

written by a Catholic priest and largely administered by Catholic laymen, had been drafted mainly to avoid open conflict with the Legion, to shape scripts and edit finished films in such a way that they would avoid its 'C' (or condemned) rating, which effectively triggered a Catholic boycott. But the shrewd Martin Quigley, publisher of exhibitor trade journals, friend of Cardinal Spellman among other princes of the church and, in fact, the man who had invented the code almost two decades earlier, was proposing just such a rating.

He probably felt he had no choice. As an adaptation of a famous and much-honored play, one that anyone could see represented an expansion of all previous definitions of what was acceptable subject-matter on stage and screen by a new generation of artists, *Streetcar* was a more than usually visible enterprise, one on which the Catholic moralists were obliged to take a stand. Moreover, as a lapsed Catholic, Tennessee Williams was, for them, an irresistible target.

Equally significant was the temper of the times. Both the Code administration and the Legion were beginning to feel what would ultimately become an irresistible pressure for change. Foreign films, full of material forbidden to American movie-makers, were proving to have a large appeal to the most loyal members of the shrinking movie audience – adolescents and the older, more educated crowd who were beginning to accept the notion that film was an art. Moreover, within the American industry itself there was a growing sense that the presentation of more openly erotic material and the use of more realistic language were a requisite for survival. On the high road, movie people argued for this loosening of outdated standards in the name of artistic freedom; on the low, they could see it was a way of differentiating their products from those of their great new competitor, television. This discontent also encouraged the Catholics to take a stand here and now, on this eagerly anticipated work.

So, with Feldman and the studio in collusion, an editor was set to work behind Kazan's back, trimming the picture to Legion specifications. These were men for whom accommodating censors was a normal aspect of business. Particular attention was paid to the relationship between Stanley and Stella, for their unquenchable sexual heat seemed to the churchmen as great a threat to morality as Stanley's brutal, unhinging rape of Blanche.

Kazan repeatedly challenged Feldman and Warner Bros, seeking to put some spine into them. He even confronted Quigley directly, arguing that 'Williams had his own morality, that he was – and his film was – an example of art serving a strong moral personality.' But all remained unmoved. Kazan recalled Quigley insisting over and over again on 'the preeminance of the moral order over artistic considerations.' Ultimately, Kazan appealed to the court of last resort, the public. He wrote a letter to the *New York Times*, exposing the issue.

All of this was unavailing: the picture was cut, though perhaps not as seriously as it might have been. But the censorship was unavailing as well: the vividness of Williams' characters and the force of his language and, yes, his morality, could not be blurred or blunted by the censors. Stanley Kowalski and Blanche Dubois are modern archetypes. And, from the moment this movie went into general release, so was Marlon Brando.

That moment, however, was more than usually delayed by the lengthy process of reaching accommodation with the censors. Something like a year passed between the completion of principal photography and the film's premiere. Ultimately, of course, *Streetcar* would become a major critical and commercial success, culminating in no fewer than twelve Academy Award nominations, including one for Brando, though Hollywood, teaching the bumptious boy a lesson, withheld his Oscar (and Kazan's) while awarding the prize to all of the film's other major players (Vivien Leigh, Kim Hunter, and Karl Malden). But in the meantime Brando was granted one last year of freedom from full-scale movie stardom; one more year in which he could continue to employ the strategies he had more or less successfully employed to evade the responsibilities that had been thrust on him when he attained theatrical stardom.

Right However much he hated the character of Stanley Kowalski, the role brought Brando instant stardom when *A Streetcar Named Desire* was finally released, following its censorship problems, in 1951.

CHAPTER FOUR

GOLDEN AGE

Looking back on 1950 with such perspective as five decades may afford, we can see that as the period began Marlon Brando was, all unknowing, already embarked on one of those rare, brief cycles of good fortune that few actors ever enjoy – a period when everything they do turns out to be the right thing to have done. This process began for Brando with *The Men*, released in July 1950. *Streetcar*, when it finally emerged from its trial by censorship in the fall of 1951, would hugely enhance it. Thereafter, *Viva Zapata, Julius Caesar, The Wild One,* and, in 1954, the culminating *On the Waterfront* would, each in its way, confirm his uniqueness and his archetypicality – those seemingly contradictory qualities that are the basis of great and authentic stardom.

Brando pores over a script in the theater. Learning his lines would become more and more of a problem as his career went on, leading to some extreme strategies.

Right The menacing Johnnie in *The Wild One* (1954). In retrospect this may seem the least of Brando's early films, but in terms of his career it is among the most important.

For all of these were films that combined serious intent with conscientious craftsmanship; all were films for the press and public to conjure with, however they fared critically and at the box office; and all were films that burned at least a few powerful images permanently into the mind.

In 1950, whatever satisfactions he felt about his work in his first two films, Brando could sensibly retreat to New York after completing *Streetcar* and pick up his old life, as if nothing had changed. He did rent a somewhat more spacious apartment than before (though it was still a cold water flat), taking in two new room-mates. One was Wally Cox. The other was Russell. Russell the raccoon, that is. The creature has become a legend within the Brando legend – a messy, nasty little guy who appears to have been the only animal utterly insusceptible to Brando's famous way with them. He bit. He scratched. He clawed. Unpredictably. Eventually, he drove Cox out of the apartment. Finally, even Brando gave up on him. But for a couple of years the actor and the animal were inseparable. Brando even brought Russell along when he went west to shoot his next movie.

That, however, was a winter and a spring away. For the moment he filled his days and nights in his accustomed fashion: large groups of friends gathered to goof off with him; a number of young actresses appeared and disappeared in his life; The Actor's Studio continued to claim his largest professional interest. There he studied direction as well as acting. He staged the first act of *Hedda Gabler* (resetting it in a crumbling Southern mansion – perhaps in tribute to Williams's influence), and he appeared in one well-recalled acting exercise as the aged Professor Sebryakov in *Uncle Vanya*, wearing pince-nez, stooped under the weight of years and the many volumes he carried for his entrance. What people remembered from the performance was what, increasingly, one would remember from his later, more public works – a breathtaking behavioral moment. Trying to juggle his books and get at a pad and pencil, Brando's professor would drop first one volume, then another in an inventive, comic, and finally quite touching display of the character's absent-minded unworldliness.

While Brando idled, however, his mentor Elia Kazan was, characteristically, hard at work on what would turn out to be the least well remembered, but in some respects the most interesting of Brando's early films, the one that would eventually be known as *Viva Zapata*. In Kazan's account, he had first thought of making a film about Emiliano Zapata, the Mexican revolutionary, as early as 1944. Zapata's peasant background stirred his imagination – he drew an analogy between the unyielding harshness of Morelos Province and the equally bleak landscapes of Anatolia from which his own Greek family had emigrated in roughly the same period. Finally, he found a political metaphor in Zapata's life that awakened his controversial instincts. In Kazan's reading of that life, Zapata voluntarily renounced power after the revolution succeeded. He retreated to his home ground, oversaw land reform there, and was assassinated by troops loyal to the very government he had helped put in place. Kazan, whose youthful flirtations with Communism had long since turned to liberal anti-Communism, saw a parallel between Zapata's fate and that of the idealists who had supported the Russian Revolution and had then been betrayed by Stalin in its aftermath.

The idea of doing a movie about Zapata was not a new one. It had been proposed to MGM as early as 1938. Shelved during the war, the Zapata project was revived in 1947, by producer Jack Cummings, one of Louis B. Mayer's nephews. He began envisioning Ricardo Montalban in the lead and engaged the Stalinist writer, Lester Cole, to draft the screenplay.

Alas for Cole, the project did not move far beyond this preliminary stage, for just as he was setting to work on his first draft screenplay he was summoned before the 1947 House Un-American Activities Committee hearings on Communism in the movie industry. He became, of course, one of the Hollywood Ten. MGM almost immediately dismissed him and joined with the other studios in blacklisting him and his cohorts.

By this time Kazan had discovered that John Steinbeck shared his enthusiasm for the Zapata legend; indeed, the novelist had been approached by a Mexican company to write a script based on it

Right A 1950 portrait for *Life* magazine by Philippe Halsman, who later recalled that before the shoot Brando enjoyed a breakfast of seven poached eggs.

in 1945. Kazan prevailed on him to attempt a screenplay on speculation, with the understanding that he, a hot property in Hollywood at the time, would help sell it. When it was done, in 1950, he brought Steinbeck and his first draft to Darryl F. Zanuck, chief of production at Twentieth Century-Fox. By this time, Fox, perhaps because Kazan had been expressing interest in Zapata for so long, possibly for other reasons, had acquired MGM's Zapata material for $60,000.

On the basis of Steinbeck's first draft script, Zanuck gave him a $20,000 advance, with a promise of $75,000 more if a revised scenario went into production, and Kazan and the writer headed for Mexico to scout locations and the possibilities of co-operation with Mexican film union leaders in the film. They were turned away by the unions. Communists had a dominant influence in these organizations, and they had long since appropriated Zapata (whose historical relationship to Marxism of any kind is dubious) for their revolutionary mythology. They were not going to let a pair of anti-Stalinist leftists, whose work would not treat the party line kindly, exploit a treasured symbol.

Clearly, the Zapata project was acquiring subtexts long before it had a generally agreed-upon text. The Steinbeck-Kazan version, as it finally evolved through several drafts, marks the first (but also the last) attempt by the anti-Communist left to respond to their sectarian enemies by showing, albeit metaphorically, how Stalinism inevitably corrupts the revolutionary process. In other words, though no one connected with the project saw it as such, the effort to recount on screen the story of a man whose life is so enigmatic that its few known facts are open to almost any interpretation, comes to seem in retrospect a symbolic turning-point in the socio-political history of American movies.

There is, of course, an irony in this: neither at MGM nor at Fox did any executive care much about the political games their hirelings were playing. Except for the war years, when their Popular Front rhetoric suited everyone's needs, Hollywood's Stalinists had always been forced to speak in metaphors, and their bosses knew that almost without any conscious effort on their part those

could be muddled and blunted by the very process of picture-making – rewriting, reshooting, re-editing. Their interest, ever and always, was in simple, straightforward story-telling.

But it was another habit of the moguls' minds that saved Kazan's project. That was their dislike of having their wills thwarted by outsiders. When it became clear that there was no hope of assistance from Mexican sources for *Zapata*, Kazan feared that Zanuck would cancel the film. It was a risky venture economically, and some subvention from below the border would have alleviated those risks. Moreover, Mexico and the rest of Central and South America were obviously an important market for this picture. Without the endorsement implied by official sanction of the production, those markets might well be adversely affected. But Zanuck was not going to be intimidated by far-away figures with strange-sounding names. The Texas side of the border could easily double for Mexico, he suggested. By this time, Kazan was convinced that the House Un-American Activities Committee would soon summon him to testify on his leftist past, and he told Zanuck that public exploration of his political past might taint the picture. Zanuck then called in a pair of high-ranking Fox executives and asked them if people on the lot perceived this enterprise as 'Communistic'. Assured that no one did, Zanuck indicated that he was not going to tolerate meddling from Washington either. If any meddling was to be done, it was Darryl Francis Zanuck who would do it.

And he did. As soon as he had given Kazan the go-ahead, he began complaining about the director's ideas for casting. Brando and Julie Harris, Kazan's first choice for the role of Josefa, Zapata's bride, were made to film a test in New York. The production chief complained that he couldn't understand either of them. Zanuck also thought that, at $100,000, Brando was overpriced, since he did not believe that *Streetcar* would turn out to be the sensation it would soon become. The spectre of Tyrone Power was raised. Or, as an alternative, Zanuck proposed Anthony Quinn (who eventually worked in the picture – and won a supporting actor Oscar – as Emiliano Zapata's brother, Eufemio).

With Anthony Quinn, Lou Gilbert and Harold Gordon in *Viva Zapata* (1952), the story of the Mexican revolutionary Emiliano Zapata. To give an edge to their performances, director Elia Kazan sowed distrust between Brando and Quinn, who played his brother, Eufemio.

In order to obtain Zanuck's consent to Brando, Kazan had to give up on Harris and accept contract player Jean Peters in her stead. Even so, once the picture began shooting the head of production kept up a steady chorus of complaint: Kazan was falling behind schedule; he didn't like Brando's moustache; he still couldn't understand him. And so on.

To begin with, Brando took seriously the issues of make-up and accent. The former went much further than the matter of his mustache. His coloring was extremely dark, he had the make-up man flare his nostrils and impart a slant to his eyes. In fact, he quite closely approximated the image of the revolutionist as it had been stylized in portraits and murals by Diego Riviera and the other Mexican radical painters. Brando worked equally hard on his accent; it was not the usual matter of erratically stretching heez ees. His vocal manner was much richer and subtler than that. To put the point simply, he was not giving an impression, he was attempting a characterization. For the first time

on screen, but scarcely the last, he was entering Paul Muni country.

But these were superficials. It is the spirit of his performance, disturbing to others besides Zanuck at the time, that imparts much of the movie's continuing claim on us. He was not a conventional revolutionary firebrand – there is no reckless *machismo*, no beloved roguishness here. Rather, this is a performance in which a pair of more interesting forces are in conflict. On the one hand, Zapata is shown to be a man harboring personal as well as idealistic ambitions; his attraction to Josefa is to some degree based on her middle-class status and the opportunity she offers for him to rise above his station. On the other hand, Brando's Zapata is full of the peasant's watchful wariness and the illiterate's sense that words can be used to spin an entrapping web. (One of the film's more touching scenes is the wedding night of Emiliano and Josefa, where he asks her to teach him to read, since he fears the educated leaders of the revolution he is joining: 'My horse and my rifle won't help me.')

The touching scene on their wedding night in which Emiliano asks his bride, played by Jean Peters, to teach him to read — knowing that as an illiterate he will be helpless in the political struggle ahead.

1952

Brando got some help on the part from Anthony Quinn. Their relationship was edgy, but Quinn is, after all, half-Mexican, and he had almost as a birthright certain attitudes that Brando needed to absorb. And Kazan, justifiably, took some credit for at least one aspect of his star's work. 'I spoke a few words of help: "A peasant does not reveal what he thinks. Things happen to him and he shows no reaction. He knows if he shows certain reactions he'll be marked 'bad' and may be killed." And so on.' But, as the director observed, no one entirely directs Brando: 'You release his instinct and give it a shove in the right direction.' He would, in those days, get the idea before it was fully enunciated, turn away, think about it and then take it further than the director imagined he might, perhaps further than the actor himself could predict, since, as Kazan put it, 'His gifts go beyond his knowledge.'

This anti-revolutionary revolutionist was also a very Fifties kind of a figure – although, this early in the decade, we were perhaps less aware of that than we would be later, after we had seen many a good man in the movies, and in popular fictions of all sorts, turn his back on large enterprises, the better to tend his own garden. But it may be that Brando's Zapata was the first to articulate that message, in the process implying the exhaustion of the old left's energies as well as its metaphors.

Kazan and Steinbeck were surely not so prescient that they saw, as of 1951, that the behavior of their principal character was going to prove generationally predictive, that young people would soon learn to distrust great ideas, great causes, great men. But the two did understand that conscience seeks belief, requires it as a bulwark against selfishness and anarchy. So they gave Zapata this speech to his followers: 'You're always looking for leaders, strong men without faults. There aren't any. They change. They desert. They die. There are no leaders but yourselves. A strong people is the only lasting strength.'

It works dramatically, in the context of the movie. And as a generalization it is indubitable. One might even translate it into the politics of the moment without too much discomfort. What in fact seems most interesting about the movie is its quite specific and quite sophisticated criticism of the Stalinist mentality. Indeed, nothing offered in popular entertainment in that era of no-nothing anti-Communism, compares with it. I don't think most of us noticed it, so focused were we on Zapata's struggles with his conscience. In any case, most of us were not then politically shrewd enough to know what to make of the character known as Fernando. But he does carry much of what Kazan and Steinbeck most urgently wanted to say politically.

Played by Joseph Wiseman, he appears out of nowhere, wearing a Gringo suit, carrying a typewriter, and looking for some native unrest to turn into a full-scale revolution. Given his way with words and his love of war, he seems for a while to be a Trotsky-like figure. But no, as the story develops, he takes on a more Stalinesque outline – while Zapata, of course, becomes something like this revolution's Trotsky. Like his model, Stalin, Fernando is not quite at the center of the revolution's ruling councils. Rather, from its fringe he constantly whispers an evil realism into the ears of its principal leaders. It is he who proposes the assassination of the liberal leader of the provisional post-revolutionary government, Francisco Madero (read Kerensky), whose execution is one of the film's masterful sequences. And after Zapata exiles himself from leadership it is Fernando who understands that, like Trotsky, a man of Zapata's popularity cannot be tolerated as a potential rallying-point for 'counter-revolution'. He is present when Zapata (who, it is hinted, is aware of what awaits him, and may welcome death as the ultimate release from the temptations of temporal power, the ultimate means of asserting spiritual power) is lured into his final, fatal ambush – another magnificent directorial set piece. Be that as it may, without this wily antagonist, Zapata's martyrdom would not be nearly so effective. We need Fernando's worship of power to ennoble Zapata's rejection of power.

And the film's conclusion, with Zapata's body being dumped with a resonant thump on the wellhead in the center of his town square, while peasant women in black watch impassively, and its coda, in which his beloved white stallion is seen galloping free in the hills, symbol of a spirit free at last of the world's constraints and importunities, is, indeed, tragically and romantically potent.

The picture was reviewed reasonably well, largely because of the reputations of its writer, director, and star for serious work, and, like Quinn, Brando was nominated for an Oscar, though he did not win. It also opened well, but it had weak legs and disappeared from the theaters quite quickly, even though it remained a staple in the revival houses throughout the decade.

For all its metaphorical relevance, the picture seemed distant to most people, and not romantically colorful enough to make up for that defect. Kazan and Brando were ambivalent about it as well in the final analysis. Kazan believed that he had not yet mastered the movie medium, that he was still more a director of actors than of the camera and action. But he was not, at the time, a reliable witness to his own work, for soon after the picture was cut he had his first direct encounter with the House Un-American Activities Committee investigators; and he would spend the winter and spring of 1952 agonizing over whether or not to name the other members of The Group Theater's Communist cell of two decades earlier. This, ultimately, he would do, for what he believed were good and sufficient reasons.

As for Brando, he has always maintained a certain reserve about *Viva Zapata*. The longest statement from him about it that I've been able to find is: 'Zapata was a hard characterization, which I don't think I fulfilled. It was a good workout.' Brando has never been a political sophisticate, and it is possible that he was unaware of the film's specifically anti-Stalinist subtext until it was pointed out. It also seems likely that he might have been dismayed to discover he had been used to mouth a seemingly establishment viewpoint.

In other words, as part of the most troubled passage in Kazan's life the film was in some measure tainted both for him and for the actor, who at this time regarded the director as a mentor. We have the testimony of Brando's next director, Joseph L. Mankiewicz, that when it came out in early summer of 1952 that Kazan had voluntarily given the committee a list of his Group Theater

Communist associates Brando was stricken by the news. Mankiewicz, who was also a friend of Kazan's, recalls the actor coming to him on the set virtually in tears over Kazan's action. With a picture to finish, and with a more sophisticated knowledge of the sectarian wars of the left, Mankiewicz remembers telling Brando not to judge his mentor too quickly or glibly, that Kazan's political activities should have no bearing on one's judgement of him as an artist.

The film on which Brando and Mankiewicz were working was *Julius Caesar*. And it was very much the product of the 'new' Hollywood. Its producer, John Houseman, was a famous man about the theater and movies. He had been Orson Welles's partner in the Mercury Theatre, and his name had since been associated with a number of literate, distinguished film and theatrical projects. When Dore Schary, a sometime screenwriter and producer noted for his serious, socially conscientious work, replaced Louis B. Mayer as head of production at MGM, he almost immediately recruited Houseman and charged him with making 'prestige' projects.

Caesar was on Schary's agenda when he hired Houseman. It was, in fact, a project that had interested several movie people, among them David O. Selznick, who had registered the title with the Motion Picture Producers Association, which forced Schary to wait until that claim expired before proceeding. It was probably Welles's famous modern-dress *Julius Caesar*, at the Mercury before the war, that stirred this interest, since it demonstrated that the play, which of course offers obvious opportunities for cinematic spectacle, could be read as anti-totalitarian in intent. In any case, by the time Selznick's title registration ran out in 1952, Schary, oppressed by management duties, had to abandon hopes of producing the film personally. But he also saw the possibility of reusing the sets and costumes created for quite another sort of Romanesque spectacle, *Quo Vadis?*, thus drastically lowering the cost of a *Julius Caesar*, and so he turned it over to Houseman. Mankiewicz, who two years in succession had won both writer and director Oscars for *A Letter to Three Wives* and *All About Eve* (an achievement

1953

Brando, as Marc Antony, delivers the funeral oration in the Forum in *Julius Caesar* (1953). Opinions were divided about his performance. Some, including John Gielgud, thought he was just imitating Olivier.

Left On the set of *Julius Caesar* with John Gielgud
(Cassius), James Mason (Brutus), Dore Schary, head of
production at MGM, and Louis Calhern (Caesar).
Right Studying the script. For his role as Marc Antony,
Brando also studied recordings of the great English
Shakespearean actors, and he probably put more effort
into this than into any other role.

unprecedented and still unduplicated), was not only a
logical choice to direct but one sure to impress observers
who had read in Schary's ascension at conservative Metro
an omen that times were changing in Hollywood.

True to his Mercury heritage, Houseman wanted to use
as many American actors as possible in the production,
and, remembering how well Brando had handled the big
climactic speech in *A Flag is Born*, was inspired to
suggest him for Marc Antony, much to the initial dismay
of Schary, Hollywood gossips, and, perhaps at first,
Mankiewicz as well. He was in London, signing John
Gielgud for Cassius and thinking seriously of testing Paul
Scofield as Antony, when Houseman cabled him.
Actually, Houseman's idea was an excellent one. For
Antony is, after all, a man trying to sort out his loyalties,
decide what a good man must do in a confused situation.
It is, ideally, a young man's part, and very right for this
particular young man. Nevertheless, all agreed that
Brando would have to prove his ability to handle
Shakespearean verse, and he agreed to make a recording
of the role's major speeches.

Brando wanted the role. According to Mankiewicz, he
studied closely the recordings of great English
Shakespeareans before making his own record, which he
played for the director at his New York apartment. 'You
sound like June Allyson,' Mankiewicz told the actor.

Apparently Brando redid the record, for both Houseman
and Schary were impressed by whatever was forwarded to
them, and Brando was quickly signed for the film.

He was never more caring in his approach to work.
Everyone was impressed by the seriousness with which
he addressed his role and the deference he accorded his
fellow players. He took a particular shine to Louis
Calhern, whose weary and nervous Caesar is one of the
film's ornaments. Gielgud, in a television interview,
offered an affectionate portrait of Brando on the set: 'He
was very self-conscious, nervous. He used to come on the
set looking perfectly wonderful in this sort of tomato-
colored toga and straight fringe [bangs] with a cigarette in
one corner of his mouth. Then he'd take it out and put it
behind his ear to show he wasn't being posh. He was
awfully afraid of being sent up silly in his costume.'

Houseman remembered Gielgud, the modern theater's
reigning master of Shakespearean melody, as enormously
helpful to the entire cast with questions of speech. Later
Gielgud would wish Brando had asked for his help with
his great scene, the funeral oration over Caesar's body in
the Forum. Though he has since revised upward his
opinion of Brando's work, he thought at the time 'he was
just imitating Olivier'. Houseman, on the other hand, was
grateful for the unflagging energy Brando brought to a
sequence that required him to do bits and pieces of a very

taxing speech over and over again so that it was covered from every angle an editor might want, and so that the crowd reaction shots, vital for its success as a movie scene, could be made.

Perhaps because of Houseman's something-for-everyone casting (besides those already named, James Mason, then at the height of his broody-romantic phase, contributed a very well-judged Brutus, and Deborah Kerr and Greer Garson played small, wifely roles, while most of the character parts were filled by familiar players), perhaps because everything about the movie was crafted with such obvious conscientiousness, the film received very supportive reviews. It also did well at the box office. Many critics indeed read the film exactly as they were supposed to, as a sign of the movies' new 'maturity'.

One is now a little less sure of one's first response both to the film and to Brando's performance. Mankiewicz is a man who idealized the theater and could not quite bring himself to a full cinematization of his *Julius Caesar*. Much of his staging has something of the theatrical about it, which is sometimes effective, sometimes not. We often see his sets as sets, that is, as stylizations of reality – and as rather underpopulated sets, at that. The staging of Caesar's assassination requires, on film, an intimacy and a horror that Mankiewicz backs away from, and the crowd massed for Antony's funeral oration is not well handled either. The rabble's volatility never seems as dangerous as it should. The Battle of Philippi, too, is thin and perfunctory. Budgetary restrictions surely hampered the director, but it must also be admitted that this kind of movie-making was not in those days Mankiewicz's strength. He was much more comfortable and effective in the more tightly wound scenes of the conspirators plotting and at his very best with Mason's Brutus on his sleepless, guilt-ridden night before Philippi.

As for Brando, this is the most problematical of his early performances. His own modest evaluation was that he 'gained ground as an actor – not so much in end performance'. But for all the conscientiousness of his study, the visible thoughtfulness of his performance, it still does not quite work as well as it might. Knowing his uncanny skills as a mimic, one can't help but think

Gielgud's first reaction to it was very largely correct. Whether or not he was, in fact, doing his well-practised Olivier imitation, this surely is an actor imitating other actors acting, never quite getting inside this character by means of his own devising.

Over the years it has become a cliché to regret that Brando did not attempt more of the classical roles. And it may be that, had he overcome his natural laziness and his understandable fear of these parts, he might have become, technically, a more reliable actor, possibly even a 'great' actor in the conventional mode. But it may also be that his only brush with Shakespeare showed him the limits of his gift.

Still there was no lack of paths open to him. In this period Brando was offered a number of interesting projects. What he chose to do was *The Wild One*. Not exactly elegant. But topical, and, as Brando saw it, capable of being a force for enlightenment. Besides, he'd get the chance to ride his Hawg on screen. For the film was based on a magazine account of a weekend when a motorcycle gang effectively siezed possession of little Hollister, California, terrorizing its citizens. Most important, the picture (which was produced by Stanley Kramer) had this to recommend it: it was the first major movie to confront the seismic rift that slowly, surely opened between the generations in the 1950s.

Even before this decade, twentieth-century American adolescents and post-adolescents had always seemed a little different. They had talked in curious, briefly indecipherable slang, danced to new and different jazz drummers. But everybody always said, tolerantly, 'they'll grow out of it,' which, of course, they generally did. Now, seemingly overnight, they were like aliens – irredeemably so, menacingly so.

'Juvenile delinquency.' Suddenly the phrase was on everyone's lips. There were senate hearings and best-sellers on the subject, and the newspapers were full of tales about gangs rumbling, usually with one another but, of course, dangerous to nice people who happened to get caught in the middle. The conventional explanations were: divorce and/or two-paycheck families, which led to neglect of the kids; affluence, which either put enough

THE EARLY YEARS

BRANDO

For his second film, Brando reprised his Broadway performance in Tennessee Williams's play, this time with Vivien Leigh as Blanche Dubois. The role of Stanley Kowalski, with its blend of menace, black comedy and near-parodistical maleness, immediately established Brando's screen image.

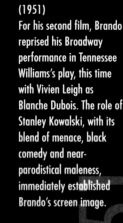

Two ages of Brando.
Left: the young stage
actor of the 1940s.
Below: the mature if
troubled screen star of
the 1960s.

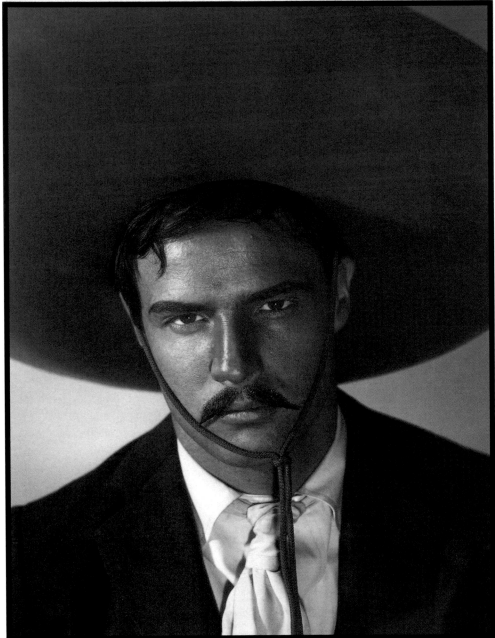

Viva Zapata (1952)
In his second
collaboration with
director Elia Kazan,
Brando's performance
as the Mexican
revolutionary captured
the watchful wariness of
the peasant. Producer
Darryl Zanuck, who had
wanted Tyrone Power for
the part, said he couldn't
understand Brando and
didn't like his moustache.

1952

On the Waterfront (1954)
In his third and last film with Elia Kazan, based on Budd Schulberg's screenplay about dockyard racketeers, Brando played Terry Malloy, small-time boxer turned bum, who develops a conscience and finds the moral strength to take on the mob. 'If there is a better performance by a man in the history of film in America, I don't know what it is,' wrote Kazan.

COLUMBIA PICTURES presents
MARLON BRANDO

On The Waterfront

AN ELIA KAZAN PRODUCTION

MALDEN · LEE J. COBB with ROD STEIGER · PAT HENNING _{and} introducing EVA MARIE SAINT
AM SPIEGEL Screen Play by BUDD SCHULBERG Music by LEONARD BERNSTEIN Directed by ELIA KAZAN

The Wild One (1954)
The role of Johnnie, the menacing leader of a motorcycle gang which took over a small Middle American town, gave Brando the opportunity to undergo the first of his many ritual beatings — and to ride his Hawg on screen. 'Hey, Johnnie, what are you rebelling against?' 'Waddya got?'

Desiree (1954)
Forced by Zanuck to play
Napoleon in 20th Century
Fox's historical love story,
Brando responded with a
performance that was
technically unimpeachable
but lacked all emotion.
Director Henry Koster had
envisaged a loud-mouthed
dictator, but Brando's
Napoleon is perhaps the
least fiery in screen history.
Remarkably, the film
outgrossed *On the
Waterfront*.

1954

1955

Guys and Dolls (1955)
Brando approached the role
of gambler Sky Masterson
with some trepidation, as it
involved singing and
dancing. There was also
both tension and technical
incompatibility between
him and co-star Frank
Sinatra, but it was not
Brando's contribution which
marred the film. He and
Jean Simmons both sang
with authentic feeling.

1957

Sayonara (1957)
The subtlety of Brando's
performance as Lloyd
Gruver, the Southern
serviceman who courts and
wins the love of a Japanese
dancer, in the face of
official disapproval of
interracial relationships,
won him
an Academy Award
nomination.

1958

The Young Lions (1958)
In Edward Dmytryk's film
of Irwin Shaw's ambitious
novel of the Second World
War, Brando played a
blond-haired Nazi, Christian
Diestl, who grows
disenchanted with Nazism,
and with war in general, as
the film progresses.

The Fugitive Kind (1960) Although the film was based on *Orpheus Descending*, the autobiographical play that Tennessee Williams had written with Brando in mind, he was miscast in the role of the guitar-pickin' singer Val Xavier, which allowed no room for the development of character.

One-Eyed Jacks (1961) Brando's directorial debut, made possible by Stanley Kubrick's departure, was a quirky revenge western, in which he played an outlaw, the Rio Kid, who finally gets even with his treacherous older partner. Meticulous if indecisive as a director, Brando created a gritty, original and beautiful film, but never directed again.

1962

Mutiny on the Bounty
(1962)
Brando was the dominant
figure in the making of
MGM's spectacular action
adventure, which nearly
bankrupted the studio. He
made himself widely
unpopular, and his
reputation suffered, but his
portrayal of Fletcher
Christian as a drawling fop
whose gradual conversion
to principled rebellion
surprises even himself was
brave and original.

The Chase (1966)
In Arthur Penn's flawed thriller about a Texas town going out of control on a Saturday night, Brando played a decent, liberal-minded sheriff — leaving the rebellion to a young Robert Redford. Penn, who lost control of the editing process to producer Sam Spiegel, lamented the fact that marvellous improvised scenes between Brando and Angie Dickinson did not survive.

1966

The Sixties saw Brando in a
mid-career trough. Whether
it was because of bad
advice, bad instincts or just
plain bad films, his work
had become less eccentric,
witty and dangerous. The
films were more modest
and routine than those of
the Fifties, and he seemed
to have repressed much of
his energy. In addition to
his career and ideological
confusions, his private life

money in young people's pockets to permit them freer range than ever before, or made those who didn't have it envious enough to try getting it through criminal means. Much of juvenile delinquency, and most of its more violent manifestations, were indeed motivated by class (and racial) envy and involved kids for whom traditional education was irrelevant: most of the work they could imagine being allowed to do was enervating and hopeless.

Apparently the movie's original script made some of these points quite firmly, and stressed the notion that the rootlessness and alienation of motorcycle gangs were not subject to amelioration by conventional means – psychiatry, social work, tinkering with school curricula, that sort of thing. The original intent, so Brando thought, was to show citizens of the occupied community responding unprogrammatically and non-violently to their threatening invaders. He thought they would be seen coming one by one to an emotional understanding of these troubled toughs.

No way the Breen office was buying that line. To begin with, the film's original script seemed to imply that there was something institutionally wrong when a society was producing youths of this kind, and social criticism of that sort did not go down well with Breen and the other Catholic conservatives on his staff. It smacked of covert leftie propaganda, just the sort of thing Congressional committees were currently determined to root out. If

one looked at this story of heartland Americans confronting an invasion by alien forces one could see that, in its original form, its bleeding heart was in quite the wrong place.

Rewrites were in order. The result is the confusion of motives still visible today. *The Wild One*'s opening sequence, with Johnnie (Brando), astride his machine, in sunglasses, cyclist's cap and leathers, leading his gang down the road to town, is wonderfully charged with menace. So is the vrooming, stunting establishment of their beach-head on Main Street, and their slouching, sneering take-over of the town café, which is (a) owned by the town's cowardly constable and (b) managed by Kathie (Mary Murphy), his daughter and the love interest. In these passages Brando is, yes, hell's angel – beautiful, insolent, seductive: Joe Breen's, all of Middle America's, worst nightmare suddenly made manifest.

The café is the setting for that famous exchange in response to Kathie's question about the gang's motives: 'Hey, Johnnie, what are you rebelling against?' 'Waddya

1954

Tame by today's standards, *The Wild One* (1954) enhanced Brando's reputation and was the first film to confront the seismic rift that opened up between the generations in the Fifties.

got?' It is also the setting for Johnnie's almost equally famous attempt to explain to the girl that, no, they are not exactly looking for a picnic spot: 'Man you're too square. I have to straighten you out. You don't go to any one special place . . . you just go to . . . the idea is to whale, to make some jive. Do you know what I'm talking about?'

Well, no, not exactly. Evidently Brando, unhappy with the rewritten script, improvised this and much of his other dialogue. But she got the general, thrilling idea. The trouble is that the movie doesn't develop it. On closer acquaintance with the Black Rebels, their sins all turn out to be against decorum, not against the Ten Commandments. They drink beer on the streets, swagger a bit under its influence, talk too loudly, but they are without the kind of hair-trigger unpredictability needed to maintain their menace. Moreover, Laslo Benedek's direction quickly settles into a kind of cool formalism, stand-offish and objective.

Nor does the narrative have the kind of erratic pulse, constantly surprising and alarming, that would keep us edgy. It heads smoothly, conventionally toward quite predictable confrontations. The arrival of a rival gang predicts imminent violence, which gets serious when its leader, Chino (Lee Marvin), is jailed and his gang goes on a rampage. As we know he will, Johnnie rescues Kathie from their depredations, then is himself mistaken as a possible rapist and savagely beaten by town vigilantes. This was the first of the many ritual beatings characters played by Brando would absorb in his films, punishment for being an outsider *and* sensitive – a hip messiah in the pop mythology of the time. After that, as he tries to leave town, one of the citizens throws a fire iron at him. He loses control of his bike and accidentally kills an old man, after which a lynch mob gathers. He is rescued by the arrival of the county sheriff, strong and sensible – authority with its best face on. In his calming presence Kathie testifies that Johnnie was not a menace but her savior, and another citizen testifies that it was a townie, not a biker, who threw that offending iron. In other words, everyone shares more or less equally in guilt for this unfortunate incident. Johnnie is ordered to leave and never return, which he does – still inarticulate, still

unable to put words to his feelings about what has happened.

This tale is, then, mostly a series of accidents and misapprehensions. About all it proves is that mutual mistrust – especially when there are a few bad apples in the barrel – is a sad, possibly preventable thing. It takes neither the radical view that middle-class America could use a good shaking up from Johnnie and his kind, nor the reactionary one that they are animals in need of the whip and the cage. Either one would have been preferable to the ameliorative inconclusiveness of the movie that finally emerged on the screen.

In one of his subsequent comments on the picture, Brando was right in his overall assessment of the film: 'We started out to do something worthwhile, to explain the psychology of the hipster. But somewhere along the way we went off the track . . . instead of finding out why young people tend to bunch into groups that seek expression in violence, all that we did was show the violence.' But out of some modesty or perversity, he also got one aspect of the film wrong. Discussing his own character with another journalist, he said: 'This was a man so possessed with inner struggle and strife that he was almost beyond the realm of articulating his feelings and almost not caring any more. I wanted to show that underneath all those things you could find a yearning, a desire to feel love – but so twisted and wrenched by disappointment that it no longer had the face of love. I wanted to show that gentleness and tolerance is the only way to dissipate the forces of social destruction. Well, it didn't come off at all . . .'

But, of course, it did. Or, anyway, his intentions did. For, in effect, he was following his own agenda in *The Wild One*, acting in the film he wanted to make, subverting as best he could the compromised movie everyone else was doing. For all the twistings and turnings that had been imposed on *The Wild One*, for all the compromises voluntarily made, Johnnie's dangerousness – the only true menace in the movie – remained obvious. And he neither apologized for it nor explained it. He leaves the picture as inarticulately as he entered it. Here and there around the US municipal

Right Brando and his biker gang looked like trouble, but the intention of the film, following a succession of rewrites, was less obvious.

moralists were outraged that he and his gang were not seen to be more firmly punished, and some fears were expressed that the film might prove to be an incitement to riot among its adolescent viewers. In Britain, indeed, censors banned the film outright for something like a decade and a half.

Thus was the last link forged in the bond between Brando and those of us who were and would remain his most devoted audience. For *The Wild One* accomplished what none of his previous pictures had: it took the screen image of a character that had first been glimpsed crippled, and then presented to us in variously exotic, distancing settings – the Vieux Carré, Mexico, ancient Rome – and thrust it, in full health and vigor, into completely familiar territory, where he confronted what were for us completely recognizable (if melodramatically heightened) issues. Judged by conventional critical standards, *The Wild One* may be the least of his early movies. But in terms of Brando's career, it is probably the most important of them. All he needed now to confirm his status as the greatest star of his generation was a role that was well within both his range and the range of his developing audience's sympathetic expectations in a film that was incontrovertibly well-made and thematically compelling; something everyone could take seriously, had to see. In short, what he needed was *On the Waterfront*.

He almost didn't get it. For the history of that film's development was vexed, if not, as it must sometimes have seemed, hexed. It begins with another script about longshoremen, called *The Hook*, which Elia Kazan and Arthur Miller developed in the late Forties, but never sold. In part this was because it seemed insufficiently anti-Communist in outlook to people like Roy Brewer, the red-baiting head of the International Alliance of Theatrical and Stage Employees. Miller and Kazan dropped the project, and then, after Kazan testified about his past associations in the Communist Party, they dropped (for a time) their friendship as well. In 1952, unapologetic about the correctness of what he had done, Kazan sought out Budd Schulberg, the novelist, who had also identified former comrades to the

Left Beautiful, insolent and seductive, Brando was truly hell's angel – Middle America's worst nightmare suddenly made manifest.

investigators. Schulberg was also unrepentent and, like Kazan, he remained a man of the left. But on their first meeting the two men discovered that they had more in common than their politics. The writer had also spent some time developing a script about working life on the New York docks, basing his story on newspaper articles about union corruption there, for which a reporter named Malcolm Johnson had won the Pulitzer Prize, and to which Schulberg had acquired screen rights.

Kazan liked Schulberg's screenplay, and while the director was busy with other projects Schulberg supplemented Johnson's work with research of his own. Eventually, he introduced Kazan to a man named Tony Mike deVincenzo, who had once been a hiring boss on the piers, until he objected to the corrupt practices of the dockyard racketeers. Blacklisted by the mob, he was reduced to selling newspapers on a street corner. Subpoenaed by the Waterfront Crime Commission, he testified against the hoodlums.

Kazan immediately drew an analogy between the experiences of Tony Mike after he testified and some of his own experiences after 'naming names'. Here was the core to the story he had been looking for. As he put it, 'I did see Tony Mike's story as my own, and that connection did lend the tone of irrefutable anger to the scenes I photographed and to my work with actors. When Brando, at the end, yells at Lee Cobb, the mob boss, "I'm glad what I done – you hear me? – glad what I done!" that was me saying, with identical heat, that I was glad I had testified as I did . . . I'd not forgotten nor would I forgive the men, old friends some of them, who'd snubbed me, so the scene in the film where Brando goes back to the waterfront to "shape up" again for employment by men with whom he'd worked day after day – that, too, was my story, now told to all the world. So that when critics say that I put my story and my feelings on the screen to justify informing, they are right.'

All movies, all fictions in any form, that have the initial impact and the lasting resonance of a work like *On the Waterfront* are animated by a personal passion of the kind Kazan describes. Indeed, it is fair to say that this movie would never have been made if Kazan and Schulberg had been moved by lesser motives. For Kazan's old friend and supporter, Darryl Zanuck, having encouraged them for months, did an abrupt turnaround when a final script was delivered to him. Thereafter, in quick succession, most of the other studios passed on the project.

But Schulberg and Kazan happened to be staying at the Beverly Hills Hotel, across the hall from the legendary freebooter Sam Spiegel. Emboldened by strong drink and strong anger, the writer-director team hauled him into their suite and started pitching their story. For reasons that remain baffling, Spiegel was interested. In a matter of weeks he had the financing together, and most important of all, it was Spiegel who brought Brando to the project.

He had first thought of Frank Sinatra, a native of Hoboken, who was in some respects right for the part – right enough for Kazan to agree to the casting and to meet with Sinatra regarding wardrobe. Both men believed a commitment had been made. Whereupon Spiegel began talking to Brando, who at first said he would not work with Kazan, because of his testimony, then began to weaken under Spiegel's persuasiveness. With Brando in the lead, Spiegel could get more money from Columbia, the studio that had finally agreed to back the project, for, despite Sinatra's recent success in *From Here to Eternity*, Brando's was a more bankable name. Finally, Brando agreed to take the part, permanently alienating Sinatra from all concerned.

Once Brando had signed, Spiegel insisted upon rewrite after rewrite. But Kazan believes that Spiegel's insistence on keeping the story moving, on the relentless building of tension, was one of the factors that made the picture work, and he also admits that he and Schulberg would have been satisfied with a lesser script. That said, the producer's cheapness once shooting began infuriated everyone, especially since the locations were the docks and slums of harsh Hoboken, which offered no amenities; the season was a bitter cold winter, with temperatures hovering around zero much of the time. Plenty of anecdotes stress the camaraderie of the company, bound together by the difficult conditions they shared, possibly by the fact that the principal cast was composed entirely of actors in the Stanislavskian tradition, from Group

Theater veteran Lee J. Cobb to Eva Marie Saint, an Actor's Studio student making her film debut. There was no compromise with the marquee in any of this casting.

Nor was there any compromise with reality. Kazan had been trying to free himself from studio sets since he began making movies, and now that effort paid off spectacularly. Similarly, he had been experimenting with the use of non-professional actors in small parts and as extras, and now his 'atmosphere' had an authenticity rarely approached by an American director. In other words, *On the Waterfront* was, if nothing else, the culmination of a stylistic trend in American film, a trend that Kazan had been leading, and which had been gathering force since the end of the war.

But, of course, *Waterfront* was something else. It is as a narrative, spare but unsparing, of an unlikely young man coming to moral consciousness, that it achieved not only its initial impact but its lasting value. The question of what constituted correct political behavior in the McCarthy era has lost its urgency, as has the issue of union corruption. What abides is the relentless, really quite unsentimental story of how Terry Malloy ceased to be 'a bum' and became a good man.

When we meet Terry, a former small-time boxer, he is hanging around the docks, existing on favors thrown him by mob boss Johnny Friendly (Cobb) and by his brother Charley (Rod Steiger), who is a lawyer for the racketeers. One of the errands he performs for them consists of unwittingly luring one of their opponents into a death-trap. Later, meeting the dead man's sister, Edie (Saint), the first glimmering of conscience begins to dawn – as does love, of course. Encouraged by a waterfront priest (Karl Malden), Terry moves painfully into opposition to the mob, which kills Charley when he cannot buy his brother's silence. Ultimately, Terry bears witness against the criminals, is ostracized by other dockers, then savagely beaten by mob goons (perhaps the most famous of Brando's ritual beatings). But, staggering from his wounds, he leads the contingent of longshoremen who witnessed his anguish past Johnny Friendly and his cohorts, thus claiming one free dock for free men.

On the Waterfront (1954)
proved to be the final film that
Brando made with Kazan.

Reduced to outline, it is a not entirely original movie story, except for its setting. What grants it its singularity is its playing. The hint of sexual heat underneath Saint's prim Catholic schoolgirl demeanor; the unctuously patronizing manner of Steiger's Charley, not quite covering the clammy fear in which he has lived his life; the awkwardness of Malden's priest when he tries to be a regular guy, not quite disguising his zealot's fervor – all of this is marvelous work, and all of it is stylistically of a piece, which is a great rarity in American film. And the star is completely with them, in no sense set apart. The delicate blend of untutored courtliness and boyish cockiness with which he woos Edie; the grief that plays across his face as she questions him about her brother's death, and the full realization of what he has done, and what it now may cost him; the gentleness of his famous final confrontation with Charley, full of pleading and puzzlement, as he tries to come to grips with his brother's betrayal – these are among the most privileged moments in our movie heritage. 'If there is a better performance by a man in the history of film in America, I don't know what it is,' Kazan wrote in his autobiography.

And yet there is this curiosity about the performance. Search though one may, it is impossible to find any detailed comments about his work from Brando. This possibly betokens, of all things, satisfaction with it. There were a few gripes about the working conditions, an allusion to some personal unhappiness that upset him at the time, but no self-criticism, and no criticism that the project had failed to live up to its promise.

His co-workers were more forthcoming. Eva Marie Saint, for example, was voluble about her affection for him. 'I'm on a one-woman crusade to right the wrongs said about Marlon Brando,' she told a reporter later, in an interview full of anecdotes about his kindness in seeing that she was wrapped in blankets against the cold, or giving her back-rubs to relieve tension. He seems to have indulged in a certain amount of jokey, arm-punching camaraderie with Kazan, but the latter is careful to say that his best direction, as far as Brando was concerned, was non-direction – letting him find his own way into a scene. One famous bit of business, picking up a glove dropped by Saint in one of their early getting-acquainted scenes, was, he says, an improvisation that arose when it slipped out of her hand by accident. The back-seat confrontation between Brando and Steiger, which had to be shot on a stage, with stage-hands rocking the shell of an auto to simulate movement, was worked out by the actors with no guidance from Kazan, according to the director. And it worked out so well in the playing because the mechanics of the scene were simple and controlled, thus undistracting to them.

But of the sources of Brando's greatness in this movie, no one present at the creation has spoken, even speculatively. It may be that Brando saw in Terry Malloy's coming to awareness of his power to do right an analogy to his own coming to awareness of the power of his gift. One may also speculate that now, in his sixth movie, he had fully absorbed the screen actor's craft. Possibly, too, the experience of working for the first time in a movie in New York, with actors and craftsmen who were part of the tradition that had formed him, may have had a liberating effect on him. But none of that quite solves the mystery.

All one can certainly say is that *On the Waterfront* represents a kind of apotheosis for the American theatrical tradition to which its leading creators owed allegiance. It represents the first entirely successful and

Two major confrontations for Brando's Terry Malloy in *On the Waterfront*. *Opposite* A violent clash with mob boss Johnny Friendly (played by Lee J. Cobb). *Left* The reproachful conversation in the taxi between Terry and his brother Charley (Rod Steiger).

1954

After a savage beating, Terry Malloy is helped to his feet by Edie (Eva Marie Saint) and the priest (Karl Malden), for a final, decisive gesture of defiance.

thoroughly embraced translation to film of The Group Theater's aesthetic: the presentation of 'real' people within an authentic representation of their milieu in a narrative that requires them to come to grips, whether they know it or not, with abstract social and political ideas that quite definitely engage and concern the audience.

And just as its theorists had long since proposed, it was the acting manner The Group had propagated that both assured the illusion of reality and, at the same time, permitted it to transcend the particulars it was dealing with, granted its characters a humanity, a universality that to this day remains recognizable and emotionally riveting.

Kazan, whom they had once patronized, but who had even before this become their most successful, therefore somewhat resented, envoy to the larger world, had done it. And he had done it employing the young actor another apostate, Stella Adler, had found and tutored, but whom they now had no choice but to see as their champion. There was irony enough in that. But what must have been more deeply galling was the fact that *On the Waterfront*'s political subtext was anathema to many of the old Group soldiers and to their newer recruits as well. Worse, it was precisely because the Stanislavskian ideals of performance were so perfectly realized by a company that contained representatives of their oldest and youngest generations that this subtext was rendered palatable. By the end of *On the Waterfront* one really didn't give a damn what the film was saying.

For *On the Waterfront* was more than an unrestrained critical and commercial triumph. It became the occasion on which the show business establishment at last extended full-scale acknowledgment of the ethic and the aesthetic of its former opposition. The picture won three of the four prizes offered by the New York Film Critics and went on to win seven Academy Awards. Brando, on the Oscar telecast, allowed himself some awkward horseplay with Bob Hope, and gave an acceptance speech that was all a Middle-western parent could hope for, brief and modest: 'This is a wonderful moment, and a rare one – and I'm certainly grateful.' It was also, perhaps, the moment of maximum power both for Brando and the tradition he exemplified. What remained of opposition to the Stanislavskian ideal was not perhaps swept away, but henceforth it would be on the defensive. From this moment on actors and serious observers of the theatrical enterprise in this country have had no choice but to define performance, and the judgement of performance, within the terms of the fractious, often schismatic movement that had developed around the Russian's theories.

But, as a modern philosopher has observed, 'The moment of maximum power is the moment of maximum danger.' For if the performances contained in the film assured the ascendency of an acting style, the film itself did not predict a further development of the realistic trend that had been the most interesting and promising development in post-war American film, a true expansion of its range. Quite the opposite: it would soon become painfully clear that *On the Waterfront* represented a one-off culmination for that style of movie-making, at least as far as the mainstream producers were concerned. No one attempted to imitate its manner, build on its success. In other words, Brando – and all the actors who were already beginning to crawl out from under his overcoat – would be, for the remainder of this decade and much of the next (until the arrival of younger directors like Martin Scorsese), largely bereft of the stylistic context their approach to their art, their manner, required. They would become characters in search of *auteurs* who did not exist, or could not function consistently, in the movie world as it was now being reconstituted. And Marlon Brando, as the leader of that school, would feel the impact of the movie industry's fear and cautiousness in the later 1950s first. And hardest.

In an obviously posed picture, Brando defends his Oscar from the avid grasp of Bob Hope. The next time he won the Best Actor award there would be no such genial horseplay, indeed no Brando.

CHAPTER FIVE

AGE OF ANXIETY

After several years in which it seemed that Brando could not put a foot wrong, he increasingly found himself in the wrong films. On the sets of *Desiree* (*right*) and *The Fugitive Kind*, with Anna Magnani (*above*).

Given the films Brando had completed prior to 1954 – all of them filmed in black-and-white in the traditional aspect ratio, all of them made by men whose spirit was not mainstream Hollywood, all of them in one way or another examples of the better nature of late Forties, early Fifties American film-making – Brando had every reason to suppose that he could continue as he had: dropping in on the industry every year or so to do something at least potentially gratifying, something he (and his followers) could justify his presence in, no matter how it finally turned out. He did not see that, with fewer pictures being made (by the end of the decade the number of movies produced in the US would be halved), more was staked on the economic performance of each individual and increasingly expensive) movie, making production executives increasingly cautious, anxious to hedge the large bet each movie represented. And he could not discern that the kind of film-making he had done was in the process of disappearing (at least for the moment; it would reappear after roughly a decade).

Certainly he did not realize that his own stardom, sealed by the success of *Waterfront*, was in itself limiting, preventing him from taking the chances that a younger actor might have taken. Finally, he could not possibly have seen that new controversy in which he found himself embroiled was predictive of things to come.

But it was. And here Darryl Zanuck took a direct role in determining Brando's fate. As of 1954, the actor owed Fox a picture, and Zanuck was adamant that Brando report to work on the one the studio had chosen for him. This obligation was essentially an accidental one, an add-on to Brando's old *Viva Zapata* contract. At the time Brando had been reluctant to sign away even such a relatively small piece of his autonomy, but it seems the ever-practical Kazan prevailed on him to do so. After all, Fox had never asked Kazan to make anything but serious films, and he could not imagine Zanuck making an untoward imposition on an actor like Brando.

Kazan reckoned without Hollywood's mid Fifties crisis. That is to say, he reckoned without enterprises like *The Egyptian*, which was based on a best-selling historical novel (Hollywood was then much taken with the fancy that adaptations of commercially successful fiction lured a 'pre-sold' audience into theaters), and believed to hold possibilities for exotic spectacle and spiritual uplift. Brando – not unreasonably – thought it was tosh. But he left New York for Hollywood just days after completing *Waterfront* for costume fittings and rehearsals, determined to fulfill his obligation as painlessly as possible. Then, suddenly, he decamped for New York. It seems likely that the ferociously demanding Michael Curtiz, a crude man but often an effective director (*Casablanca* and *Mildred Pierce* are among his estimated 178 titles), scared Brando off. Putting it mildly, he was not a man known for his ability to communicate with actors about the nuances of their performances. Fox sued for $2 million, claiming that was the sum it would lose on pre-production costs if Brando continued to renege on his contract.

While this wrangle proceeded, Brando was suddenly presented with an authentic crisis. His mother, while visiting her sister in Los Angeles, had collapsed, desperately and, as it turned out, terminally ill. He returned to Los Angeles to be with Dodie during her final illness, which she bore with great gallantry (Brando would later tell friends that she had taught him how to die).

Stella Adler thought he took his mother's death very well, but she also predicted, correctly, that the death of this 'heavenly, girlish, lost creature' would change her son. 'She was the symbol of many important things – her passion for purity, her attitude toward animals, earth, and music . . .' There was, now, in Brando a new cynicism in his comments about routine movie work and an upsurge in his commitment to good causes outside the realm of his art.

It must be said, however, that other factors contributed to the restlessness and lack of focus he began to demonstrate during this passage. By this time Marlon Sr had become something more than the man who handled his allowance. He was a full-scale business manager, whose chief investment on his son's behalf was a cattle ranch in Nebraska. It was a constant drain on his resources and a constant strain on his relationship with his father, which, though outwardly pleasant, was never to be resolved in affection. Finally, there were romantic problems. While making *Viva Zapata* he had met the Mexican actress Movita (Castenada), and they had been keeping more or less steady company ever since, though that term is a relative one where Brando is concerned. The number of women with whom he was linked in these days is quite uncountable. Apparently, though, while he was shooting *Waterfront* she began insisting on marriage. This occasioned a break-up that was very troubling to Brando, who had obviously found in the older woman – she was nine years his senior – some sort of stabilizing influence. Now he was involved with a much younger woman, Josanne-Mariana Berenger, a nineteen-year-old French model he met in New York and took back with him to Los Angeles. Eventually, much to the titillation of the press, they would announce their engagement, though they never would marry.

Movita, the actress whom Brando had met while working on *Viva Zapata* and, after his divorce from Anna Kashfi, eventually married in 1960, when she too was pregnant.

Brando as Napoleon in *Desiree* (1956). Whether through unsympathetic direction, sulkiness on the part of the actor, or perverse casting by Darryl Zanuck, to whom Brando owed a film, this was his first truly unsatisfactory screen performance.

1956

Clearly, there was much on his mind at this point, and he did not need the continued enmity of Darryl Zanuck. Nor did he need the expense of settling his dispute with him, so a compromise was arrived at. Brando was forced to commit to yet another future Fox film. *The Egyptian* would go ahead, and Brando would play Napoleon in *Desiree*.

One cannot quite understand what Zanuck was thinking of. He was often a bully, and he particularly liked giving outlanders little lessons in Hollywood power politics. He may well have been making sure Brando understood the mores of a community of which the production executive was one of the unquestioned grandees. On the other hand, Zanuck was rarely a fool. Indeed, he was, arguably, the shrewdest studio chief in town. He was not a man who would, in normal circumstances, waste an asset like this – the services of a hot young star – on something as inappropriate as *Desiree*. One has to believe he was operating out of panic.

Desiree, too, was an adaptation of a best-selling historical novel, its eponymous heroine (Jean Simmons) being a young woman who meets and falls in love with

Napoleon when he is a young officer, and whose sister
marries his brother, Joseph. Desiree moons about after
him for the rest of the movie, even entering into a loveless
marriage with an agreeable and civilized brother officer,
General Bernadotte (Michael Rennie), in order to stay
close to Napoleon. Occasionally Napoleon returns her
interest in the rather distant and diffident manner Brando
affects in the role. Ultimately it is Desiree who persuades
him to make his final surrender, and accept exile.

It is a ludicrous film, entirely characteristic of the kind
of big, slow-moving machines that were beginning to
lumber across the movie landscape. Moreover, Brando
was for the first time directed by one of those stolid
professionals who have ever been the backbone of
Hollywood mediocrity. Henry Koster was a civilized,
gently spoken émigré, who had directed numberless mild
and sentimental little comedies. *Desiree* was his reward
for the success of *The Robe*, his previous picture, and,
unfazed by whatever problems the new Cinemascope
technology presented, he brought it in on budget. As it
turned out, he was something of an amateur Napoleon
scholar, too.

Brando was agreeable enough with Koster and the rest
of the company when work was not at issue. There were
no temperamental outbursts, no signs of overt
rebelliousness. His mood was, rather, devilish. An
anecdote seems to characterize his spirit. It finds Brando
staring soulfully, unspeaking, into a fountain on one of
the sets. What is it? What's the matter? Koster inquires.
Silence. Entreaties. More silence. Until, finally, the actor
confesses he is wishing for something. What? the director
asks, eager to get his star back on his feet and his shot
made. 'I wish this fountain were full of chocolate ice
cream soda,' comes the sober reply. Why? Long pause.
'Because I like chocolate ice cream sodas.' Another
pause. And a general bust-up.

The camera got nothing so amusing from Brando.
Kindly, one might suggest that he seems to have modeled
his performance on one of those solid English character
actors who had often been found in Hollywood historical
epics over the years. He is crisply spoken, technically
unimpeachable, and utterly absent emotionally. Unkindly,

Brando in relaxed mood on the set of *Desiree*. Although the film was uninspired,
one positive aspect of a generally unhappy episode was the rapport he struck up
with Jean Simmons, with whom he would very soon be working again to much
better effect.

one might propose that Brando merely sulked his way
through the role, staying just this side of legally
actionable insubordination. But, for whatever reasons,
this is perhaps the least fiery Napoleon in screen history.
'I had an idea about how Napoleon should be played,'
Koster later recalled. 'As a real extrovert, as a loud-
mouthed dictator.' He met endlessly with Brando off the
set, argued patiently. And got nowhere. Koster assumed
that Brando was simply too 'introverted' to play the role –
and it certainly seems that Brando stressed the 'shy' side
of his nature in his dealings with the director.

Koster was the first director Brando had encountered who was settled in the ways of Hollywood, unquestioning of its routines and unquesting about trying to exceed the apparent limits of a project. So Koster was the first director, but by no means the last, to be tested and to a degree victimized by Brando's need to define their relationship. Brando could not tolerate menacing reserve – anything that smacked of his own father's style. On the other hand, heedless hackery and easy amiability were also anathema to him.

Kazan unquestionably knew best how to deal with him. In manner, he was more sympathetic elder brother than father, a collaborator who was neither a dictator nor a patsy. Everything that Brando is, Kazan has said, 'is available to a director – if he agrees with you.' The director's job is to engineer that consent, by carefully psyching out the actor, determining, often through indirect means, where he is coming from, where he thinks he is going. Above all he must listen to the actor's interpretive ideas, take them seriously, incorporate what he can of them into the film; otherwise the actor's careful psychological preparation, from which he derives his sense of professional security, is rendered meaningless.

Deep in his heart the director may regard this as nonsensical, even an infringement of his own authorial prerogatives, but he had better create the impression that he is playing along. Now, of course, decades of experience have taught directors this trick of their trade. But in the Fifties and Sixties it was a new one. Nevertheless, the men who later worked with Brando most happily – Arthur Penn, Francis Coppola, Bernardo Bertolucci – all mastered it. The others have endured much misery at his hands, and have brought out the worst in him – the kind of behavior that would eventually make studios shy away from him as a trouble-maker.

For the moment, however, no great harm was done, either to *Desiree* or Brando's reputation. Its critical reception was predictably patronizing, though *Desiree* actually outgrossed *On the Waterfront*. And, by and large, everyone forgave Brando and understood that there were things that actors in Hollywood had to do. If anyone was unforgiving of Brando it was Brando himself. For, in

interviews about the movie, that note which would soon become characteristic when he discussed movies made under conditions that offended him – a note of defensive cynicism – crept into his conversations for the first time: 'Most of the time I just let the make-up play the part.' And: 'Movies, to me, are a way of making a living. Any satisfaction one gets beyond that is gratis.'

From afar, Stella Adler commented: 'Marlon was discovered as a personality before he discovered himself as an actor.' To which one might add: he was discovered as a personality before he had a personality, that is to say, a firm sense of his own identity. The muddled boy, that curious combination of the hard and the yielding, who had come to New York in search of himself only a decade earlier, had not resolved any of his primal conflicts. They had merely been subsumed by the agreeable persona of the aspiring actor – earnest, idealistic, embracing poverty as he purely pursued his art. It had served him quite well for a time; it was both good copy and a sufficient explanation for his behavioral oddities as he rose to fame. But the usefulness of that persona in sustaining him as a star of the magnitude that he had now become was obviously limited.

In time, all his old, pre-Hollywood suspicions about the possibilities of doing anything worthwhile in the movies, now reinforced by what he saw as embittering experience, would surface, along with many a dismal comment about the childishness and social inutility of acting as a profession. His defenses eventually came down to these: a man has to make a living somehow, and sometimes, however inept it is as art, a movie can do some good in the world. In other words, the not entirely misplaced bleatings first heard at the time of *Desiree* would grow louder and more commonplace as the years wore on. It should be added that much of the reviewing that greeted his work from this point on in his career did him no favors, perhaps precisely because it arose from the same source as his self-criticism, which was unreasonably heightened expectations of him.

Guys and Dolls, the film he went into very quickly after *Desiree* wrapped, provides an excellent case in point. He was probably charmed into taking a job in the movie

adaptation of Frank Loesser's truly wonderful Broadway musical by this ingratiating telegram from Joe Mankiewicz, who had, after all, seen him through another anxious reach: 'UNDERSTAND YOU'RE APPREHENSIVE BECAUSE YOU'VE NEVER DONE MUSICAL COMEDY. YOU HAVE NOTHING REPEAT NOTHING TO WORRY ABOUT. BECAUSE NEITHER HAVE I. LOVE, JOE.'

Brando would later be quoted as saying that producer Samuel Goldwyn's offer came at a moment when, understandably, he wanted 'to do something in a lighter color'. He also confessed that he was scared of attempting to sing anywhere outside the shower, but then added, unexceptionably, 'I think it's part of an actor's job to do new things.' Very reasonable, very sensible.

And aside from a certain tension between Frank Sinatra, who played Nathan Detroit, proprietor of New York's 'oldest established permanent floating crap game', and Brando, playing that highest-rolling gambler, Sky Masterson, production went smoothly. The singer was still aggrieved by the fact that he had lost the *Waterfront* role to Brando, and since he was notoriously an actor who was best on the first take while Brando still needed his several groping, mumbling read-throughs, there was an explosion after their one long scene together, in which

Detroit is required to consume a slice of cheesecake while attempting to con Sky into a sucker bet. At the end of a day of many takes, Sinatra cried: 'These fucking New York actors – how much cake do you think I can eat?' For his part, Brando was dubious about Sinatra's choices as an actor. Too romantic, he thought, too ingratiating, not enough toughness and street smarts. At one point he urged Mankiewicz to speak to Sinatra on this matter. 'You first,' said Mankiewicz. Or words to that effect. Brando, it is said, lost some of his regard for the director because of this refusal. Still, he and Sinatra worked in parallel sub-plots, which rarely merged, so their animosity did not often affect the production.

But Brando is marvelous in what is probably his most underrated performance this side of *Mutiny on the Bounty*. It is Sky's function, in the scheme of the story, to seduce Miss Sarah (Jean Simmons), leader of the Salvation Army-like 'Save-A-Soul' mission (he has a bet with Nathan that he cannot get her to accompany him to Cuba), and Brando plays the gambler with great delicacy. There is just the slightest roughness to his tone, but he enunciates with the thoughtful precision of a man who needs to think about the niceties of grammar and pronunciation. His movements and gestures also have the

1955

Reunited with director Joe Mankiewicz, Brando was a revelation in *Guys and Dolls* (1955). His sensitive acting as gambler Sky Masterson made for a believable relationship with Jean Simmons' soul-saving Miss Sarah (*left*), while his 'Luck Be a Lady' number (opposite) was the film's outstanding production number.

studied grace of a man learning to mind his manners. There is something touching about him, and precisely because there is nothing studdish about him we can see why this genteel lass might take him to heart. In other words, he makes an essentially unbelievable relationship believable. He is more than a diamond in the rough; he is a diamond in the midst of a self-polishing process.

His dancing is minimal, more a question of choreographed movement than sets of combinations; but his singing, much criticized at the time, is a revelation. His voice is light, but true, and in fact reminds one of those other splendid non-singing singers, Fred Astaire and Gene Kelly. It is movie singing, not stage singing, and the more effective for being so. Indeed Brando's 'Luck Be a Lady' number, in which he bets $1,000 apiece for the 'souls' of the entire Broadway gambling fraternity (if they lose they have to report to Miss Sarah's mission and participate in a revival meeting, thus redeeming the pledge he made to her in order to lure her to Cuba), is the only production number in the show with something like the vitality and tension of the stage production. For the truth is that Mankiewicz's production is, again, underpopulated and very stage-bound. Not for a minute do we feel we are in Damon Runyon's juicy, juking, jiving New York. The film is dry, distant, essentially passionless.

Despite its decidedly mixed critical reception, *Guys and Dolls* grossed some $9 million on its initial release, and was the top moneymaker of 1956. Here was further evidence, as far as the industry was concerned, that Brando might be, next to William Holden, then the beau ideal of middle-class masculine virtue, the most important male movie star, and perhaps Holden's necessary opposite.

He went next to what is surely the most appalling movie he made in this decade, *The Teahouse of the August Moon*. It is easy to see what attracted Hollywood to it: based on a popular novel it had been a great Broadway success, and was thus another 'pre-sold' property. As for Brando, who campaigned for the role, it offered an agreeably liberal-minded, live-and-let-live message and the opportunity for radical off-casting. Hidden beneath a deep coating of make-up, speaking in a sometimes incomprehensible

Brando's performance as Sakini, the Japanese interpreter and handyman, in *The Teahouse of the August Moon* (1956), was a technical tour de force in an otherwise banal film.

accent, he was Sakini, a comically sly Okinawan interpreter and handyman to the post-war American occupation forces. There is a nice scuttle and scurry about him as he simultaneously obliges and subverts the soldiery, and their plan to bring western-style democracy to a venue where it is not entirely appropriate. 'Okinawa very fortunate. Culture brought to us. Not have to leave home for it,' he says at one point, and that pretty well captures the vacuous flavor of the film.

The movie is full of that sort of pseudo-comic pseudo-wisdom, as Sakini takes in hand a bumbling Captain

Frisbe (Glenn Ford) and helps turn his wayward and childish native charges – they are patronized unmercifully by the unwittingly racist script – into what a Pentagon plan wants them to be: incipient capitalists. Of course, this is accomplished by nefarious means: a network bootlegging potato brandy and the institution of the title, a Geisha house. First the hopelessly square Frisbe embraces their free-spirited example. Then a dotty psychiatrist (Eddie Albert), and finally even the commanding officer, Colonel Purdy (Paul Ford, in his patented, and usually enjoyable, specialty as a Babbity blowhard), are won over.

In the end, Brando's performance is hard to judge, partly because its context is so overwhelmingly banal. He is lively in the takes director Daniel Mann – with whom he did not get along – finally printed, and as insinuating as he can be in the circumstances, but one is conscious only of technique. His Sakini is, ultimately, a kind of parlor trick, an impression of a foreigner, not a true performance as one. Needless to say, he got generally more favorable reviews of his work here than for *Guys and Dolls*, largely because most critics had nothing to compare it to, except, perhaps, other Oriental impersonations by western actors.

Brando addressed the issue of race from the opposite perspective in *Sayonara*. It was based on a novel the director Joshua Logan encouraged decent-minded James A. Michener to write. (Logan had, of course, been the co-adapter and director of the author's *South Pacific.*) He had in mind something that would help Americans appreciate Japan's traditional performing arts, which might in turn serve as the basis for another musical. What Michener produced was more a plea for racial tolerance, with special reference to the American policy of discouraging marriage between the occupation forces and Japanese women and Japanese disapproval of such matches. Michener, who was himself married to a Japanese woman, crafted a story in which an American jet pilot, Lloyd Gruver (Brando), an ace in the Korean war, meets and falls in love with Hana-ogi (Miiko Taka). She is a dancer in the Takarazuka Opera Company, an all-female music hall troupe, whose management assiduously promoted the

idea that its members led a convent-like existence, the better to devote themselves to their art. A parallel story, involving an enlisted man, Kelly (Red Buttons), living with a Japanese woman (Miyoshi Umeki) ends in tragedy – mutual suicide, because they are prevented from marriage and he is about to be shipped home.

Trouble afflicted the company before it arrived in Japan, some of it arising from Brando's dissatisfaction with the script (he did extensive rewrites, most of which were unused). Once in Japan, the situation deteriorated further. The Japanese entertainment conglomerate that had promised Logan permission to shoot with its Noh, Kabuki, and Bunraku puppet companies, suddenly insisted on renegotiating its deal. The Takarazuku people remained adamantly opposed to the project, and there was much criticism in the Japanese press, which feared that the Americans would travesty revered cultural institutions.

In the event, Logan was forced to recruit players from outside these institutions, and Takarazuka became the fictional Mitsubayashi Company. As far as a westerner can judge, he treated Japanese theatrical traditions respectfully, though, of course, they function mainly to provide atmosphere, a touch of exotic spectacle, helping to justify the length of what turned out to be an interminable movie. Michener's original plot underwent one significant change, too. Instead of parting in the final reel (hence the title *Sayonara*) Gruver and Hana-ogi defy custom and marry, thus providing a happy, exemplary ending instead of a downbeat, but possibly more realistic one.

Brando's performance, however, is remarkable. He insisted on supplying Gruver with a soft Southern accent, implying that the racial prejudices love encouraged him to overcome were profound. But what's best about his work is its curious blend of amiability and discomfort. His Gruver is, at heart, a good ole boy eager to please and perhaps as surprised as anyone to discover that he is causing displeasure. But he is also a West Point graduate, his nature stiffened and stifled by discipline, and Brando plays this conflict with great subtlety. When we meet him he is engaged to marry the daughter of an air force

With co-star Miiko Taka in Joshua Logan's *Sayonara* (1957). Brando was disappointed by the sentimentality of the film, which had been intended as a serious plea for racial tolerance.

1957

general. She is a nice, spirited girl, and her parents are comfortable, middle-class people, none of them remotely deserving of disapproval or even disappointed hopes. Brando's scenes with them are marvels of awkwardness, of eye contact avoided, of sentences swallowed half-finished, as he strives not to hurt them unduly, yet to communicate his shift of heart. At one point, trying to explain what has happened to him, he picks up a throw pillow, studying it, picking at it as, haltingly, he attempts to say hard things in a soft voice. The scene is heartbreaking in its behavioral authenticity.

So are the scenes between him and the woman he insists on addressing with over-politeness as 'Miss Ogi'. He falls in love with her from afar, and wins her attention largely by sitting in a park and eyeing her longingly as she and her troupe trot back and forth between their dormitory and their theater. His struggle between discomfort and persistence is charmingly done. Somehow you believe that this modest (and protected) woman might, against *her* will, feel the force of *his* will, despite the distances separating them. When, at last, they get together, his innocent eagerness to learn, to enter her world, has both a boyish sweetness and a gentle masculine force.

Unlike Kelly, however, Gruver never attempts to embrace fully the customs of an alien culture. He retains the stance of a sympathetic observer, and he retains those aspects of his American maleness that are essential to his self-definition, which is, of course, why he avoids Kelly's tragic fate. His reaction when he discovers his friends' bodies is a brilliant, and extremely effective, example of suppressed emotion, of throttled rage. It is of a piece with the long display of reasonableness that preceded it, in which he was seen patiently working through channels on behalf of their marriage, believing that common sense and common decency would win them their hearts' desire. (True to the developing spirit of his screen character, he does subsequently absorb one of his ritual beatings at the hands of a Japanese mob, outraged by the love-death of Kelly and Matsumi and looking for a foreigner to blame.) But given the tentative, compromising way he has played Gruver, there is a just irony in this development, and, of course, it all helps give dramatic strength to his final break with convention, his marriage to 'Miss Ogi', which, because he is a war hero and she a theatrical star, receives media coverage, and thus becomes an exemplary moral act.

With its earnest effort to portray what was then an exotic culture respectfully, thus imparting to the film an air of expensive and 'beautiful' spectacle, with its careful attempt to preach racial amity in romantically approachable terms, *Sayonara* is a paradigm of Fifties movie-making, Fifties American culture. But it is to a degree redeemed by Brando's performance, for which he received another Academy Award nomination (though of course it was Buttons and Umeki, so cute and so sad, who actually got the Oscars).

Typically, Brando was unhappy with *Sayonara*. He made his unhappiness manifest in the article, previously mentioned, written for the *New Yorker* by Truman Capote, which caused something of a sensation at the time and, perhaps more than any single journalistic item about him, revised public perceptions of Brando. In those days, the magazine and its middle-brow audience liked to affect an air of smug superiority to popular culture in general, and Capote was obviously determined to play to this attitude when he invaded Brando's hotel room in Kyoto on a night when the star was restlessly confined there with some minor ailment. In the manner that the 'new journalism' would soon make *de rigueur* in celebrity profiles, the novelist set a scene of slightly squalid indulgence. The overweight actor is discovered among carelessly discarded clothes, unconsumed snacks, 'deep-thought' books, and the manuscript pages of a screenplay on which he is avoiding work. In the course of the evening he orders excesses of food, downs excesses of drink, indulges in excesses of self-pity and self-loathing.

Brando was dismissive of a project he had once found promising: 'This wondrous hearts-and-flowers nonsense that was supposed to be a serious picture about Japan.' But his contempt ranged farther and wider than his current work. Take the theater, for instance. 'What's so hot about New York?' the actor inquired rhetorically at

one point. 'Anyway, what would I be in? There aren't any parts for me.' This momentarily caused Capote to lose ironic distance, for this was still the Fifties, still a period in which literary people like Capote felt obliged to regard Broadway as somehow culturally superior to the movies. In any event, Capote interrupted the flow of his article to list a number of suitable theatrical enterprises that he knew had been offered to Brando, making special reference to *Orpheus Descending*. Tennessee Williams had written this for Brando, whose refusal to play in it had sabotaged its chances, and sabotaged some of Brando's reputation with theater-minded people, who saw this as evidence of his final 'sell-out' to Hollywood.

This, in a sense, Brando indirectly confirmed. In his first press conference in Japan he had made a very winning speech, saying he had undertaken *Sayonara* because 'it strikes very precisely at prejudices that serve to limit our progress toward a peaceful world'. Since he was able to decorate his remarks with references to Oriental religion, which he had indeed studied, and even to such cultural traditions as flower arrangement, he had been helpful in easing some of the tensions surrounding the production. Now, to Capote, he insisted on applying his justification for appearing in *Sayonara* to his entire movie career – and to his abandonment of the theater as well. 'You can say important things to a lot of people. About discrimination and hatred and prejudice.' And so on.

Here, for the first time, a new theme in Brando's public reflections about his art surfaced. Perhaps movies could not, in their nature, offer him satisfaction as an actor. But they could be, as he put it, 'a factor for good', for 'moral development'. For the moment, he indicated, this potential was sustaining him as he toiled on *Sayonara*. He had formed his own production company, Pennebaker (his mother's maiden name, and considering what her ideals meant to him, a not insignificant choice), intending to produce films that would 'explore the themes current in the world today'. His salary from the present silly venture would, if nothing else, provide money 'to put in the kick' for Pennebaker's more purely intentioned ventures.

Capote got some sport out of the fact that, together with someone known only as Murray, Brando was occupying

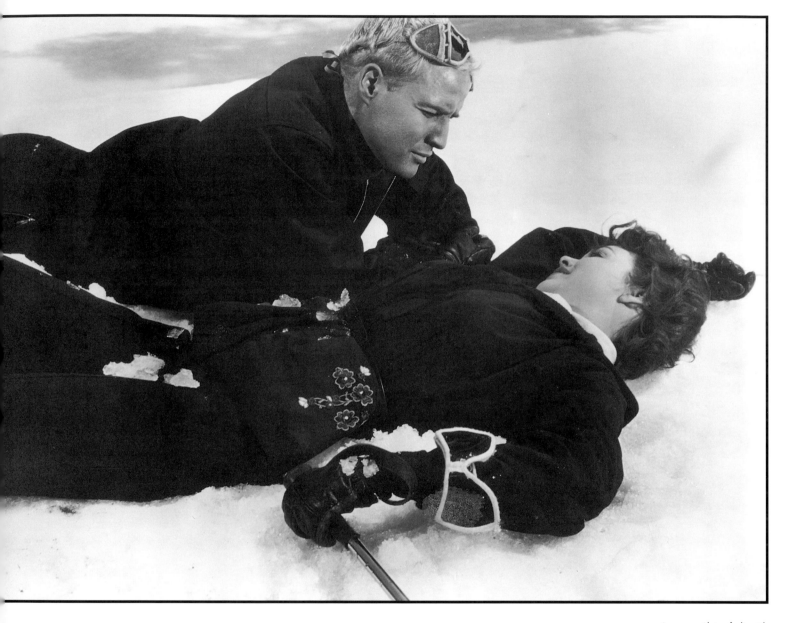

A pre-war Alpine frolic with Barbara Rush in *The Young Lions* (1958). Brando played a Nazi, she the girlfriend of an American (Dean Martin) whom he would later meet on the battlefield.

1958

some of his spare time in Japan writing the script for what he intended to be his first independent production. Capote was amused to discover this was to be, of all humble things, a western titled *A Burst of Vermillion*. It seemed not to occur to him that the form had long since proved itself to be metaphorically capacious, capable of handling all sorts of pointed themes, often more subtly and interestingly than films that attacked important topics more directly. He was, of course, dismissive of Brando's claim that the project would, indeed, address the subject of racial prejudice in its own way.

One is, perhaps perversely, sympathetic to Brando's rather innocent idealism, but from here on, almost all of his professional problems, problems that would by the early Sixties vitiate both his powers of choice and his powers as a performer, all stemmed from his insistence that his movies should make some usefully uplifting statement about matters of high concern. When he was thwarted on this point he would become balky and unreachable. In other words, he would act on, act out, the attitude Capote observed – perhaps in part because others, too, had responded as the writer had, patronizingly, sneeringly.

He worked ceaselessly in these days, and moved on quickly to another prestigious, 'serious', and morally upstanding project, the adaptation of *The Young Lions*, Irwin Shaw's best-selling attempt to encompass the entire experience of World War Two within a single volume. It was a novel both sober and slick, an attempt by an esteemed writer of short stories to realize one of his literary generation's great ideals, 'the big book'.

The story traces the lives of three young men: a poor American Jew, Noah Ackerman (played in the film by Montgomery Clift); an ambitious entertainer and politically uncommitted show business figure, Michael Whiteacre (Dean Martin); and, as Shaw originally wrote him, a Nazi true believer, Christian Diestl (played in a controversially different spirit by a blond-haired Brando). Their lives are coincidentally, but not unpersuasively, intertwined. Diestl meets and flirts with Whiteacre's girlfriend (Barbara Rush) at a Swiss ski resort, where he is an instructor, in the last days of peace. Ackerman and

Whiteacre meet at their draft board, where the latter is trying to get a deferment. They will soldier on through the war together, and just after liberating a concentration camp, they will confront Diestl in combat.

All three are, as a result of their wartime experiences, changed men by that time. But the movie Diestl is also a changed man from the character as Shaw originally envisioned him. He had portrayed him as a man mildly sympathetic to Nazism in peacetime who becomes more and more committed to Hitlerism as the war proceeds. The idea was to contrast his shrinkage of conscience with the developing moral awareness of his American counterparts (particularly Whiteacre) under the impress of battle. A lesson in the differences between the possibilities offered by a free society and those presented by a totalitarian one was thus proposed. The movie entirely reverses Diestl's development. As the film develops, he grows more and more disenchanted with Nazism, with war in general. In other words, his moral growth, instead of being contrasted to that of his American counterparts, parallels it.

Brando has often been accused of imposing this change on the movie. But the film's director, Edward Dmytryk, and its screenwriter, Edward Anhalt, both thought that with the war over a decade into the past it was perhaps more fruitful to make the film less of an anti-Nazi tract and more an anti-war piece. Besides changing Christian's character, they also changed the climactic combat scene. In the novel the Nazi kills the Jew and then the Wasp kills the Nazi. The movie permitted Ackerman to survive, and leaves in doubt whether he or his friend killed Christian, who, in this version, fires no shots at them at all.

Brando, who had been recruited to the project because it would enable him honorably to repay yet another contractual debt to Fox, agreed with these revisions, and he became their chief public defender. For example, when the production was on location in Germany, he told a press conference: 'Irwin Shaw wrote his great book while war hatreds were white hot. We hope they have cooled. The picture will try to show that Nazism is a matter of mind, not geography; that there are Nazis – and people of goodwill – in every country.'

In any case, Shaw was infuriated by the revisions, and he came to Paris as shooting began, arriving not long after a waiter in a restaurant spilled a scalding pot of tea in Brando's lap, causing third-degree burns around the genital area, and briefly hospitalizing him. When he came back to work he was not in the best of moods – especially for a television interview that David Schoenbrun of CBS set up with him and Shaw. 'Any problems with the characterization?' the correspondent asked, not entirely innocently. No, said the actor. Yes, said the writer. Shaw then accused Brando of changing the role because he wanted to appear sympathetic on the screen. Brando replied that Shaw knew nothing about the character. 'It's my character,' Shaw replied hotly. 'I gave birth to him. I created him.' 'Nobody creates a character but an actor,' Brando replied. 'I play the role, now he exists. He is my creation.' The conversation deteriorated still further. Shaw called Brando 'stupid', and raised his fists to him.

Subsequently, Shaw was chastised by Hemingway himself for caring so volubly about the matter. 'What you do,' said Papa, 'is sell your book to the movies, go to the bar, and take a drink. You don't think about the movie, you don't look at the movie, you know it's going to be a piece of shit. The idea of selling a book to the movies is to make money.'

The conflicts attending this production now seem rather academic. *The Young Lions* is, finally, a popular fiction. Its characters are archetypes in a schematized story, and its best quality is its relentless narrative pressure. To the degree that the movie kept that up it served the novel reasonably well. Since its story could sustain with equal logic either the author's moral or the one that replaced it on the screen, it really does not make much difference what the movie actually said.

Moreover, all concerned had reason, in the end, to thank Brando. This is not sloppy work. It is, in fact, more interesting than Montgomery Clift's, which is a version of his performance in *From Here to Eternity* – another sensitive barrack-room outsider. In Brando's long absences, while the Ackerman-Whiteacre story is pursued, one misses him. His performance in the opening passages, with Whiteacre's fiancée, is very good, soft and

tentative, and patient in his attempt to avoid conflict, get on with his seduction. 'I sink ve should not discuss zis,' he says as politics rears its ugly head at a New Year's Eve party, 'because I don't know all the answers, you don't know the answers. Political discussions go 'round and 'round.'

This is a character unformed when we meet him, therefore with somewhere to go emotionally as the film proceeds. Building this kind of a line was something Brando was often more attentive to than his scripts were. Yet this line, which leads toward his reformation and ultimate martyrdom, is walked ambiguously. Indeed, it is possible to see what happens to Diestl more ironically than the arguments about this character might lead one to think. At the start of the war, you can sense his pleasure in his fine new uniform. You can sense his confusion when a Frenchwoman rejects his advances: he is not, as he sees it, personally responsible for the ugliness of occupation, and he is genuinely puzzled to be a victim of prejudice. When he protests against totalitarian methods ('I don't think it's possible to remake the world from the basement of a dirty little police station') it is as a 'good' German, correct and fastidious, not a political radical.

You can sense his confusions beginning to reach a resolution when he is ordered to participate in a massacre on the African front, but you can also sense a desire to compromise those confusions, to retain an outward show of loyalty, whatever levels of disgust he is reaching inwardly. He does, finally, toy with the idea of desertion, after his friend Hardenburg (Maximillian Schell) is grotesquely wounded and inveigles Diestl into providing him with the means to commit suicide. But even then, confronting his comrade's slatternly wife with news of her husband's death, there is a marvelously Germanic rectitude about him. This character may eventually turn his back on the evils of Nazism, but he is always loyal, humanly and rather touchingly so, to the larger cultural tradition that formed both the light and the dark sides of a national character. Even in his final moment, when he aims his gun at Ackerman and Whiteacre, you feel it is possible for him to shoot out of that larger, good-soldier's sense of duty. He does not, firing instead a shot in the air,

An off-screen
conversation with
Montgomery Clift,
one of Brando's
co-stars in *The
Young Lions* and
his only serious
rival among his
generation of
actors.

which reveals his presence. This may or may not be an act of suicide, but it is surely an irony, and one that is in keeping with the tormented and never quite emotionally resolute character Brando has given us.

The hunger Brando had expressed to Capote, and would go on expressing, for moral leadership or, anyway, for film roles that would instruct the world in right behavior, ill became him. He was, if anything, the poet of our ambivalences, the not-so-secret sharer of our dubiety about all those cocksure voices, amplified by the media bullhorn, who always seemed to know what they were doing and what we should be doing – about the Cold War, about mental health, about family life, about what did and did not constitute a good society and what programs were required to create one.

What, then, was Brando doing? Groping for words, I think, metaphors for his inchoate discontents. And not finding the right ones, finding exactly the wrong ones. When he finished *The Young Lions*, Brando paused in his career. It would be over two years before he appeared on the screen again. It is appropriate for us to pause as well, and reflect on his recent accomplishments. He had appeared in five movies since *On the Waterfront*, an average of one a year. All five had been major commercial successes. But all five had been based either on a best-selling novel or on a long-running Broadway play, all of them in their origins mainstream works. All of them, save *Guys and Dolls*, had embodied sincere, but comfortably stated, messages: against war or racism, in favor of peace and tolerance – something of which we could unquestionably approve. Setting his ridiculous Napoleon and his unfortunate Sakini aside, Brando's work in three of them, whatever their overall creative failures, whatever his own dissatisfactions, whatever his own trouble-making on the set, was, finally, worthwhile.

The great thing about all these performances was the factor that had first distinguished Brando's work from most of the movie-star acting that had preceded it, derived from his insistence on letting his characters grow. His comings to consciousness, even in these big mainstream movies, continued to be more interesting than those of other movie protagonists precisely because, in

the films' early passages, he was unafraid to portray foolishness, moral blindness, even stupidity. He made sure we understood that most heroism begins in anti-heroism. Or at least non-heroism.

And yet, increasingly, what he was doing was discomfiting to many of us, and not just those who shared his theatrical generation's ambitions for him. I think he felt what we felt, but could not, any more than we could at the time, articulate his disappointment at what he was doing. Moreover, though his native intelligence and his intuitions are first-rate, he is not a man who is much good at formulating formal arguments for or against a course of action, nor does he seem to have any capacity for the kind of analytical thinking required to bring a movie from idea to script to finished form. Or to criticize it coherently. Finally, it was not in Brando's nature to express his feelings directly. In effect, when he expatiated on the subtextual matters he thought his movies should be taking up, he said 'politics' when he meant to say 'lostness' or 'loneliness' or possibly even 'existential pain'.

And now he wished to serve as his own producer, to act decisively and forthrightly on his own behalf, risking that which was the hardest thing to risk, open wrathfulness on the part of others when he dared to manifest his wishes

Anna Kashfi, whom Brando married suddenly in 1957 after shooting *The Young Lions*. Their acrimonious divorce two years later was followed by a series of custody battles, lasting many years, over their son Christian.

Directing the highly
original western, *One-Eyed
Jacks* (1961). Brando's
work was painstaking and
imaginative, but he shot
far too much film and the
task of cutting it was
beyond him.

1961

and needs openly. It puts it mildly to say that he was not really a good candidate to exercise the kind of creative autonomy that some other stars of his stature had begun to wield in this decade. But it was also obvious to him that he had to try, as, indeed, his work on the 'western' that so amused Capote and Pennebaker's acquisition of other properties had indicated.

When he finished *The Young Lions* in late 1957, Brando meant to get serious, at last, about independent production. He was, however, distracted by, of all unlikely occurrences, marriage. Just weeks after finishing his picture he suddenly wed Anna Kashfi, in a match that was a disaster from the start and would have consequences that reverberate to this day, since Christian Brando is their issue. Their courtship, however, was desultory until she was stricken with tuberculosis and Brando – characteristically – took pity on her helplessness, becoming a devoted visitor at her bedside. She was surely Brando's type: a small, dark, exotically attractive woman who claimed to be of Anglo-Indian background. Unfortunately, as soon as the press announced their marriage, her father, a man named Callahan, living in England, stepped forward to proclaim that she had been born there, had no Indian blood, and had not, to his knowledge, ever set foot on the subcontinent. She stuck to her story, but Brando was outraged by her duplicity, and, though she was pregnant, they separated. There was, it seems, a brief reconciliation when the child was born, but thereafter their relationship deteriorated into scandalous animosity. Hers was an addictive personality, and a vindictive one, and their battles over custody of their child persisted for years, and included dramatic abductions. No outsider, of course, can calculate what harm may have been done the boy by this miserable chain of events, but it cannot have been minor.

Be that as it may, Brando was surely even less focused than usual when he addressed the problems of creating a screenplay for the film that was eventually to be known as *One-Eyed Jacks*. Aside from the fact that both scripts contained characters of Mexican extraction, there seems to be but a small relationship between this western and the one that so amused Capote in 1956. The new project was

at least initially based on a novel by Charles Neider called *The Authentic Death of Hendry Jones*. The novelist did a first-draft screenplay for producer Frank Rosenberg, who submitted it to Brando, who, in turn, committed to it in a matter of days – unprecedented decisiveness for him. Of course, there would have to be rewrites . . .

And then the fun began. Having liked, for obvious reasons, Stanley Kubrick's great pacifist film, *Paths of Glory*, Brando eagerly agreed to him as director. Calder Willingham, whose novel about military school life, *End as a Man*, may have recommended him to Brando, was signed on as screenwriter. Now, for months on end, they met virtually every day to work on the script at the handsome, but not overwhelming, home Brando had recently purchased on Mulholland Drive, near Coldwater Canyon. In time, Willingham was dismissed, to be replaced by Guy Trosper, and finally, when disputes over casting arose, Kubrick decamped.

It might have profited all concerned to consult Capote's *New Yorker* article, which had appeared by this time, for in it Brando had insisted that he only meant what he said about forty per cent of the time, and he had also offered an estimate of his attention span – seven minutes. There is no reason to doubt either figure, and both were relevant to these discussions. Hollywood people are accustomed to assume that whatever the star says is definitive, not to be trifled with, and so rush to do his bidding, which in this case must surely have resulted in many a spitballed idea getting written into this or that draft of the script – or at the least leading to many wasted, confusing hours of discussion. The limit of the star's ability to concentrate must, similarly, have led to the abandonment of promising lines of attack before they were fully explored, as well as the failure to resolve many another issue presented by the story line.

Yes, of course, Brando's hand was all aces in a game where the deck was inevitably loaded in his favor. And the script, if we can judge it by that portion of it that finally made it to the screen, surely reflects many of his preoccupations. Essentially, *One-Eyed Jacks* is a revenge

Right The Rio Kid escapes from jail in *One-Eyed Jacks*. This brooding character can be seen as the juvenile delinquent that Brando didn't get to develop fully in *The Wild One*.

western. Two gunmen, the Rio Kid (Brando) and Dad Longworth (Karl Malden), make a fine living robbing Mexican banks. One day, however, they are ambushed by mounted police. One of their horses is lamed, and they flip a coin to determine who will ride away on their remaining mount in search of another. Rio loses and Dad never returns. Rio spends five years in a Sonora jail. Escaping, he and his confederates learn of a 'cheesebox' bank in Monterrey, where coincidentally Dad, having gone straight, is the sheriff. As it turns out he is married, and with a beautiful stepdaughter named Louisa (Pina Pellicer). Rio, pretending that he too escaped capture, claims no grudge against Dad. But, of course, he intends to rob the bank, kill Dad, and seduce the girl. However, he kills a man who is mistreating a bar girl, and Dad administers a brutal flogging (the most sadistic of all Brando's on-screen beatings) and then breaks his gun hand. Rio and his gang retreat to a picturesque fishing village up the coast where he recuperates. He returns to rob the bank, is jailed, and sentenced to hang. But Louisa smuggles a derringer in to him, and he escapes, finally kills Dad, and promising to return to the girl, who is now carrying his child, he rides off.

Dad. Dad. Dad. A smooth, well-spoken, pious man. Highly respected in the community. Yet a man with a secret life. A betrayer of trusts. And unconscionably cruel to his Kid. Who is inarticulate. A young man putting a hard face on his sensitivities. A young man who, despite his rough manners, is quick to defend the defenseless. Eventually Kid kills Dad. What could the uncredited author of this screenplay have been thinking about? One resorts to irony only to avoid belaboring the obvious.

It must be judged a perfectly serviceable, even enjoyable, tale as far as the unknowing public was concerned. And if *One-Eyed Jacks* only incidentally took up the kind of obvious moral issues that Brando had so often insisted he wanted to address in movies, it did take up, metaphorically, the kind of psychological issues that were of moment to Brando. It might well have been, in the end, a satisfying experience for him, and one that might have opened opportunities to express himself in his own way on the screen.

But then he decided to direct the picture himself. The job *was* open. Rosenberg demurred. And it seems likely that his backers at Paramount entered some questions about the idea. Brando was not, after all, an unknown quantity. He was a type that had always, and not incorrectly, frightened production executives. But . . . well, he was a star. Look at those grosses. So greed came into play. And also hope: maybe if we give him a good cameraman . . . a smart AD . . . a solid production manager. And a darker thought: chasten his arrogance, teach him a lesson. How much can it cost? He whom Hollywood would humble, it first indulges. It is, perhaps, the most basic law of the business. Brando didn't see any of that. 'I've got no respect for acting,' he declared. And: 'Acting is a bum's life in that it leads to perfect self-indulgence.' And: 'You get paid for doing nothing and it all adds up to nothing.' Heigh-ho, the director's life for me.

A two-month shoot stretched to six months. A two million dollar budget went to six. A million feet of film were exposed, 250,000 feet printed – six times as much as usual in the first instance, more than three times as much as usual in the second. The rough assemblage of the work ran close to five hours. Brando was meticulous – you'd have to give him that. He waited hours for the right light, or for the cloud formations to reach their most photogenic proportions. He covered every sequence from every imaginable angle. But eventually, it is said, cast and crew were standing around on the set, helping him decide on an ending by putting alternatives to a democratic vote.

And when Brando got all this stuff back to the cutting-room, he despaired of it. Cutting a film, especially one with this much exposed footage, requires the patience of Job, and the concentrated eye of a pointillist. The directorial temperament is not, usually, the actor's temperament. Good, bad, or indifferent, a director has to be decisive, keep things moving. Actors, by contrast, like to examine alternatives, let someone else decide what to keep, what to throw out. Brando, in fact, abandoned the task and took another acting job. Costs, of course, continued to mount as post-production crept along for months more than was customary.

In the end *One-Eyed Jacks* did not return its negative cost, let alone the additional nine million dollars it cost to place it in release. And yet it is an achievement of sorts. It *is* a beautiful film – the decision to shoot the last half of the western by the seaside in Monterey is both original and productive of wondrous imagery. Much of the dialogue has a gritty, period quality to it. Malden, given a chance to do evil – an opportunity not vouchsafed him before – relishes it. Brando himself is marvelously broody; this is perhaps the juvenile delinquent he didn't get to develop fully in *The Wild One*. Yes, the movie is self-evidently self-indulgent. And, yes, it has its *longueurs*; and, yes, in effect, it has two climaxes, the first of which, the flogging and its aftermath, is by far the stronger. Brando's chief objection to the finished film, an ending in which he and Louisa do not die, is irrelevant. There was no tragic inevitability implicit in this script; no reason, therefore, why a little hint of eventual romantic reunion is unacceptable, after the Kid has out-run the posse pursuing him for the shooting of Dad.

But, of course, Brando made his post-partum blues public. Directing, he now said, is 'like being an emotional traffic cop'. And (ludicrously): 'I'm a businessman. I'm a captain of industry – nothing else. Any pretensions I've had of being artistic are now just a chilly hope.'

Certainly any hopes he had of being a director were, for the foreseeable future, frozen. And it is too bad. *One-Eyed Jacks* was for a time a cult film, granted that status by those who remained faithful to Brando's promise. With the passage of time, it seems better than that. The western was the one traditional genre that prospered in the Fifties, a place where a certain toughness of mind and spirit could still flourish. *The Gunfighter* and *High Noon*, *Winchester '73* and *Shane*, *The Searchers* and *Rio Bravo* – whatever their defects, these films exercise a claim on movie history and our affection. *One-Eyed Jacks* belongs among them. And in its quirkiness it is not the least of them.

The work for which its star-director deserted it need not detain us long. *The Fugitive Kind* is the movie version of the Tennessee Williams play, *Orpheus Descending*, which Brando had long been criticized for not doing. Now it was to be brought to the screen with Anna Magnani, the very

actress he once claimed 'would have wiped me off the stage', in the original Broadway production. Williams insisted that the work, despite its roots in classical myth, was emotionally autobiographical. Certainly he had been persistently loyal to it, since it was a reworking of his first produced work, *Battle of Angels*, which closed out of town in 1940. It is a high-pitched melodrama, in which Val Xavier, a guitar-pickin' singer wearing a snakeskin jacket, symbolic of his freedom from convention, finds an underworld on earth when he wanders into a small town and takes up with a storekeeper's lusty, middle-aged wife, enjoys a flirtation with a nymphomaniacal heiress, and comes to a brutal end.

Brando is miscast in this role, despite Williams's long-standing passion to place him in it. And that may account for Brando's equally long-standing resistance to it. For he is, in effect, the Blanche Dubois of the film, a delicate soul set upon, ultimately martyred by the cruel world. Since his sensitivity, played as unworldly innocence, is established at the outset, the pleasure of seeing him come to consciousness – a movement that defined all of his best previous work – is denied us, and denied the actor as well. Aside from a well-written opening courtroom monologue, which outlines Val's background and character, and which Brando does with poignant simplicity, the movie is most of the time one of those insanely miscalculated ventures that at first creates laughter and then an appalled silence. It is said that Williams was hissed as he left the New York premiere, and its grosses were said to be not just minor, but humiliatingly so. It is also said, however, that Brando received a million dollars for his services – if so, it was the first time any actor received a seven-figure salary, thus a significant milestone on the way to Hollywood's present wildly inflated pay scale. It was obviously enough to return Pennebaker to a semblance of solvency. In addition the work repaid whatever debt Brando may have been thought to owe Williams and the theatrical tradition that had formed him. It also provided an excuse for avoiding it in the future.

Was Brando's movie career now in trouble? Not really. The largest cost to him was that work on this film,

5

1962

together with his delays in finishing his western, prevented him from taking the leading role in *Lawrence of Arabia*, which Sam Spiegel offered him – certainly proof of his continued viability. One might even imagine the mogul community imagining that he had learned valuable lessons from *One-Eyed Jacks* and *The Fugitive Kind*. All he needed to do was return to what industry leaders still believed was the main line. If not *Lawrence*, why not *Mutiny on the Bounty*? Superficially, it represented the same wisdom. Based on a beloved best-seller and a movie that everyone remembered as wonderful, it offered spectacle and romance, action and exotic adventure. And a fine part for a man with a rebel's image: Fletcher Christian, leader of the morally defensible mutiny against the sadistic Captain Bligh; Clark Gable's old role. Best of all, from its point of view, MGM, which was financing the project, owned all rights to all three of the Charles

Nordhof-James Norman Hall historical novels about the *Bounty*.

Brando was interested. And he offered producer Aaron Rosenberg a little suggestion. Might not the work be made more meaningful to modern audiences if it went on past the point where the first film had stopped, showed something more of the mutineers' life on Pitcairns Island than the original film had (it stopped short of Mr Christian's early death)? Rosenberg agreed to accommodate the star's ideas.

It was his first mistake, though a rounding off, in some way, of the original film's conclusion was surely worth a try. That redoubtable craftsman, Eric Ambler, the espionage novelist, took a first crack at the story. His work was deemed unsatisfactory. Thereafter, five other writers were employed on it, running up a bill for story costs alone of some $237,000. Eventually, the company

With Trevor Howard, Gordon Jackson and Richard Harris, his often exasperated co-stars, at a dramatic moment in *Mutiny on the Bounty* (1962).

set forth for the South Seas without a finished script. And without a finished *Bounty*. The shipwrights working on the authentic reproduction fell some six weeks behind schedule. That was only the beginning of the technical difficulties that plagued the production. The weather and the seas were more changeable than they were supposed to be, so there was trouble matching shots in sequences. And, since the seas were also running high, many sequences were slow, dangerous going.

The lack of a finished script didn't help matters. With approval over its finished form, Brando wrangled endlessly over it with the director, the gentlemanly Englishman Carol Reed, a fine director who had never before undertaken a production on this epic scale – though it is doubtful whether even a tough, resourceful veteran of large-scale action films could have handled this combination of problems. In the confusion, needless to say, bored and anxious actors began to fall out. Richard Harris, playing John Mills, Christian's co-conspirator, and Trevor Howard, playing Bligh, both became testy with Brando – to put it mildly. He remained, for the most part, in good spirits. This was his introduction to the South Seas, and he was genuinely enraptured by the handsome natives (he began an affair with Tarita, who was playing the role of an island princess, and he would eventually have children with her, and marry her as well) and by a lifestyle that suited him philosophically – languid and unconcerned with getting, spending and celebrity.

Still, twentieth-century reality, or at least the motion picture industry version of it, was always near at hand. When a production manager put together a revised schedule, indicating that after months on location the picture still needed 139 days to complete, the picture was shut down and the company returned to Los Angeles to work on interiors and backlot sequences. Rosenberg, Brando, and Reed were called into executive conference, and when Reed, now ailing from kidney stones and exhaustion, could not in conscience promise to finish the film in the hundred days the studio now mandated, he was asked to leave (or perhaps volunteered to). In any case, most of the footage he shot was scrapped. Brando was outraged. He had had his differences with Reed, but

for the most part he had been a good and patient father figure. To replace him, Rosenberg signed Lewis Milestone. He had made great films in his day (notably *All Quiet on the Western Front*), but his reputation had diminished over the years. This was principally because he had not always been wise in his selection of stories, for his craftsmanship, even on rather ungrateful projects, remained bold. The trouble was that he was now in his late sixties, not in entirely good health, and, even in the best of circumstances, not someone who enjoyed talking things over with his actors. Confronted by a star in an advanced state of the sulks, Milestone responded in kind. Very quickly they were communicating solely through intermediaries – if at all. This was Milestone's recollection, some years later: 'Right or wrong, the man simply took charge of everything. You had the option of sitting and watching him or turning your back on him.'

The return to Tahiti was no return to paradise; it was production hell. The same troubles that afflicted the company on its first visit – the weather and the seas – recurred, and this time large numbers of people were hurt (and one was killed) in a sequence in which a small boatload of deserters is pursued, on Bligh's orders, by a party in native war canoes. Before the picture was wrapped, Milestone quit and solid George Seaton shot the concluding sequence, Christian's death. For this the actor bedded himself on two hundred pounds of ice so that he could duplicate authentically the death tremors he had witnessed at his mother's bedside.

By the time it was finished, the *Mutiny on the Bounty* negative cost some $20 million, double the original budget, and with another $7 million tacked on for prints and advertising, it was bringing MGM dangerously close to bankruptcy. In the long months between completion of principal photography and release of the film, stories about the troubles on set, already widely rumored, began leaking to the press. And, somehow, Brando seemed responsible for all of them. That he had caused some delays is unquestionable, but the fact is that the really costly mistakes of this production – those stemming from the unfinished script, the delay in ship construction, the ill-scouted and at best very difficult location – could not fairly be blamed on him. Rather obviously he was being scapegoated by studio executives, who were using the supine showbiz press, as they often did, to help them. The journalism finally reached such a level of viciousness that Brando felt obliged to bring a libel suit against one publication and its writer.

The public had long understood Brando to be a difficult chap, and, in any case, public knowledge that the star was being paid what was in those days a huge sum, $1,250,000 against a percentage, did not increase sympathy for him inside or outside the industry. When the picture was released, it was not Brando's performance that was reviewed, but his reputation, and most of the notices were negative, if not downright defamatory. The distrust and dislike of Brando felt by older, more conservative critics and audience, and *haut* Hollywood, until then silenced by his success, could now safely spew forth.

At first prejudiced glance, Brando's performance was clearly not Gable's – and that was held against him. But, in fact, it was a much better Fletcher Christian. Gable's Christian had been a stolid, no-nonsense, very American sort of hero. Brando first appears as a drawling fop, with a dandy's red cape swirling about him, a handkerchief tucked in his elegant sleeve, handsome ladies on his arm, talk of a swell country weekend on his lips. He infuriates Bligh, an officer up from the ranks and sensitive to class slights. Since the *Bounty*'s mission is to collect samples of breadfruit, thought to be useful in feeding the masses, Brando is languidly contemptuous – 'halfway 'round the world on a grocer's errand'.

It is a delicious performance, wonderfully comic, and socially acute (his accent perfectly placed, he is clearly of the squirearchy); and its beginnings – once again – leave the actor somewhere to go. Indeed, what can eventually be read as rebellion begins as upper-class needling. That Bligh has a corrupt side and a sadistic streak comes almost as a surprise to Christian, and the principled opposition to the captain that develops in him, as evidence of misconduct piles up, comes as a surprise to him, too. It is, at first, unimaginable to him that he might become the leader of a mutiny. He conducts it, when finally he must, with impeccable manners. And he seeks most earnestly to convert it into something else, not just an end to wretched conditions, but a beginning of a better alternative.

Indeed, Brando's playing of the tragic last passages on Pitcairn, with his shipmates falling into moral disarray, his hopes coming at last to nothing as the *Bounty* burns in the harbor, completes the thoughtful arc of his performance. His own line is almost strong enough to compensate for the fact that the dramatic line he insisted on for the movie remained essentially intractable, imposing on it a whimpering conclusion. Yet he does not lose our sympathy. 'I did what honor dictated, and that belief sustains me,' he says, before adding, still with something of the wicked dandy about him, 'except for a slight desire to be dead.' If the rest of the actors – giving much more conventional performances – had been up to him, and if his directors had imagined a way to key this elephantine enterprise to his eccentric work, they might yet have pulled off an artistic coup. Or anyway a cult classic.

It would have been useless at the time to point any of this out, such was the hue and cry about Brando's brave and original performance, which, taken together with the stories that had preceded it, and the commercial failure that followed, did irreparable harm to his career and perhaps to his self-regard. What might have been seen as the great climax to this phase of his career was instead seen as its nadir, the bad end which so many had for so long predicted. He would be many years recovering from this fiasco.

But let a good and wise director, soon to enter Brando's life, have the final, and more nearly accurate, word. Said Arthur Penn, some years later: 'Hollywood loves to elevate someone to stardom and then start tearing him down. When you have someone like Brando, who is a superbly creative human being, I think they are terrified of him and I think that was probably the case on *Bounty*. Personally, I thought his performance was a terrific work of art.'

Right Brando as the reluctant mutineer Fletcher Christian. His wrangling over the script made Carol Reed's job difficult, but he was outraged when the gentlemanly English director was replaced.

CHAPTER SIX

FOOLISH SEASON

In 1966, Pauline Kael, considering Brando at mid passage (he was then forty-two), summoned no less an authority than Ralph Waldo Emerson to help her define the issues her favorite actor was then confronting. 'Thou must pass for a fool and a churl for a long season,' the Transcendentalist sage had advised the American artist a century before. Kael added this gloss: 'We used to think that the season meant only youth, before the artist could prove his talent, make his place, achieve something. Now it is clear that for screen artists, and perhaps not only for screen artists, youth is, relatively speaking, the short season: the long one is the degradation after success.'

Taking the role of Grindl, the lecherous Indian guru, in Christian Marquand's *Candy*, was just one of the strange career choices Brando made in the Sixties. But he was a great sight gag.

Right Equally bizarre was his pairing with David Niven in *Bedtime Story*, a comedy about the rivalry of two gigolos on the French Riviera. However, Brando admired his co-star and said he could learn from actors like him.

She likened the development of Brando's career to that of the typical hero of a typical movie, at first discovered to be in some way atypical, either more idealistic or more cynical than the norm, then forced by the mechanisms of the plot to be either raised or lowered until he seems to share the values common to the audience. Brando's entire public life, says Kael, follows that line, except that, desperate to escape from ordinariness, he had chosen 'to become an eccentric, which in this country means a clown, possibly the only way left to preserve some kind of difference.'

One trouble with that argument is that Brando always *was* a weirdo, long before anyone ever heard of him. Surely his 'eccentricity' deepened with the passing years, but the overall evidence is that he consciously chose to stress that side of his nature less, not more, in his Sixties work. This is almost perverse given the decade's larger social currents and trends within the movie industry. After all, black comedy was increasingly 'in', and there really was a sexual revolution going on. Both were matters that should have interested Brando the actor and Brando the screen character. Apparently, most of the time, he didn't feel like being funny or sexy in public. It is also likely, as we shall see, that his response to roles was dulled by his inability to connect consistently with directors who would create for him the kind of atmosphere that he needed for his work. Time and again we find him beginning movies in good spirits, contributing good moments to them, then withdrawing emotionally.

It is convenient to blame his troubles on Hollywood crassness and insensitivity and on a malevolence particularly directed at Brando. Depending on your point of view, Hollywood is either a closely knit community, jealously protective of its own rather conservative social standards, or it is tribal in a harsh and primitive sort of way, quick to banish individuals whose weaknesses seem to endanger the tribe's welfare. Its behavior is particularly vicious toward box office leaders who become laggards – especially if, like Brando, they were not, when they were on top, notably sensitive to local standards of *politesse*. One does have to take tables at

charity functions, pay elaborate tribute to prominent dolts and nincompoops, 'put back in' (as a favorite local saying has it) to an industry that has treated you generously. All of which says nothing of its natural fear of singular and rebellious talents.

His enemies, however, may not have been as important in shaping (or misshaping) Brando's career as his friends were. Hollywood's business style is a curious mix of the avuncular, the confrontational, and the careless – all quite transparently obvious. What happened to Brando was not that anybody asked him to 'sell out'. Or forced him to. It was that attempts to rescue his suddenly faltering career by perfectly well-meaning people produced dismal unintended consequences.

It happened like this: in the wake of the *Bounty*'s disastrous voyage, it was apparent that Brando required a safe harbor in which to lay up and repair damages. And MCA, his long-time agents, were now in a position to provide one. In 1959, the agency, in a complicated deal mainly predicated on its need for production facilities for television programs it was packaging for clients, had taken control of Universal Studios. The business plan was to use TV as a source of profits, steadying the company against the higher risks inherent in feature production, and as a place where new talent could be developed, old talent pastured. They determined, as well, to make their theatrical films on a carefully cost-controlled basis. Jay Kantor, Brando's trusted agent, became a highly placed production executive at Universal, and he offered the star a one-picture deal for the modestly priced Pennebaker production of *The Ugly American*, as Brando's first picture after *Bounty*. Soon thereafter Universal bought Pennebaker for a reported $1 million, in a deal that obliged Brando to make a certain number of films for the studio on a non-exclusive basis.

Brando was not the only MCA client who found a home at Universal, but he was probably the one least likely to succeed at a studio committed to cost-conscious, genre-oriented production. On the other hand, the studio had no desire to sabotage him, and had every motive to return him to success. Brando may have imagined he could make this arrangement work for him in another way, since it provided him with financial stability while leaving him free to embark on other more ambitious or more 'personal' projects. One can discern, in at least half the films Brando did in the Sixties and early Seventies, reasons why an actor of his background would take them on. That almost all of them failed, often ludicrously, to fulfill their promise does not invalidate his enthusiasms. Neither does the fact that some of his directors failed to fulfill their promise to provide him with the creative atmosphere he required, failed to listen to him, take his ideas seriously.

It was now possible to impute to his renunciations, and ultimately his degradations, a certain martyred nobility. But even so, for his core audience, the disappointments were acute. It was not just that he was working in bad pictures; that could be the luck of the draw, or an inevitable balancing out of his average. It was that for the most part he was working in *cheap* bad pictures.

For, with just a couple of exceptions, his Sixties movies did not have even the commercial ambitions of his second-phase films. They were mostly – to the degree that the term was still applicable – program pictures. Whether at Universal or elsewhere, his films were routinely made, generally by directors who turned out not to be first-class; by other craftsmen of no great distinction; with supporting casts of the most modest attainments. They were designed primarily to keep studios and distribution systems humming – well, no, busied, since Hollywood could not be said to have been humming in this period (box office receipts reached their all-time low in 1962; attendance was cut in half, and fell below 20 million per week, for the first time, in 1967).

Finally – and this was perhaps the most grievous of all defects in a time when Brando himself, and most of his natural, middle-brow audience, were galvanically politicized by the Civil Rights struggle and the war in Vietnam – only two or three of them were endowed with any sort of contemporary social or political relevance. At a moment when one might have expected Brando's social consciousness to be rewarded with the kind of work he had the right to expect, he suddenly seemed in every respect irrelevant.

Like many of us in this period, Brando suffered not merely from career confusions, but from personal and ideological confusions as well. His private life, not to put too fine a point on it, was a mess. He divorced Kashfi in 1959, and finally married Movita at a secret ceremony in 1960, because she, like Kashfi before her, was pregnant. In 1962 they, too, separated, more or less amicably. But there was nothing amicable about his relationship with Kashfi. Their custody battles over their son, Christian, continued on into the 1970s: throughout this period they were in and out of court, asserting their claims on the boy. To complicate matters still further, by 1970 Brando had fathered two more children with Tarita.

It seems worth recording his remarks to Capote a few years earlier on the subject of love: 'What other reason is there for living? Except love. That has been my main trouble. My inability to love. . . . I can't love anyone. I can't trust anyone enough to give myself to anyone. . . .' It was not an uncommon confession from a man of his age and background, especially one who was in the midst of a twenty-year course in psychoanalysis. Nor was his relationship with his children unique, just rather more complicated than most, given their varied maternal backgrounds and his unique status in our celebrity hierarchy.

Like a lot of successful, preoccupied men, Brando appears to have been an affectionate and indulgent father, but often a very distant one. Christian, for example, seems to have had everything he needed, except the things a child needs most – emotional and geographical stability. In those periods when Brando did have custody of him he was often left in the care of Brando's women friends or of his sister Fran and her husband in Illinois. There were spells in boarding school, too. How could his father expect the boy to grow up untroubled? The practicalities of the situation were daunting. This was especially so because Brando now embraced political activism, becoming more than ever a restless wanderer on behalf of the causes that stirred him. This was not entirely uncharacteristic behavior among performers during this period. And, of course, there was nothing especially compelling going on in Brando's career.

Brando the political activist. On an anti-apartheid platform in London he questions a South African Indian about race relations in his country. On the left is the critic Kenneth Tynan, then artistic adviser to the National Theatre.

He travelled widely in support of the Civil Rights movement, abandoning his reclusive ways for extensive public appearances. Among them, prominently, were the Selma, Alabama, and the Washington, DC, civil rights marches of 1965. After Martin Luther King's assassination in 1968, he walked through Harlem with New York mayor John V. Lindsay, in a successful attempt to calm riotous unrest. A month later he was in Berkeley on a more controversial mission – an appearance at a memorial service for a member of the Black Panthers, slain by police. In this tragic year, he went everywhere, even into the jungle of the talk shows – the last place one expected to find him – on behalf of the movement. He seemed to want to take on himself all the guilt of the white race for all the inequities visited on the blacks. He even tithed a percentage of his income to the Southern Christian Leadership Conference.

At the same time, he worked for UNICEF, attempting to make a documentary about starvation in India. Later, in the mid-Seventies, his concern for the fate of American Indians brought him to Wounded Knee, to the Menominee Uprising in Wisconsin, to many a fund-raiser for the cause, and, at the height of his involvement, to stage-managing his famous non-appearance at the 1973 Academy Award broadcast at which a surrogate rejected his *Godfather* Oscar as a frivolity not to be countenanced when most native Americans were discriminated against, kept in dire poverty, and grievously under- and misrepresented in film and television.

Until this later period, when his passions seemed to run away with him, Brando the activist was almost as singular as Brando the actor. But in the opposite way. For unlike many of the other performers who thrust themselves forward as spokespersons for this or that cause, he caused almost no controversy. In the Sixties, he took positions, contributed his presence, but almost never made pronouncements. He did not strike revolutionary poses in public. His manner, instead, was very much that of less famous liberals, quietly, self-effacingly bearing witness to the things he believed in. Nor did his involvement with the Civil Rights movement lead him, as it did so many other celebrities, to noisy opposition to the war in Vietnam. To put it simply, he was no Jane Fonda.

To trace Brando's course through the Sixties is to trace a course many followed, albeit less colorfully: from political engagement via support for the Civil Rights movement to disengagement when its fervor, but not its capacity for making careful distinctions between allies and enemies, was taken over by the anti-war movement. A spirit that, for a moment, held the promise of erasing many class distinctions, was transformed, through violence and the crudest kind of media manipulation, into a spirit that exacerbated those distinctions. It was at this point that Brando's involvement with the Indian rights movement became his primary public issue. By then no one was paying much attention to Marlon Brando, and until his re-emergence in the Seventies as a leading spokesman for, and a significant contributor to this movement, he kept quite a low profile. There was a moment when, devastated by the murders of Martin Luther King and Robert Kennedy, it was rumored that he might abandon acting altogether and devote himself entirely to quasi-political activity. On the other hand, there was also speculation that he might withdraw from *all* forms of public life. He has himself said that he was, by that time, 'paralyzed with hopelessness', but he attributed that to the hunger and misery he had seen on his travels in the Third World. It also seems likely that the disarray of his career contributed to the distinct air of withdrawal that hung about him in the last two years of the Sixties and the first two of the Seventies.

Whatever his reasons, it was in 1968, that watershed year in recent American politics, that, after a search that had taken him to Mexico, Bali, and Thailand among other locales, he bought Tetaroa, a circular atoll consisting of thirteen small islands thirty miles north of Tahiti. He had first glimpsed it during the making of *Bounty*, and now he imagined that it might be a place where he and his family could achieve self-sufficiency and survive the nuclear holocaust that recent events had convinced him would soon come. As late as 1976, he still thought world devastation was likely. He told a journalist visiting him on Tetaroa: 'The end is near, if not at hand.'

One may reasonably speculate that he was over-dramatizing, justifying a decision that was not in some respects very practical. Tetaroa may be a great place to lie low, but, quite literally, it lies low, about five feet above sea level. His hopes for a vacation hotel were

spoiled by flooding – and importunate guests. With a shudder he would recall 'Middle-aged ladies from Peoria telling me, "Mr Brando, we loved you as Napoleon" for Christsake.' In more recent times he has devoted himself to experiments in aquaculture, and the islands are also, apparently, a notable sanctuary for tropical birds.

If we look more closely at Brando's movie work in this period it becomes obvious, however, that within the increasingly limited options available to him it was the actor in him, not the political idealist, that he was usually trying to satisfy. By and large his choices only make sense if we look on them as opportunities either to stretch his gift or to find an environment in which it could function comfortably. In particular he appears to have agreed to the majority of his projects because the directors already attached to them promised to create the kind of working conditions he required. This, I believe, is the hidden theme of his professional life in the decade following the *Bounty* debacle.

On the surface, the first of these films, *The Ugly American*, seems to defy this argument. As it worked out, whatever interest the film has derives not from its rather commonplace 'message', but from Brando's performance in it. Based on a best-selling novel thought at the time to be 'controversial', *The Ugly American* tells the story of an American ambassador's education in Third World politics. An intellectually arrogant newspaper proprietor, Brando's Harrison Carter MacWhite, is appointed US ambassador to fictional Sarkhan, in Southeast Asia. He is questioned at his Senate confirmation hearing on his friendship with a Sarkhanese named Deong, who served with him in the guerrilla war against Japan during the Second World War and has emerged as leader of the opposition to the American-supported government. He looks like a Commie to the Know-Nothing solons. MacWhite responds with a bland lecture: Americans have got to begin seeing issues in the non-aligned nations in terms other than black and . . . red. Deong, he is sure, represents a third force in Sarkhan we must carefully, with reason and dignity, woo away from Communism.

Arriving in Sarkhan, and reviving this friendship, MacWhite begins to feel less sure about Deong. They fall

out when, against Deong's advice, MacWhite reroutes his pet project, the so-called Freedom Road, financed by American dollars, so that it aims directly at a section of the country controlled by Communists. Just as his friend predicted, this does not look like economic development to the Reds. The Communists launch an attack on the road's dedication ceremony, destroying in the process a children's hospital. The ambassador is now convinced his friend is behind the attack, but no, the government tells him Deong is targeted for assassination by the Communists, who need him for a martyr. They do kill him, but his dying words are anti-Communist, pro-American. Even so, the guilt-ridden and thoroughly chastened MacWhite resigns. He is last seen delivering one more lecture – this time on American television – urging Americans to aid in the development of Third World nations, not because it is a way of fighting Communism, but because it is the humanitarian thing to do. His line was standard issue among enlightened liberals at the time, endlessly set forth on all the better editorial pages and Sunday morning discussion programs.

What's worse, though, is that the movie never escapes its origins in a social science novel (one of its authors was a political scientist). Its main character and situations had been invented to make an essentially abstract point, and so never achieved human interest. The film as a whole does not address this defect. Directed in a rather academic style by George Englund, who was a partner in Pennebaker, it is visually monotonous.

It is also unconvincingly acted, except, on occasion, by Brando. He plays MacWhite, especially in the early passages, as an Ivy League twit – all drawling nasality and condescension in his hearing room appearance, all false self-confidence when he arrives in Sarkhan and attempts to fire up his weary and cynical diplomatic staff, all false *bonhomie* when he tries to re-establish his friendship with Deong. A dapper, smooth and above all vain man, he is often fussily busy with his pipe, smugly tamping and stoking it as he offhandedly delivers his high-minded opinions.

Left In *The Ugly American* (1963) Brando played an arrogant newspaper proprietor who is appointed ambassador to a Southeast Asian country and receives a chastening education in Third World politics.

At the time the performance drove Andrew Sarris crazy. Obviously aware that Brando's company was the producer of record, the critic made the not illogical point that the film was 'designed to make Brando the center of attention at all times.' He guessed that weakish actors were deliberately cast so that Brando could effortlessly outshine them. Fair comment. Especially about a man who may have felt a need, at that moment, to reassert his star power as forcefully as he could. On the other hand, he sometimes has about him the air of a man rather desperately trying to save the show. But whatever motivated Brando, one must insist that if *The Ugly American* has any interest at all after some forty years, that interest derives from Brando's canny observation of a social type and his attempt to portray a man losing misplaced confidence and coming to fuller, truer consciousness of himself and the world. In other words, for whatever reasons, in *The Ugly American* he was an actor acting. And an actor thinking.

Against the accumulated wisdom of the ages, I maintain that Brando sustained that attitude even unto his next film, *Bedtime Story*. 'Say it ain't so, Marlon' was the common response to this venture at the time, and it has passed into the annals as the common consent nadir of his career. But this much should be said for *Bedtime Story*: it's a pretty solid farce, full of lively, original comic invention, and it is directed with more conviction than a lot of Brando's other movies. More important, precisely because he had never played farce before, and was intrigued by its techniques, it energized Brando. He admired his co-star, David Niven, for his graceful comic ways, and was on record as thinking he could learn something from *movie* actors of his kind (Tracy and Grant were mentioned), men who know how to hold back and then 'dart in' to make their points. His other co-star, Shirley Jones, reported the set to be a happy one, with Brando having 'a good time', despite worries about a recent weight gain, which led to more than usual concern about his lighting and make-up.

His commitment shows in the movie. Even those who admire his generally under-valued work in *Bounty* and *The Ugly American* must admit that there is a

Bedtime Story (1964) was the nadir of Brando's career, but the set was a happy one, he enjoyed the company of David Niven and found the techniques of farce intriguing.

certain tightness about him in these films, something occasionally too studied, too self-conscious in the pursuit of his effects. In this movie he is relaxed, cutting loose, overtly rather than covertly clowning.

In *Bedtime Story* Brando is Freddy, a GI stationed in Germany but with a sideline in conning young women out of small change, usually with

a story about needing funds to pay for an emergency operation required by his 'Grosse Mutter' (Brando puts a nifty comic spin on that phrase). When he invades the Riviera turf of Lawrence (Niven), a much more elegant operative, preying on much richer – and older – women, that fastidious fellow reacts defensively. Freddy is a potential competitor, of course, being younger and more obviously sexy. But he also lowers the tone of the neighborhood.

Pretending to bring Freddy into his business as an apprentice, Lawrence in fact tries to abuse him into voiding the field. In one particularly good sequence, Brando is required to play Lawrence's mad younger brother, helping him to get rid of a lover determined to marry the latter and bring him back to Oklahoma with her. Love me, love my brother Ruprecht, says Lawrence, who then brings her to a cell where Brando, affecting an underslung jaw, is soon tossing food around and swinging from the rafters like a demented ape – and an awfully good impersonation it is. Soon both men are in pursuit of Shirley Jones's Janet, believing her to be the heiress to a soap chip fortune, which it turns out she is not. In aid of his effort, Brando is next pretending to be a paraplegic, traumatized by a disastrous love affair (as if that cross-reference to a past triumph is not enough, he also has a line in which he carefully refers to himself as 'a bum', with just a hint of Terry Malloy in his tone). He's good at the physical comedy in this passage, and at comically turned self-pity.

Set aside for the moment the thought that this is not the sort of thing people expect to find their great actor playing at. It was also not the sort of thing we were supposed to think was funny – and still aren't. Lonely women preyed on for their money are a subject for pathos, not laughs. Nor are crazy people and cripples comfortable subjects for jokes. Nowadays, all of these minorities have lobbies. But even back in the Sixties, we knew it just wasn't tasteful to base comedy on these unfortunates.

The spirit of farce has, of course, been strangled in these toils; it's an anarchic form that requires treating the pitiable with the same contempt it visits on the powerful. *All* things human must be alien to it, or else it loses its animating force and (depending on your point of view) descends or rises to satire, which is a form of special pleading. Certainly *Bedtime Story* was strangled in the several varieties of nice-nellyism with which people responded to it, and as a result comedy was effectively denied Brando thereafter, though he has gone on looking for chances to play it.

True, Pauline Kael thought he was funny in *Morituri*. But he's going to the same well he went to in *Bounty* and *The Ugly American*, giving himself some room to grow by coming on in the early sequences in less than heroic guise. He's not a fop or a twit this time, but he is amusing at first glance as Robert Crain, an epicine pacifist, and a German living above World War Two's battles in India.

When British Intelligence, represented by Trevor Howard, first tries to recruit him, he responds, in the flutiest of tones: 'I think I have all I could possibly want. I have my books and my music and my mother's art collection, and a visit from a beautiful lady from time to time. And what I value most, my privacy.'

No dice. He is told he'll be turned over to the Germans if he doesn't sail aboard one of their freighters to make sure it does not deliver its cargo of rubber to Europe. The captain (Yul Brynner) is an anti-Nazi merchant seaman; the first officer is a devoted party member, a familiar kind of war movie fanatic; the crew is composed of criminals, some of them political, some of them the usual menacing riff-raff. Crain's main assignment is to disarm explosives that have been placed so as to destroy the ship in case it is about to fall into Allied hands – which he accomplishes in the film's only really suspenseful and entirely successful sequence.

The problem with the movie is that it aspires to being something more than a thriller. Brando is burdened (or perhaps burdened himself) with more than one speech of this nature: 'All wars are idiotic. I'm not concerned about this war. I don't care who wins or loses it. I am concerned about the Gestapo. You have no idea what they are capable of.' Worse, though, is its heavy traffic in heavy irony. It belabors the fact that Crain must befriend the Nazi first officer in order to advance his mission and pretend contempt for his natural ally, the civilized captain. And then it heads toward an even heavier irony. For the ship takes on, from a Japanese submarine, a group of American POWs and a young Jewish woman, Esther (Janet Margolen), who is being returned to Germany and certain imprisonment in a concentration camp. When Crain's cover is blown, his only hope is to foment a mutiny and he seeks Esther's aid. This poor damaged creature has already been forced by Nazis to have sex with her brother and with seventeen soldiers. Trying to help out by recruiting the American prisoners to Crain's side, she is forced to submit once again to gang rape, which drives her to insanity (eventually, mercifully, she is killed in the fight for control of the ship). This is simply too much. Irony has now darkened to horror, and the modest genre base of the movie simply cannot sustain those notes.

Brando may have felt this. Reports from location, which most of the time was a rented tramp steamer moored off Catalina, have him staging a near-mutiny of his own. He had accepted this project, which was not a Universal film, in part because its director, Bernard Wicki, was the sort of person people were telling him he should work with – young, artistically ambitious (he had just done *The Bridge*, a much-admired German anti-war drama), unbeholden to Hollywood habit. As so often happens, people had mistaken a gloomy manner for authentic artistry. Brando unloosed one of his colorful metaphors to summarize his feelings: 'Making this movie has been like pushing a prune pit with my nose from here to Cucamonga.' At least he was able to secure small roles for his old pals Wally Cox and William Redfield.

Undaunted, Pauline Kael was still advising him to look for directors of this ilk *after* seeing *Morituri*. Equally undaunted, Brando continued to follow that advice, signing to make *The Chase* with Arthur Penn, who was the most interesting American director of the Sixties. He had worked in live television, made a name for himself in the theater with his productions of William Gibson's *Two for the Seesaw* and *The Miracle Worker*, made a particularly intense film adaptation of the latter as well as the lively, original *Mickey One*, which was less a gangster movie than a *Nouvelle Vague*-ish commentary on the genre. He was just two years away from making that great touchstone movie of the era, *Bonnie and Clyde*.

Penn was not the only attractive aspect of *The Chase*. Lillian Hellman, to many a great lady of the theater, was adapting the piece from a novel and a play by Horton Foote, who was one of a group of promising younger playwrights live TV had helped bring to prominence and whose writing was particularly attuned to actors of Brando's generation. The producer was Sam Spiegel, who had now added *The Bridge on the River Kwai* and

Lawrence of Arabia to *Waterfront* and *The African Queen*, making him possibly the most successful independent of the time. Finally, an interesting cast was chosen. It was not exactly all-star, but it included three strong younger women (Jane Fonda, Angie Dickinson, Janice Rule), solid supporting players out of a variety of traditions (E. G. Marshall, Henry Hull, Miriam Hopkins, and Brando's sister Jocelyn), and three promising male newcomers (James Fox, Robert Duvall, and, in his first important movie role, Robert Redford).

In short (and on paper) *The Chase* was everything *Morituri* was not – a big, 'important' movie that attracted large anticipatory interest from press and public. It promised, as well, a serious examination of significant contemporary issues. For when Bubber Reeves (Redford) escapes from prison, and makes his way back to his home town in Texas – where Brando is the sheriff, a decent, liberal-minded man trying to keep the lid on everyone's unreasonable passions – he awakens, in a single night, all sorts of class and sexual enmity. The story offered the possibility of a metaphorical examination of a topic much on everyone's mind in the wake of John F. Kennedy's assassination – the American propensity for violent outcomes. For Bubber, like the murdered president, is finally killed for no good reason, except that he stirs inchoate anxiety and envy and (perhaps) because he happens to be in Texas.

That metaphor was, Hellman insisted, an imposition. Her original intention had been 'a modest picture about some aimless people on an aimless Saturday night'. One somehow doubts this protestation, given Hellman's Stalinist past, and some aspects of the film itself, which makes much of the way the town's leading citizen – a banker, of course, with a decadent family – instigates the tragedy by trying to protect its interests and respectability.

But there is certainly plenty of evidence that the script was 'mauled about and slicked up', as Hellman put it, for three other writers were called in to work on it by Spiegel. And then, as is usual in such circumstances, the producer, whom the writers are trying to satisfy, becomes the film's *de facto* author. 'What happened . . . was, of

THE LATER YEARS

BRANDO

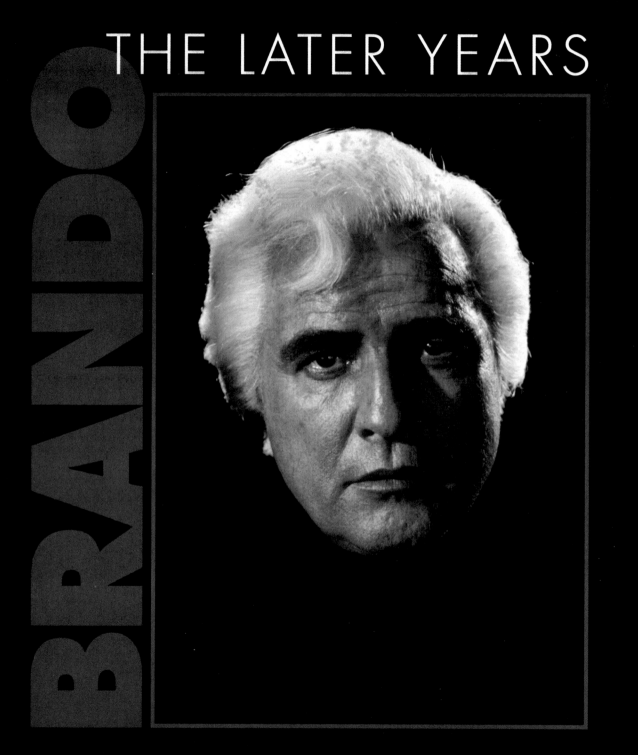

1966

The Apaloosa (1966)
In a claustrophobic western,
also known as *Southwest to
Sonora*, Brando played a
saddle tramp locked in a
feud with the Mexican
bandit who had stolen his
horse. The director was
obsessed with gimmicky
camera angles at the
expense of character, and
Brando responded with a
sulky, mumbling
performance.

1967

The Countess from Hong Kong
(1967)
Brando felt privileged to be
asked to work with the
revered Chaplin. However,
the attempt to recreate the
verbal delights of 1930s
comedy on an ocean liner by
a director stuck in an even
earlier period proved an
embarrassment. Brando,
playing an ambassador with
a glamorous stowaway
(Sophia Loren) in his
stateroom, had to replicate
every gesture and expression
that Chaplin prescribed.

The Night of the Following Day (1969)
The only consolation about his last and worst film for Universal was the presence of his old friends Richard Boone and Rita Moreno. Brando played a blond, jive-talking chauffeur in a chic, empty story about a kidnapping. It was another commercial failure, though not one of the reviews was harsher than his own verdict.

1969

The Nightcomers (1971)
Playing Peter Quint, an Irish
servant, in Michael Winner's
prequel to Henry James's
story 'The Turn of the Screw',
Brando rediscovered some of
his old energy in scenes of
sexual cruelty with Stephanie
Beacham's repressed
governess. 'The most hard-
working actor I've ever met,'

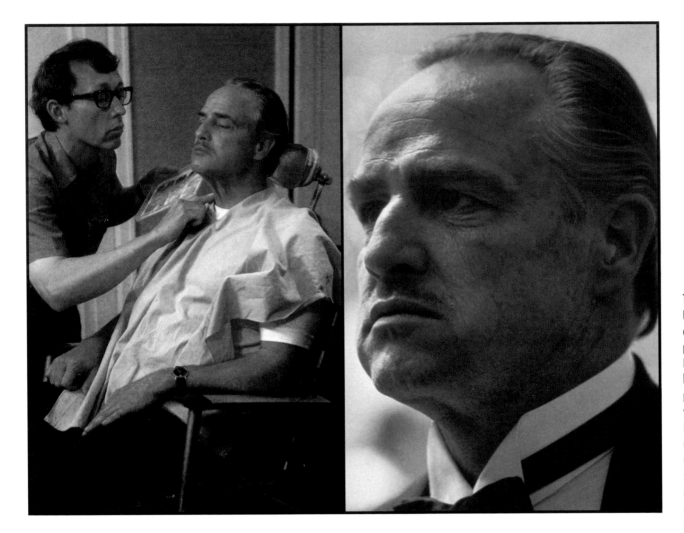

The Godfather (1972)
In one of his most celebrated roles, Brando played the Godfather, Don Corleone. There had been concerns about him playing someone twenty years his senior, and Brando had taken the unusual step of undergoing a screen test for the role. That convinced him that he could play it, and the outcome was the biggest hit since *Gone with the Wind* and an Academy Award for Best Actor.

1973

Last Tango in Paris (1973)
Brando's comeback
continued with an artistic,
scandalous *succès d'estime*.
Director Bernardo
Bertolucci's working method
suited Brando, allowing him
to indulge his free-
associational humour, while
the sustained improvising
as a man in a mid-life crisis
forced him to reveal more
than his outer skin.

Reunited with director
Arthur Penn, and working
for the first time with his
neighbour and admirer
Jack Nicholson, Brando
gave the best comic
performance of his career
as a monstrous,
schizophrenic lawman.
However, critics and public
alike were not ready for a
comic horror western.

1976

1978

Superman (1978)
His days of real acting now over, for fourteen years Brando made only the occasional brief guest appearance. In 1978 he played Jor-El, the wise, white-haired father of Superman, who at the beginning of the film rockets his son into space to save him from the destruction of the planet Krypton.

The Formula (1980)
Playing a powerful industrialist engaged in a murderous conspiracy, Brando wore a hearing aid — in fact a radio receiver through which he was fed his lines. 'I'm not an actor and haven't been for years,' he now admitted. 'I'm a human being — hopefully a concerned and somewhat intelligent one — who occasionally acts.'

1979

Apocalypse Now (1979)
In Francis Ford Coppola's muddled epic, Brando played Kurtz, the army officer who has gone native somewhere up-river. With his head shaved, and photographed in shadow to disguise his girth, he turned in an incomprehensible performance. Witnesses recalled that 'script conferences' between him and Coppola included him hanging from palm trees tossing coconuts at the director.

1980

1989

A Dry White Season (1989)
A brief appearance, in just
two good scenes, as an
idealist-cynical lawyer
fighting apartheid in South
Africa was enough to earn
Brando another Academy
Award nomination.

The Freshman (1990)
In his first substantial role
since *The Missouri Breaks*,
Brando gave a comic
reprise of Don Corleone. His
charming performance also
contained one of his
singular, treasurable

The Island of Dr Moreau
(1996)
f recent audiences have been
hocked by the sight of the
ageing Brando, admirers
lready had been by the
ense of waste when
ontemplating his overall
ecord. In spite of the weak
ilms and the lapses into self-
parody, however, few actors
have provided as many
moments of really great
cting.

1966

With Angie Dickinson in *The Chase* (1966). Director Arthur Penn described Brando as 'one of the most maligned guys in the history of movies ... He has an abundance of gifts and he makes those purely and prodigally available.'

course, the center of the film . . . moved out of my hands and clearly into Sam Spiegel's hands,' Penn said recently. Thereafter, 'I was essentially in the position of a functionary . . . nicely paid to work with all these wonderful actors.'

Still, one of the actors was Brando, and to Penn he was a revelation. One of the reasons the film has remained an embittering experience for the director, who said he was 'dysfunctional' for a period after it was finished, was that 'wonderful, wonderful stuff . . . scenes that [Marlon] improvised with Angie Dickinson, scenes that he improvised with this great company of absolutely superb actors . . . are just not in the film.' This is doubtless one

reason Spiegel broke his contract with Penn, which called for editing to be accomplished in New York, and took the negative with him to London. The producer knew, of course, that Penn would fight to insert these improvisations into the picture.

What we have here are all the elements of a big picture disaster: bickering authorial egos; a producer intellectually incapable of forthrightly solving the project's creative issues and relying on his natural deviousness to solve its human issues; a good director working on his first mainstream production and not knowing how to assert command of it. The result is a film uncentered in every possible way that presented itself to audiences as an almost random succession of melodramatic sensations. (The broadest of these is Bubber's murder. Having been rescued from a lynch mob, he is killed as Brando's Sheriff Calder leads him into the jail, with the scene staged so as to imitate the footage of Lee Harvey Oswald's murder by Jack Ruby.)

There being no more interesting way to read the movie, one is forced to read it as Kael did: superior Northern liberals looking down their noses at Southern peckerwoods. My dear, what can you expect from such . . . primitives.

The first New York screening of the film was a disaster, with a packed house in a Broadway movie palace hooting and talking back to the screen. The critics treated it with similar derisiveness. They did not focus their contempt particularly on Brando, and, indeed, his performance (or what's left of it) comes across as workmanlike; his developing belly, which he was at pains to let hang out, suited the part, he worked up a good Texas accent, and he accepted another of his ritual beatings.

No one paid a lot of attention to that aspect of his role that is unquestionably one of the things that drew Brando to it – the irony of a Southern sheriff going against mythic and media type and being the one representative of authentic liberal values in the piece. And few knew what Penn and the other actors did: that Brando worked harder, with less complaint, public or private, on this film than he had on any other for years.

There is irony and instruction to be found here. For this role and this film were not better – were in many respects worse – than material on which he had exercised far greater contempt in the past. To be sure, Spiegel was unhappy with him: he sneered that Brando needed to feel tortured in order to work, and now 'had to pseudo-torture himself to function'. And Brando, disgusted by the producer's, and the studio's, constant attempts to raise the film's quotient of violence, was heard to mutter: 'Fuck 'em. If they're going to be so stupid, I'll just take the money and do what they want and get out. I don't give a damn about anything.'

We have observed before Brando's inability to say what he means, condemning a movie for its failure to take up

serious issues when, in fact, what's bothering him is a failure to provide him with the working conditions he requires. But the capacity to insist on your due is an essential requirement of the movie star's profession: 'they' (corporate Hollywood) will run roughshod over you if it is lacking. All the great ones – Davis and Cagney in their bold ways, Stanwyck and Grant in their more subtle ways – have had it. But Brando just can't bring himself to assert his skittish ego on his own behalf – nice Middle-western Wasp boys are not taught that skill; are, indeed, taught that people who have it are not 'nice'. In any case, he felt obliged to wrap his professional unhappinesses in high-sounding principles: the unworthy self stifled and held blameless for asserting its needs.

Now here he was in a movie that, more than most, failed its promise, failed it laughably, in the process becoming a textbook case in how movies should not be made. And yet Brando said almost nothing critical about it. There can be only one reason why: the working conditions suited him. He became, in Penn's view, the great saving grace of *The Chase*.

'I think Marlon Brando is one of the most maligned guys in the history of movies. . . . Brando is an eminently fair guy. And perfectly accessible and decent and available. He has an abundance of gifts and he makes those purely and prodigally available. . . . He's not just saying the lines, he's never, never dogging it. He's out there working. He loves the work, he loves the process. He doesn't like the economics. He doesn't like the environment. He doesn't like being a star. . . . But he does love the work.'

Uncanny, isn't it? This perversity. But it was Penn himself, working with actors the only way he knew how, who perhaps unknowingly created the atmosphere that brought out the best in Brando: letting him consult his instincts and find his way into a part, letting him fool with Hollywood's sacred text, the shooting script, a document that is, of course, often the end product of foolings-with by far less talented people.

This is, I think, at the heart of Brando's career problem: there just were not enough Kazans and Penns to go around, not enough directors who shared the values of the

Brando (*right*), photographed on the set of *The Appaloosa* (1966) with Paul Baxley, his stunt double for the scene in which saddle tramp Matt Fletcher is dragged behind a galloping horse.

acting tradition that had formed him. To put it another way, his struggle was not so much to say what he wanted to say, but to say it in the manner he wanted to say it.

Brando continued his search for sympathetic, empathetic direction. In his next two films, neither of which need detain us long, he went first with another young director whose early films seemed promising, and then to one of the most revered of the old masters for help. His reward was still more frustration.

Sydney J. Furie was a Canadian-born director who had made two stylish films in the 'swinging' London of the early Sixties – *The Leather Boys* and *The Ipcress File*, the former a youth gang film, the latter an espionage thriller. They seemed, especially the latter, very hip, though there was nothing about them to suggest that Furie was just the right man to direct a western. Still, sometime in 1965 he and Brando found themselves in Utah, pretending it was Mexico and the southwestern American border, and trying

to make something significant out of a story – *The Appaloosa* – about a man whose horse is stolen by a Hispanic bandido named Chuy played by slick John Saxon. Brando's character, a saddle tramp named Matt Fletcher, has a terrible time recovering his property from him, an effort complicated by his growing need to extract a young woman named Trini (Anjanette Comer) from the bandit's clutches.

This time Brando's ritual punishment for daring to exist consists of being tied to a rope and dragged through a rocky stream and scratchy sagebrush by a galloping horse. More memorable is a hand-wrestling contest Chuy obliges him to engage in: there are scorpions on the table, waiting to sting the loser's hand. At one point this contest is photographed from the scorpion's point of view. But then Furie's search for the odd angle is, finally, the most suspenseful element in the movie: what will he think of next? Through the horse's legs, through a tequila bottle –

these are routine views for his camera. At one point he blocks out 90 per cent of the screen with some shadowy foreground object. Brando is often, quite literally, just a shadow of himself.

This searching for dubious visual novelty when they should have been searching for his character drove Brando crazy. He and Furie argued about his make-up. They argued about the line changes he insisted on making. People on the set imagined that any day he and Furie would come to blows. They didn't. Instead, Brando sulked a lot: you can see him doing it on screen. This is one movie in which he is guilty as charged: he mumbles. It is the perfect verbal equivalent of Furie's visual murkiness. Together, they contrived to create a cinematic rarity – a claustrophobic western. It is one form, perhaps *the* one form of originality this spacious genre cannot accommodate.

All right, so much for what passed as the avant-garde in the commercial cinema. Let's try classicism. Charles Chaplin, for example, a man whose devotion to the eye-level long and medium shots was unsullied by any technique invented during the half-century between the time he first appeared in such a shot and found it good and the day he walked onto the set to direct the shooting of *The Countess from Hong Kong*.

This manner had always worked for him as a performer, permitting the camera to hold in frame all, or almost all, of his favorite subject, which was, of course, himself. Not that Brando, devotee of silent screen comedy, cared about that. He said that it would be a privilege to read the telephone book under The Old Master's guidance. He apparently did not notice that the script Chaplin presented was somewhat less original than a new edition of the phone book. For Chaplin had drafted this story in the 1930s, imagining at one time that it would be right for him and his one-time bride, Paulette Goddard.

It is the tale of a Hong Kong 'dance hall girl' – she works in a house where all the ladies are given titles – who stows away in the ocean liner stateroom of one of her customers. From there, the Countess, played by Sophia Loren, hopes to smuggle herself into America. Needless to say, the comedy revolves around attempts to hide her presence. She threatens to tell the captain she has been abducted if the customer exposes her, and he can't afford that since (1) he is in the midst of an unpleasant divorce and (2) he has just been appointed ambassador to Saudi Arabia. Naturally, enforced propinquity makes their hearts grow fonder. Inevitably, there is much slamming of doors and hiding in closets as passengers and ship's personnel threaten their secret. Needless to say, the claustrophobia here is even worse than it was in Brando's previous film.

It is perhaps necessary to add that verbal exchanges, the delight of 1930s romantic comedy, which often operated quite happily in similarly cramped quarters, were not within Chaplin's range. Brando was several times reduced to belching for laughs that didn't come. Perhaps one should also add that Chaplin had less of the onset manner Brando required than any director he had ever encountered. It was his solipsistic habit to act out, in detail, every gesture and expression he expected his performers to make and to require that they imitate him precisely. 'Chaplin's a nice old gent,' Brando told a journalist in London (where the picture was shot). 'We do things his way, that's all.' He made no public criticism of the director, who was then seventy-seven. Reviewers were not so discreet, though, of course, everyone wrote about the picture more in sorrow than in anger. Few blamed the stars for this failure; most seemed to think it was nice, even brave, of them to help the old man out.

An elderly 'classicist' (Andrew Sarris's nice word for Chaplin) having failed him as badly as the bright young things had, Brando now found himself in the company of a man who, at sixty-one, should have been at the height of his powers, but was not. Early and late John Huston created a great body of work, but now, no less than Brando, he was groping for handholds during a slippery passage. At some earlier point Brando had turned down *Reflections in a Golden Eye* on the same grounds that several other stars had – the role was that of a suppressed homosexual. But when his old rival, Montgomery Clift, died on the eve of production, he allowed himself to be recruited to an Italian location (something to do with co-star Elizabeth Taylor's tax situation and her desire to be

In John Huston's still underrated *Reflections in a Golden Eye* (1967), Brando gave a brave and masterly performance as an army officer gradually coming to face the fact of his homosexuality.

1967

The portrayal of the vain and repressed Major Penderton, trapped in the sexual closet of marriage to a flighty, sexy Elizabeth Taylor, was Brando's greatest achievement of the Sixties.

not totally impossible, dreams. Everyone in *Reflection* is certainly eccentric enough to claim Huston's concentrated attention. And though no one ever strays from the fort, there is a quest in it. To be sure, it is a devious and unacknowledged one, but, in effect, it is for freedom: escape from the sexual closets in which three of its major characters are trapped. As Major Weldon Penderton, Brando, married to Leonora, a general's flighty, sexy daughter (Taylor), but reluctantly, in great anguish acknowledging his attraction to Private Williams, a mysterious enlisted man (Robert Forster), thereby acknowledges his true nature. Brando's character is not moving toward generally approved values, but he is moving toward acceptance of a painful truth about himself. The other major figures in this drama balance the scales of desire with great delicacy: Colonel Morris Langdon, a blunt and lusty brother officer, played by Brian Keith, uncomplicatedly enjoys his affair with Penderton's wife; Mrs Langdon (Julie Harris), a hysterically neurasthenic and self-destructive woman; and Anacleto (Zorro David), the Langdon's openly homosexual houseboy, whose cheery embrace of his sexuality is the equivalent of Leonora Penderton's.

They are a horsy crowd, these military folk, and Leonora's white stallion, which only she can master, is the symbol of natural, unfettered sexual power. And Penderton's attempt to ride him is the source of his ultimate humiliation. The scene is terrifyingly staged by Huston, and it is the turning-point of the movie. After the animal throws him, Penderton beats the animal savagely. Thereafter, though, he begins to own up to what he really wants sexually, and it is his discovery that the always-lurking Williams is interested, not in him, but in his wife, that finally unbalances him completely. This leads to the film's climactic murder – of the private, who is discovered in Leonora's room, watching her sleep.

This is, obviously, a dangerous movie, walking not along the edge of intellectually fashionable absurdity, but of unfashionable hysteria. The original release prints were struck in muted gold tones, intended to soften the impulse to titter at the bold, primary

near Richard Burton, who was also filming in Italy). It did not, on the face of it, appear to be any more sensible a career move for him than it did for Huston. An adaptation of Carson McCullers' literary curiosity – a Gothic tale placed in the plain geometric confines of a Southern army post and told in a spare, straightforward prose almost worthy of Hemingway – just had to be all wrong for both of them.

But Huston's best films – the ones that constitute the main line of his career – are rather special kinds of adventures. *The Maltese Falcon*, *The Treasure of the Sierra Madre* and *The African Queen*, to name just a few typical works, are largely quest stories, involving eccentrics, ill-matched outsiders pursuing improbable, if

Right Frolicking with Ewa Aulin in *Candy* (1968). His cameo as the sexually opportunistic Indian guru was arguably the best thing in an irredeemable movie.

colors of the film's emotional palette.) But yet, it is also a film that imprints itself on the memory because of its vivid resistance to the usual. When, almost reluctantly, you return to it today, fearing that recollection has once again played you for a fool, you discover that it is actually better than you remembered. For the years have done what Huston's gold tint (long since banished from the video cassette) couldn't accomplish – cooled and distanced it, so that it can be viewed with a certain objectivity. Seen in this new light, Brando's performance, in particular, comes as a revelation.

It is, simply, one of his greatest. Begin with his accent. It is strangled Southern. He seems afraid of its softness, its sweet languidness. So he clips its impulse to that mode, treating his own voice almost as if it were a raw recruit whose undisciplined civilian ways must be stamped out in basic training. Move on to his appearance: the plastered down hair, the uniform kept tightly buttoned even when he is off duty, the ramrod posture that is never granted permission to stand at ease. Finally, consider the measured precision of his locutions when he lectures, dryly, on military tactics, his effort to reduce the passion of battle to abstract logic. There is also a curious vanity about the man. He is like a little boy playing soldier, and rather pleased by his own (as he sees it) successful impersonation of conventional, grown-up maleness (he has a lovely moment, saluting himself in a mirror). And all of that, for Brando, is only a beginning.

When the stallion runs away with him, his furious response has about it a curiously innocent quality, that of a child confronting first knowledge of the world's intractability and his own powerlessness in it. His lips widen into a pout and he blubbers like a three-year-old. There is nothing in his behavior to suggest that complexity of forces that compose an adult's rage. So the sequence becomes a confrontation with his imperfect primal self, the self that all his posturings cannot hide.

But it is, at last, his acknowledgement of what he is, what he must be, and wants to be, that is most painfully real, and touching. When he thinks Private Williams is coming to visit him, he is back at the mirror, cold-creaming his face like a happy teenaged girl. His moment

of moments is so quick that one could miss it with the smallest glance away from the screen – a quick pat of his hair as he sits, almost primly, on his bed, thinking his dream lover is drawing near, never imagining that Williams is headed for the bedroom next door. There was not then an actor in America who would have dared these moments. What is Stanislavsky's phrase? 'Public solitude.' Yes. The ability to behave in public as we do when we believe we are unobserved.

Much good it did him. The film was too rich for most critics' blood – and the general public's, too. There *was* hooting and hollering, and listings on their 'ten worst' lists by critics with such fine critical sensibilities as Judith Crist. In every sense, *Reflections in a Golden Eye* failed miserably. It seems unlikely that it can ever recover from the contempt initially visited on it, even though Huston stoutly insisted, to the end of his life, that it was one of his best works. Certainly the set, despite all the volatile temperaments gathered on it, was a happy and hard-working one. Moreover Brando never once said a word against the film – a sure sign, as we know, that he had been granted the time and space he required to do his work properly.

To do your best and to have it go unrecognized, treated as indistinguishable from your worst, is embittering. And now, truly, Brando bottomed out. His next films, both of which were belated and half-hearted attempts to catch hold of styles that were thought to be favored by the youth culture, were unredeemed even by honorable intentions. The first of them, *Candy*, appeared in 1968. Based on a book by Terry Southern and Mason Hoffenberg (the former a voguish black comic novelist), the novel had originally been published by the Olympia Press of Paris, whose list included a lot of hard-core porn and some fiction of merit (like *Lolita*). Anyway, the piece titillated the literati. The title is a play on that of the more famous *Candide*. Candy is a female innocent, exploited sexually by various archetypal fakirs of our time. Brando was recruited to the enterprise by its director, Christian Marquand, whom he had met in Paris when they were both young actors. They had remained close friends and Brando had, in fact, named his son for him. In the film he

Among the worst films that Brando made during his career trough in the Sixties was *The Night of the Following Day* (1969), the story of a brutal kidnapping.

1969

played Grindl, an Indian guru maintaining the lotus position in the back of a semi-trailer truck until circumstances offered him the possibilities of Kama-Sutrian positions. His make-up was perfect, his accent superb, his comic timing sharp. He was a great sight gag, and as such it could be argued, perhaps, that his cameo appearance was the best thing in a movie attempting – but failing – to achieve the jumbled, anarchic spirit of, say, an old Marx Brothers movie. But the argument must be resisted. The movie was god-awful.

If Brando's appearance in *Candy* can be explained, feebly, by his friendship with the director, there is no explanation whatsoever for his appearance in *The Night of the Following Day*, although it did discharge his final obligation to Universal. The film, directed by Hubert Cornfield, whose filmography contains such titles as *Lure of the Swamp* and *Angel Baby*, ostensibly concerns the kidnapping of an adolescent heiress (Pamela Franklin) by

a gang that is both inept and cruel. Richard Boone, an old Actor's Studio friend, plays the chief sadist; Rita Moreno, an old girlfriend, plays a drugged-out accomplice; Brando, with dyed blond hair contrasting prettily with his black turtleneck, appears as a jive-talking chauffeur who finally turns on the conspirators and rescues their victim. The film has a chic air about it; its pace and imagery are dreamy; and, indeed, at the end the whole story is revealed to be a (possibly precognitive) dream on the part of the victim. Brando offered the most colorful of the many bad reviews it received: 'It makes about as much sense as a rat fucking a grapefruit.'

Burn! or *Queimada,* as it was known in much of the world, did have aspirations more serious than Brando's two previous attempts, and, once again, the director, Gillo Pontecorvo, was reckoned to be just the kind of young genius with whom Brando should cast his lot. His reputation was based on *The Battle of Algiers* of 1965, and his technique in that film *was* astounding. Using hand-held cameras, grainy black-and-white film, amateur actors, and short, newsreel-like cuts, he veraciously, ferociously captured the spirit of urban guerrilla warfare as Arab revolutionaries and French Foreign Legionnaires struggled for control of the eponymous city. Pontecorvo showed, at least in this picture, a more authentic gift than most of the young directors Brando had linked with, and the actor agreed to work with him even before Pontecorvo finished pitching his (unwritten) story to him in Hollywood.

Pontecorvo's timing was excellent, for Brando had recently turned down Elia Kazan's adaptation of his own novel, *The Arrangement*. His excuse was that he was too preoccupied by the threat of racial violence in the United States, and, indeed, in 1968 his public activities on behalf of blacks reached a height. He went so far as to say that henceforth he would only do movies of 'appropriate significance'. Which *Burn!* clearly promised to be.

It is, however, one thing to agree to act (in both senses of the word) on your principles (and for $750,000) in your living-room on Mulholland Drive, quite another to act on them in a jungle location in Colombia. It is one thing excitedly to agree to do a work of high principle; quite another to attempt the specific, practical work a movie requires across the kind of language barriers existing between actor and director. That is particularly so when the director is required to supply the kind of patient emotional support needed by an actor like Brando. After a few weeks of good feeling, things started to fall apart. To make matters worse, Brando became ill with a tropical facial rash that required constant attention between shots and, of course, distracted him.

He also grew increasingly anxious about the performance of Evaristo Marquez, a local agricultural worker Pontecorvo had discovered and cast opposite Brando in the demanding role of a native revolutionary named José Dolores. Besides being utterly untrained as an actor, the man spoke almost no English, and so soaked up much of the directorial attention to which the star naturally felt entitled. Finally, Brando became convinced that Pontecorvo was exploiting and mistreating his native

cast. Things came to a head when the director required some forty-odd takes of Brando, in a scene where he was forced to stand in the hot sun while a sugar-cane field burned behind him.

Brando headed for the airport, but much of the company followed him there to plead with him to stay. He acquiesced. A little later, however, pleading illness, he decamped for good. The production shut down for months while the lawyers wrangled, the upshot being that it was finished in a non-tropical Third World country, Morocco, of all places, for a story that was supposed to be set in the Caribbean. Ultimately the film limped into the theaters with (in the US at least) twenty minutes of the director's cut missing.

Brando plays William Walker, a British *agent provocateur*, sent to a Portuguese island in the Antilles to foment revolution among the natives, so the English can take over and assure an uninterrupted supply of sugar for their tea. (Originally the island was supposed to be a Spanish possession, but the Franco government was touchy about Spain's reputation as a particularly cruel colonial power, so the film-makers ceded the place to Portugal, which historically had no presence in this part of the world, but whose boycotts of films that offended it were not as costly as those of its Iberian neighbor.) Walker finds in José Dolores a likely front man for a revolution, trains him and his men in insurgency, and soon enough the Portuguese are forced out. Asked by his revolutionary friend where he's headed next, Walker replies: 'A place called Indochina. Ever hear of it?'

Ten years pass off-screen, and Walker is next discovered fallen low and brawling in a London dive. The imperialists need him again. For Dolores has learned Walker's lessons too well, and has now gone over to the anti-British opposition. Brando returns to conduct a scorched earth campaign against his former ally, who is ultimately captured. Brando tries to save him from execution, first by telling the island's rulers that a dead martyr is more dangerous than a defeated revolutionary on the run, then by pleading with Dolores to escape, and showing him how to do so unscathed. His sometime

Right The Nightcomers (1971), director Michael Winner's crude encounter with Henry James, saw Brando exuding menace and, at last, some of his old sexuality.

1971

comrade in arms refuses; he, too, senses the power implicit in martyrdom. The film ends with Walker being assassinated as he is about to take ship from Queimada. A smile, somewhere between the ironic and the beatific, plays on Brando's face as he expires.

It is, of course, almost impossible to judge a film as drastically truncated as this one was by its distributors. Crucial sequences are quite obviously missing, and so its continuity is often incomprehensible. But it can be said that Pontecorvo is not a natural formalist. The immediacy of the *cinéma vérité* manner he affected in his earlier film, the sheer rush of its rhythms, is badly needed here, and only rarely in evidence.

This air of abstraction extends to writing and performance, too. Brando was right – Marquez lacks the technical facility to play a hero; he looks the part, but he can't act it. Brando might have filled the anti-heroic vacuum, but the film gives him no background, no motivation, nothing on which to build a full characterization. And he, for whatever reasons, invents nothing. There is a shadow of his Mr Christian in his William Walker, but only a dim one. In any case, that's not a great idea, for this figure needs to be dark and devious, and Brando manages, at most, a sort of upper-crust cynicism, touched by a sort of tragic likeability. Meant to be a modern CIA-type projected backward in history, we do respond occasionally to his growing awareness of the evil he's doing. But that's patchily shown in the film on release, and one suspects that Brando's natural sympathy for 'the wretched of the earth' interfered with his 'process' as he worked on this role. One is also sure that his disgust with the whole enterprise also daunted his imagination. *Burn!* was perhaps not a disgrace as a film, but Brando's performance was troubling in its lack of spirit.

Bad enough that this was his tenth consecutive commercial failure, but now Brando seemed not even to be trying. Directors who wanted to work with him could not get permission from the studios to employ him in anything like a major film, even at cut prices. In 1971 he was actually fired (it was a first for him) by producer David Merrick – exactly the sort of erratic egomaniac he

should never have been working for – from the Sidney Lumet production of *Child's Play*, which was exactly the kind of third-rate material (guilty doings in a Catholic boys school) he should never have been working in.

The alternative was not, on the face of it, much better. It was *The Nightcomers*. But for some curious reason it reanimated him. It is what has since come to be known as a prequel, a tale that tells what happened before a more famous story takes place. In this case what we have is an account of the previous history of Peter Quint and Margaret Jessel, the ghosts who haunt the children in Henry James's famous ghost story, 'The Turn of the Screw' (which previously had been dramatized, and turned into a movie, *The Innocents*). We learn how they died and why they exercise such a powerful hold on the imaginations of little Master Miles and his sister, Flora. Basically it is because Quint (Brando), a servant at Bly House, an English country house, likes to tie up girls – especially Miss Jessel (Stephanie Beacham), the sexually repressed governess to the orphan children. Miles, having spied on their love-making, induces his sister to emulate it with him. Quint, it must be admitted, has a certain rough and ready charm, and a willingness, which no one else has shown, to play with the lonely youngsters. Since he has love and pain, love and death all mixed up in his mind, he soon has the children nicely muddled, too. Afraid that their spoilsport housekeeper will send their friends away, the children murder them in the belief that their shades will hang about Bly House, and keep them entertained in perpetuity.

'Turn of the Screwy' would be a perfectly acceptable alternative title for *The Nightcomers*. And looked at from a purely literary point of view, it is everything James never is: coarse when it should be delicate in its language, broad when it should be subtle in its effects, openly sexual when it should suppress the impulse to reveal. (The old Production Code had given way to the new ratings system in 1968, and this movie, like many of its moment, partook of the new freedom zestfully and tastelessly; some of Brando's encounters with Beacham came very close to soft-core porn.) It is, in short, a movie of which it is extraordinarily easy to make fun. And yet

Brando is frequently very good in it. Sporting his first Irish accent, he is often utterly disarming in his passages with the children. There is no obvious note of menace in his playing, which makes him all the more menacing. For despite his talk about the big subjects, he is like a child himself, unaware of the ramifications of what he is spouting, and unaware of the effect it is having on his audience. This, of course, makes his murder at their hands the more startling, and also gives it a curiously satisfying psychological (and moral) correctness.

But the main thing about Brando's work is that it is alive, bursting with energy. The director, Michael Winner, is a cheeky, egocentric movie-maker, who, known in those days for his lack of inhibiting 'good taste', was sometimes perversely stirring. Anyway, his spirit appealed to Brando. And Brando appealed to the director. 'Immaculately professional' was his judgement, 'the most hard-working actor I've ever met.'

Confronting this film, minor and silly as it often is, one also confronts what had been largely absent from Brando's work for years – going back even to the late Fifties. That was, simply, libidinal energy. Or, yet more simply, sexiness of the special sort he had once delivered. We all know that besides driving his performances in all his best-case scenarios it is the quality that made him a star in the full popular sense. We can even see that it is what drove his only truly great performance of the Sixties, in *Reflections in a Golden Eye*, where he mobilized his sexuality implosively rather than explosively, menacing only himself with it. But now, however perversely, however parodistically, however self-satirizingly, it was out in the open again. He is not just acting sadism in his encounters with Beacham in *The Nightcomers*, he is pleasuring in it – not perhaps in the cruelty itself, but in the surfacing of a dark, but authentic, element of sexuality that is almost never represented in movies.

And in those moments we suddenly saw what had been missing in his Harrison MacWhites and his Sheriff Calders and his William Walkers. Somehow that which had first drawn us to him, that which had been the generally unacknowledged source of the anxiety he had stirred in older generations, had been tamed without anyone quite knowing it was happening – including, I think, Brando himself. Pursuing the significant, the 'appropriate' statement, he had himself been guilty of the sort of self-repression that was anathema not only to the artistic principles that had formed him, but to his best self. And, most ironic of all, he had done so in the very period when everyone, everywhere was embracing the very sexual revolution he had, in his early presence, predicted.

Bad advice? Bad instincts? Bad Karma? Or just plain bad pictures – a run of them without precedent in the annals of stardom? In the end it is impossible to say which was the most important factor in bringing Brando to the brink of being unemployable as the Sixties turned into the Seventies – and even for pushing him over the brink into being considered laughable in some unsympathetic quarters. Certainly one does not want to imply that *The Nightcomers* represented anything like a comeback, though reviewers, as if tiring of beating up on Brando, or just possibly aware that he had found something restorative in this role, were on the whole kind to him. But the movie itself was greeted with the edgy guffaws that hard-edged sex always elicits in the movies. In the US the picture was released sparingly.

But if *The Nightcomers*, a cinematic fringe-dweller if there ever was one, inevitably referred us backward to all the commercially hopeless enterprises that Brando had lent himself to since his voyage on the *Bounty* carried him to the remoter shores of the movie world, something in this movie, released exactly ten years later, also hinted at the possibility of energies gathering, spirits brightening, for a return journey.

CHAPTER SEVEN

MOMENTS OF TRUTH

Sometime in 1971 Marlon Brando appeared in the office of Robert Evans, chief of production at Paramount. Tanned, his hair lightened almost to blond by the South Seas sun and pulled back in a bun, he looked fit and vigorous. Here on business almost unprecedented for him, he was lobbying for a role, that of Don Corleone, in Francis Ford Coppola's *The Godfather*. 'I know a lot of people in Hollywood say I'm washed up,' Evans would recall him saying, 'and I know you've heard a lot of stories about me, and some of them are true. But I can play that part, and I can do a good job.'

Brando's great, contrasting performances of the early Seventies: as Don Corleone in *The Godfather* (right), based on observation, imagination and technical mastery; and as Paul in *Last Tango in Paris*, the product of painful self-exploration.

Before this meeting Brando had done something even more unprecedented for an actor of his stature; he had made a screen test. Of course, no one called it that; it was billed as a make-up test, determining whether the forty-seven-year-old actor could impersonate a character supposed to be something like two decades older. Coppola had taken a video camera to Brando's home, sat him down at a table on the terrace, and had him register a range of expressions – no dialogue. Brando darkened his hair with shoe polish, pencilled on a mustache, and stuffed Kleenex in his mouth to broaden his face. It is said that, studying himself in a mirror before facing Coppola's camera he muttered to himself: 'That's it, that's it. Mean bulldog face, warmth inside.'

Did he really find his character that fast? Obviously not in all its nuances. But he had the right idea, and he liked it. One doubts the tale that when the tape was shown to studio executives they failed to recognize Brando. But there is no doubt that he made a powerful impression on his select audience. Everybody admired Brando's reputation. The question was, could he still live up to it? And, more importantly, would he meet Hollywood's standards of discipline? No one had yet observed what we have seen: that the most important casting decision in a Brando picture – after Brando himself, of course – was settling on a director sympathetic to his way of doing things. At this point, naturally, the executives had no way of knowing that they had such a figure in Coppola, though with the beginnings already established of what was to prove an excellent relationship, the director began pressing them very firmly on Brando's behalf.

The only reason Brando has subsequently advanced for letting his eagerness for the role show was this: *The Godfather* said something metaphorically about the corporate mentality of America. To him, these gangsters instructively parodied establishment attitudes. 'To me, the key phrase in the story is that whenever they wanted to kill somebody it was always a matter of policy. Before pulling the trigger, they told him: "Just business. Nothing personal." When I read that, McNamara, Johnson, and Rusk flashed before my eyes.'

One has to believe that other, more simple factors had induced him to make tests and take meetings. For one thing, the Don was obviously a great part, richer than anything Brando had done for years – the still, menacing, motivating center of a vast, dark epic. It was also one that would provide him with the opportunity to do what he had not done since playing Sakini in *Teahouse* – hide in plain sight. This part would permit him to operate from deep cover. And while it would tax his talents, it would not unduly tax his time. For although it was a pivotal role, it was not a huge one, so his presence would not be required for the entire shooting schedule. He could be in and out in a month or so.

Finally, however, it was Coppola's attitude toward the film, and toward the actor himself, that may have been, for Brando, the project's most encouraging aspects. Paramount had optioned Mario Puzo's book even before it was finished, mostly because his asking price was low, and thus easy to write off if the book flopped. No one had imagined that it would become the mighty best-seller that it became, but even after it did, the studio saw *The Godfather* as a low-budget project – $2 million – partly because another Mafia story, *The Brotherhood*, had been one of the company's failures in 1968. It raised the budget slowly, grudgingly, but even though the book stayed on the charts for over a year, the studio remained cautious and, perhaps for that reason, had trouble finding a director. Arthur Penn, Peter Yates, Costa-Gavras, and Richard Brooks, among others, turned it down for various reasons. It was Brooks who, having read Coppola's script for *Patton*, and admired it, recommended that Paramount talk to him about the project. It is probably true that most of these men, reading Puzo's first-draft script felt, as Coppola did initially, that it was a 'hunk of trash'.

Maybe it was. But the book on which it was based wasn't – not really. It has something most popular fiction does not have – conviction. Reading it, one feels that the writer is working from inside the world he is portraying, from inside the skin of his principal characters. The more he thought about it, the more Coppola apparently realized that if the same spirit was brought to filming the story, something wonderful could be made of it. And surely, as

1972

In *The Godfather* (1972), the Don's sons embodied aspects of his own nature. Left to right: the hot-blooded Sonny (James Caan), the icy Michael (Al Pacino), and the easy-going Fredo (John Cazale).

an Italian-American who cherished his heritage, he realized that he was the man to do it. For what Evans later said about Coppola is true: 'He knew the way these men . . . ate their food, kissed each other, talked. He knew the grit.'

In any case, as he worked on the script with Puzo, who was the first person to suggest Brando for Don Corleone, some of the more sensational aspects of the story were eliminated, and a wise decision was taken to concentrate on its crucial passage: the post-war moment when the Mafia began the process of corporatizing itself, finding large-scale fronts for its activities in the respectable community. Above all, the most interesting and surprising element in the book, its insistence on the depth and passion of family relationships among criminals, was clarified and dramatically sharpened, creating at least a superficial sympathy for them. It was this, as much as the fact that Coppola was a *paisano*, that disarmed Mafia objections to the project.

It was not, however, just because Coppola appeared on Brando's doorstep with a sound adaptation of what turned out, after all, to be a hot property that the actor committed so fully to the enterprise. It was because Coppola was what he was – a young (thirty-one), passionate, knowledgeable, and articulate film-maker who had paid his dues. He had written screenplays and he had already

directed all kinds of movies. All of them had been messy and talented – qualities Brando could relate to. He could also relate to a man who was trying to do what Brando now had to do – escape the Hollywood fringe, get into the mainstream. Above all, he could relate to a spirit that was not cynical, that harbored serious ambitions not merely for himself, but for the medium, since Coppola intended to use whatever funds accrued from *The Godfather* for more idealistic venturings. Coppola, like Brando, was a seeker after truth, a man who looked as if he would patiently indulge a fellow pilgrim with whatever time and attention he needed to find his way.

And so a deal was at last struck. Brando received a small cash advance and 1.5 per cent of the gross, capped at $1.5 million. (It is said that after the picture was released Evans offered to raise the cap if Brando would permit a news magazine to do a cover story on him, which he refused at an eventual cost of who knows how many millions.) The cash was less than half what Coppola was making, and his percentage was lower, too, but it really didn't matter, since no one at this point believed the picture would be more than a routine commercial success – if that. The important thing was that in production both men remained true to the unspoken bargain they had struck. Coppola got the performance he needed, disciplined and brilliant; Brando got the conditions he required to give that performance.

Or as the director later put it: 'Before we started, I thought of him as this strange, moody Titan. But he turned out to be very simple, very direct . . . He's very tactile, he likes to touch you. He likes to be dealt with honestly, likes to feel he's listened to and told "No" when his idea is stupid, "Yes" when it's good . . . I avoided intellectual discussion, and tried to make him feel he wasn't going to be taken advantage of.'

His strategy worked. And the fact that in pre-production Coppola kept fighting to give the picture the qualities it needed was not lost on Brando either. The director persisted in the struggle for the cast he wanted, and he forced the budget up over $6 million, assuring that it would be done on location in New York and with handsomely detailed period flavor. For his part, Brando was helpful in unexpected ways. When the studio found Al Pacino's screen test too reserved and balked at casting him, Brando called Evans and told him the role of Michael, the son who takes over the Corleone empire when the Don is incapacitated, required 'a brooder', because that would give the actor playing him room to develop a character. His intervention was probably instrumental in assuring Pacino the role. Later, when the studio disliked Coppola's dailies after a few days of shooting, Brando let it be known that if the director were fired he would leave also.

But perhaps his most important off-screen contribution was as role model and inspiration for the young cast and its young director. Sure, he sometimes did not report for work on Monday, and he sometimes changed his lines (and often had his words written out on cue cards, or even on his fellow-players' persons), but he enjoyed playing morale-builder and mentor, as *The Godfather*'s godfather.

There was one last struggle with the studio over the film's length, which was close to three hours, but Coppola and producer Al Ruddy prevailed, with Evans admitting that the longer version actually played faster than the truncated one. The kind of observations that greater length permitted – of behavioral detail, of setting – were in fact vital to the movie's success. In any case, they gave

The Godfather its air of sobriety and veracity and, despite its many bloody doings, made it impossible for people to think of it as just a rattling good yarn, which at its simplest level it surely was.

If the contrast between the sometimes comic, sometimes almost sentimental presentation of the Corleone family's life away from their 'business' and the operatically staged violence of their lives on the job is the most important of the contrasts the film offers, it is not the only one. The use of light provides another. The light in the family scenes is warm and sunny, and so is the light when they go forth to conduct their murderous affairs. But when they are in conference, scheming, cinematographer Gordon Willis's palette is dark, his tones burnished. You think of corporate boardrooms, and you are not wrong to do so.

Character contrast is important, too. Don Corleone has three sons, each of whom represents an aspect of his own nature. Sonny (James Caan) is hot-blooded – a womanizer, a comedian, and openly, eagerly violent. Michael (Al Pacino) is, indeed, a brooder, an educated man, avatar of his father's hopes for respectability, and yet an icy figure who has been warmed by only one thing, family loyalty. He sets it above all else, including his own best interests. And he will enforce it at gunpoint. A third brother, Fredo (the late John Cazale), represents all the impulses the other men of the family suppress; he is soft, lazy, unmoved by passionate belief. In his good-natured need to be liked he is something of an unacknowledged burden to the rest of them. In short, there is an insinuating typicality about the Corleone family, and it works steadily throughout the picture to disarm our moral defenses. We know what they do is ultimately evil, socially costly in incalculable amounts. But they are in some respects so like us, or at least so like people we know, that it takes an effort of will to deplore them.

Actually, we envy them. Their milieu permits them, encourages them, to act out emotions boldly, without the circumspection that bedevils us in life. As an extended family they are like the rest of us, at once treasuring and sustaining bonds of family tradition and also maddened by

Right Brando's intervention helped secure the part of Michael for Al Pacino. He also let it be known, when Coppola's position was under threat, that if the director were fired he would leave also.

their inability to escape from them. But they were allowed to vent this range of emotions more boldly than we are, settle their disputes openly, without hypocrisy. The conventions prevailing in their line of work permit them, encourage them, to do what the rest of us only dream of doing. There are, one feels, no ulcers in the executive ranks of the Mafia. And – obviously – no golden parachutes for disloyal or incompetent managers. At one level the film is, therefore, a relief from the prevailing pieties about both family and corporate life, a shrewd, joyful, and finally anarchic penetration to the emotional heart of the frustrations that rule most American lives.

At the time, though, the picture's opponents taxed it for its failures (as they saw it) of conventional morality. Here is John Simon: 'Missing is the banality of evil: the cheap, ugly, petty racketeering that is the mainstay of organized crime and that neither the script of Mario Puzo nor the direction of Francis Ford Coppola could have made glamorous or palatable.' One must ask, is there not sufficient 'banality' in the capacity of the Corleones to sit down to a huge Italian feast, with the entire family gathered warmly about, immediately before or after executing a contract on some enemy? Consider only the famous cross-cut sequence in which, while the immediate clan attend an elaborate wedding, Michael Corleone's soldiers fan out across the underworld, executing all their opponents, consolidating his position. But banality isn't really the film's subject. Humanity is.

There is no better example of it than the Don's death. It comes as he plays in the garden with a grandchild. He cuts false ogre's teeth out of an orange rind, puts them in his mouth and is silently, lumberingly, humorously chasing the giggling child around when a heart attack fells him. This business was Brando's invention – he had amused his own children with the orange trick. But it has, like so much of the film, that astonishing rightness of effect that cannot arise entirely out of conscious calculation, that comes only when artists achieve an unconscious harmony with their material. Here a man who has ruled his world through fear at last acknowledges, self-satirizingly, that he knows what he has been and implies as well that his carefully cultivated

air of monstrousness was, among other things, a strategy, a put-on useful in a business that he like many another businessman may have conceived of as – yes – a game. Does this moment sentimentalize the Don? Yes. Does it also create the most chilling of all his resonances? Yes, again.

Curiously, Brando came closer to the truth about his success, and by extension the success of the movie, than any of the reviewers. A few years later, reminiscing with uncharacteristic geniality about *The Godfather*, Brando dismissed his accomplishment as an accident: 'What the hell did I know about a sixty-five-year-old Italian who smokes twisted goat shit cigars?' But then he added: 'I'll tell you the real secret: the people who plonk down six bucks to see a fantasy on celluloid actually supply their own fantasy and do a helluva lot better job . . . than I do. People lived the character of Don Corleone in their own mind's eye.'

In other words, he could only make a good guess about a Mafioso's mannerisms, but he had been around the movie business (and around life) for a while, so he knew something about the core psychology of the powerful, those aspects of it that are found everywhere in contemporary life. And he could communicate in terms all of us could recognize and employ in making our connections with his character specifically, *The Godfather* in general.

There is in his work a marvelous objectivity, a refusal to judge his character, that sets the tone of the picture, and permits us, finally, to read it in whatever spirit we choose. For what Brando gives us in the Don is a portrait of a man who has distilled his drive for power to its essence and is, of course, the more menacing by the carefully measured reserve with which he deploys the force of his will. He is all understatement; he makes people lean in to hear what he says in his thin, cracked, voice. And when people lean in, they usually bow their heads, assuming, perforce, an attitude of respect, obsequiousness. This effect is further reinforced by the dim light in which he is placed when he is conducting business. You have to strain your eyes as well as your ears to attend him.

'That's it, that's it. Mean bulldog face, warmth inside,' Brando is said to have muttered to the mirror. Finding the look of the Don helped him find the character.

Is he capable of kindness? Naturally – when it does not interfere with his larger interests. Is he sentimental about women and children? Certainly – most ambitious men are when they have a moment and the courtly emotions occur to them. Is he reluctant to acknowledge that there are people in the world who disagree with him, almost weary when he is forced to exert himself against their rebelliousness? Of course – strife is bad for business, bad for a CEO's digestion.

The unstated wit of this performance is breathtaking. Brando's Don is in every respect a recognizable man – full of contradictions, of muted, antithetical emotions that are only resolved by his drive for power. And so, while a part of our mind recognizes him as evil incarnate, another part of it must admire both his directness of intention and his delicate indirection of language when he quietly rasps what became the movie's catch phrase: 'Make him an offer he can't refuse.' Some part of us quite simply wants to be him, to exercise power untrammeled by the niceties.

It is perhaps needless to add that Brando, no less than the movie, was subjected to willful critical misunderstanding. Here is Simon again, accusing him of 'hamming things up by sheer underacting' – an oxymoron of astonishing wrong-headedness. It was not quite as amazing, though, as Andrew Sarris's assertion this was 'a role Lee J. Cobb could have played in his sleep without special make-up'. Yes, let's have evil power thump and crash about, so everyone recognizes it and draws the right, comfortable, distancing conclusions from monstrousness made clearly visible. Better still, let's revisit the classic gangster movie and revel once again in its clichés.

But, of course, such criticism is as irrelevant as it is risible. A more typical review, by *Newsweek*'s Paul D. Zimmerman, got much closer both to the truth of the performance and the truth of our response to it: 'There is no longer any need to talk tragically of Marlon Brando's career. His stormy two-decade odyssey through films good and bad, but rarely big enough to house his prodigious talents, has ended in triumph.' Especially for those of us who had long since struck what Sarris shrewdly called our 'Faustian' bargain with the actor, this performance could not be looked upon as anything but a long-delayed fulfillment. For the first time he was doing what we had imagined he would be doing at this age: accomplishing singular work in a context that was fully worthy of that work.

It is impossible to say whether Brando took his tone from the film or vice versa, but there is a remarkable seamlessness in the fit of character to context. It is equally futile to try to determine whether it was word of this performance or word of the film's richness of color and sheer narrative power, or the hope that it would at last reveal the secrets of the underworld, that powered it commercially. What is certain is that *The Godfather* was an instant success and went on to become the mightiest hit of its day, grossing some $81 million in North America in its first year of release, 1972. That was more than three times what the next most successful film took in that year. Eventually the picture grossed some $150 million, worldwide, which does not count huge television and video cassette sales.

For Brando, the irony must have been delicious: fourteen consecutive flops, the longest dry spell any major movie star has ever endured, and now, overnight, he had the biggest hit since *Gone with the Wind*. But there is no hint that he savored it. What we may somewhat more safely speculate is that it energized him, renewed his self-confidence. Around this time he granted an interview in which he allowed – and, for a man who had so often expressed his contempt for his profession, it was a major allowance – that acting, on a certain routine, 'let's pretend' level, was 'a perfectly reasonable way to make a living. You're not stealing money, and you're entertaining people.' He implied that if he could have been that kind of an actor he might have led a contented life. But, of course, he was not. He was the kind of actor, he insisted, who could not help but 'upset' himself in certain roles, had to dive down deep within himself and examine the junk and offal buried there; and that, he said, had grown increasingly difficult for him. It was on this occasion that he expressed the thought that, I think, bears repetition. 'There comes a time in one's life when you don't want to do it anymore.'

His performance in *The Godfather* clearly derives from observation and imagination, not from self-exploration or self-revelation, and so represents the glorious culmination of his long effort to become the new Paul Muni, hiding out behind accents and make-up and avoiding the dark depths he alluded to. But even before its release he could not help but know that his work in *The Godfather* was extraordinary; and could not help but feel energy, conviction flowing back into him. Possibly, just possibly, he was ready for one more dive into the blackness.

And, coincidentally, along came Bernardo Bertolucci, acclaimed director of *The Conformist* among other serious and ambitious works, offering him the opportunity to take a voyage into the depths under something like ideal circumstances. He came under good auspices, as the friend of Christian Marquand, who was then living with Dominique Sanda, *The Conformist*'s star who was committed to appear with Jean-Louis Trintignant in the project the director was now offering to Brando, *Last Tango in Paris*. There has never been an explanation of

why the Sanda-Trintignant pairing was abandoned, but one must suspect that once Bertolucci met Brando (*emozionato* was the director's word for his feelings – 'scared and excited'), poor Trintignant, such a cool, 'intellectual' actor, didn't have a chance to keep his role.

And Brando did not have a chance to escape it. Here is Bertolucci's recollection of their first meeting: 'For the first fifteen minutes he didn't say a word; he only looked at me. Then he asked me to talk about him. I was very embarrassed but I got around it. I didn't talk about him, but about the character I had in mind for the film, how I saw him in the role.' But soon monologue turned to dialogue, and Bertolucci began interviewing Brando, 'using the material that came out to construct or perfect the story in my mind. He listened carefully, and then he said "yes" right away, without asking to read the script.'

A good thing, too. For the likelihood is that little, if anything, was at this point committed to paper. Perhaps something was a little later, when Bertolucci visited Los Angeles for two weeks for further conversations with Brando. Or perhaps not. For by this time he must have known that the appeal of the project for Brando lay in its lack of pre-ordained structure, the opportunities it offered him not merely to improvise a character, but to let his own character interpenetrate a screen character. Bertolucci said at the time that he liked to create characters based 'on what the actors are in themselves', and he felt Brando's training as an actor made him an ideal candidate 'to superimpose himself upon the character in the film'.

His entire history in the movies spoke of Brando's impatience with following a script as written. And his more recent history announced an increasing reluctance to learn lines in any but the most approximate ways. Bertolucci's methods would at least free him from his recent dependence on cue cards. After all the high-toned blather about the brilliance of Bertolucci's radical new working methods, it *is* something of a comedown to suggest that he gathered in his most famous recruit because these methods suggested to Brando a practical solution to a very practical issue. Yet the thought is inescapable.

So is the notion that, however sketchy, the tale

In Bernardo Bertolucci's
Last Tango in Paris (1973),
Brando and Maria
Schneider played a pair of
strangers who, on meeting
in an empty apartment,
use it for a series of sexual
encounters freed from all
conventional restraint.

1973

Bertolucci told Brando at their meetings must have contained a powerful hint of the erotic elements that made *Last Tango in Paris* the sensation it became when it was released, and that this was, at least, not uninteresting to Brando. As early as *Streetcar* and as late as *The Nightcomers*, we have observed that the admixture of sex and violence (even if the violence is more psychological than physical) does stir something in him. In the event, of course, it delivered even more than Bertolucci promised.

Finally, though, it may be that Bertolucci's personality was the most important element in recruiting Brando to this project. He is, by all accounts, the most seductive of directors. At the time, Chris Mankiewicz, the American writer-producer, who is also the son of Joseph L. Mankiewicz, was occasionally on the set and later told a reporter, 'Bernardo is the kind of man you work for out of love rather than fear or just for the job.'

So it was, certainly, with Brando. In their pre-production meetings and on the set Bertolucci was ever the soft-spoken, youthful collaborator with his star, creating an ambiance that Mankiewicz described as charming Brando in such a way that 'he was not aware of being charmed'. The film's production manager described Bertolucci's technique as *violentandolo dolcemente* – gentle rape. The director himself put it otherwise: he understood Brando to be 'a hunter of instinct . . . he isn't capable of rationalizing.' And so, from the start, 'my rapport with him was solely emotional.' As work proceeded, the picture became, in Bertolucci's words 'a kind of psychological adventure', and one that engaged the star's attention more deeply than anything he had done in years. As time went on, Bertolucci and Brando required less in the way of verbal exchange in order to do their work, and when it was finished Bertolucci would remember 'the glances that Brando would send me. His look was full of meanings, as though he wanted to say: "Is it worth doing all this? Being actors, wanting success, performing, putting our hearts into it?" I think that it is . . . even if one must always be aware that each thing is immediately consumed, that it is already over when it has scarcely begun.'

The film now seems more of a curiosity than a precursor to anything very much. On the other hand, it did not evanesce with anything like the immediacy Bertolucci imagined it would. It caused a gorgeous ruckus: banned in Bertolucci's native Italy, the threat of censorship everywhere, twitterings in the fashionable quarters of all the world's cultural capitals.

A simple recital of the story as it finally evolved explains only the least interesting aspects of this stir. It opens with a man named Paul and a woman named Jeanne (played by the unknown Maria Schneider) meeting in an apartment that both are thinking of renting. Having checked it out, but before they have even introduced themselves, he falls upon her and she, in the modern manner, accepts him for a quick, brutal fuck. Thereafter, they continue meeting in the apartment for increasingly vivid fornications. Isolated, the domineering male and the submissive female are freed from all conventional restraint – it's the classic porn device – and the intensity and daring of their sexual feats escalate. Value-free, history-free, future-free, Paul and Jeanne furnish the apartment only with a bed, a plain table and chairs, lust and memory. For these rooms are an existentialist symbol as well as a pornographic device – a central void in the universe, to be filled in the absence of God (or whatever) with autobiography as well as sex.

Between these encounters we learn that she is involved with a young film-maker, who is recording their relationship and her biography for a documentary. He wishes to impose the spurious order of art on life. It is also revealed that the Brando character's wife has recently committed suicide, and that this has summoned both reminiscence and remorse on his part – along with the need for the affectless sanctuary the apartment and the girl afford.

Eventually there is a somewhat banal role reversal. After dancing their 'last tango' in an elegantly decadent ballroom, he proposes a conventional living arrangement to her. But she has by this time decided that she has explored to the full the de Sadian paradox that holds that in sexual slavery lies sexual freedom. He follows her to the home she shares with her parents to plead his case still further, but when he violates that bourgeois sanctuary she kills him with her father's army revolver. The film

For Brando the appeal of
Last Tango lay in its lack of
pre-ordained structure, and
the opportunities it offered
him not merely to improvise,
but to let his own character
interpenetrate a screen
character.

closes with her rehearsing her story for the police: he was a total stranger, he broke in and tried to rape me, etc.

Rather obviously, this movie could – and did – support a wide range of interpretations, or perhaps one should say over-interpretations. Confronting the picture now, after the passage of over two decades, one also feels a powerful desire to skip all that. Its abiding interest is as elegant erotica, as a significant moment in its star's career, and as a social phenomenon of its moment. But efforts to locate *Last Tango in Paris* within the landscape of traditional modernist culture require some comment, if only because they miss its essence as an experience. This is not to say that Bertolucci was unaware of his work's possible cultural resonances. He is a self-conscious artist, and the critical edifices constructed on the film have a basis in his aspirations. But the fact is that the film as it finally evolved is, intellectually speaking, strictly soft-core. It is a consequential act not in the intellectual or artistic history of our age, but in its celebrity drama.

In order to have taken up the Big Themes that Bertolucci clearly wanted to examine, the film would have needed to maintain what we must presume was its original dramatic focus, as a story of male and female equals who, as they fall into a romantic turmoil resonant with philosophical implications – can be seen as 'universals'. To have accomplished this, the movie would have had to be cast quite differently, very possibly with unknowns or little knowns or, failing that, with stars of roughly the same magnitude. In other words, once Brando had been cast, what was required was someone whose significance in our fantasy lives was equal to his. Bertolucci seems to have recognized this, for an effort was made to sign Catherine Deneuve. She had a following, and *Belle de Jour* had recently imprinted her cool capacity to portray the darker enigmas of female sexuality on everyone's mind. But being prettily tied up and lightly flogged in a Bunuel dream sequence is one thing; enduring the earthier, more realistic humiliations Bertolucci had in mind, quite another. She passed, as did some other stars of comparable stature. Bertolucci began interviewing unknowns.

Once that decision was taken, his film could not be what he had envisioned initially. Once Bertolucci decided to go with Schneider (who got the job by stripping for the camera in a test) the picture became Brando's. For even though Schneider was a lively, and pretty young woman, the best she can do in this context is play accompaniment to a recitalist in full song. The differences in their age and experience assured that no matter what the actors did, we would read Brando somewhat paternalistically. And though he was very sweet and comforting to an inexperienced actress taking on a role that would tax the resources of a more experienced performer, the fact remains that he was the star, drawing not only most of our attention but also most of the bedazzled Bertolucci's attention on the set. In modern film we determine a film's power center by observing not only who has the most lines, but also who has to take off the fewest clothes. On both counts Brando is the winner here.

This thing is the star vehicle to end all star vehicles. And that's precisely why Norman Mailer, in his famous essay on the film, registered only half-ironic disappointment in the film's sex. It may be well faked, and not without its ability to turn us on, but it is, nevertheless, quite visibly faked. As a result, it is, in his view, curiously disappointing. He wrote, 'Brando's cock up Schneider's real vagina would have brought the history of the cinema one huge march closer to the ultimate experience it has promised since its inception (which is to embody life).' Bertolucci, it would seem, understood this point. 'Bernardo wanted me to fuck Maria . . . on screen,' Brando said later. 'I told him, "That's impossible. If that happens, our sex organs become the centerpiece of the film." He never did agree with me.'

It may be that Bertolucci wanted, at last, to push the cinema on to that destiny in perfect realism he was not alone in imagining for it. But it may also be that he sensed a disappointing incongruity between the sex he was filming and the talk he was filming. In the latter sequences, we feel, no niceties have been allowed to intervene; Brando, in particular, gives the impression that he has been allowed to say anything that comes into his head. Much of his character's history is, in fact, borrowed from Brando's past – his real one and some of his movie roles, too. And it is more than possible to imagine, from what we know of the star's private conversational style, that he is speaking from the heart of his private darkness, giving us authentic insight into the life in which we had taken such an avid interest these two decades.

The verisimilitude of this dialogue is further reinforced by Brando's behavior. We have long since observed that the effort not to appear as himself in public is, perhaps, the major theme of his career – all those accents and make-ups and so on. Now, forced to appear, as it were, in his own skin, he is bereft of his usual disguises. And Bertolucci makes capital of Brando's frantic borrowings to escape not from nakedness, but from naked confession. If the actor wants to drop into an English accent or adopt the mannerisms of a bouncy adolescent, he lets him. Brando can mumble his lines or stumble on them, he can strike poses or sulk. Best of all, he can indulge his free-associational humor, which leads him inevitably toward the sexual and scatological. And the more he tries not to be Brando, the more he is Brando – in one sense at least.

And so, autobiography and behavior combine to create the illusion of guaranteeing the truth of the second major aspect of his dialogue, the sexual fantasies, which up to a point his partner must act out for him. And if, whether fantasized or acted out, these disgust, so be it. When Brando buggers Schneider's chic, saucy, *cultured* little bourgeois ass, he is buggering everything that has bugged him, all those middle-class importunings, all those demands for discipline and responsibility. When he forces her to explore his own fundament, the while describing his fancy of her copulation with a dying pig, he is saying something about the fate he would like to visit on all who have tried to probe him for his secrets these many years.

Was it honest work? I think so, in that Brando saw his own depths as polluted. What had once been a pure and authentic spirit – that of an idealistic artist, as he perhaps saw it, certainly an uncorrupted individualist – now carried the poisons of fame in his system. It was this bile that he spewed forth here, under the not entirely erroneous assumption that we, the audience, were as

much responsible for its creation as he was and deserved a sample of its bitter taste. And so what we had was the first (and so far only) performance in which the *fact* of the star's stardom – not just the idea of stardom – was the subject of the starring role.

In the formal sense, this probably was not really acting, but it was an astonishing act of self-assertion. For Brando had taken it all – his conceptions and misconceptions of himself, our conceptions and misconceptions about the same subject – and made a role of the mess. And we are not talking here about a few scribbled rewrites on the set, designed to match image and skills more closely to the demands of the writers' blue-print. No, we are talking about an organic symbiosis: something that does not, I think, exist in nature but can perhaps be used as a term of description in the unnatural world of celebrity. Brando, especially toward the end of the film, when he puts on his fallen angel mask, begs for a tragic interpretation of his efforts. And one feels like conceding it to him, if only for his death scene. Shot by his lover, done in, that is, by the bourgeoisie, Paul reels backward out of her parents' overstuffed living-room on to a balcony and, before plunging from it to his death, pauses to remove his gum and stick it to the railing. We can imagine no other actor in the history of the movies imagining that gesture, let alone playing it. Compared to it, his 'real' cock up Maria Schneider's 'real' vagina is nothing – the easy stuff, as any actor but few literary gentlemen would know.

If life were artfully organized, like a good novel, or even a good screenplay, this narrative could now come to a close, and on a triumphant note as well. For whatever one thought of the film as a whole, Brando had for the first time linked himself with an alternative school of film-making, one that proceeded in a way that was exactly the opposite of Hollywood's and, in this period when the unplanned was much admired, had taken the dangerous art of improvisation further than it had ever gone before – making up not just an isolated scene or two, but an entire character, an entire movie while he was on his feet. This was the kind of daring his talent and his spirit had promised from the start. So it seemed a culmination and a fulfillment. And his energy and commitment to the processes of this film seemed to suggest renewal, a re-engagement with a best, lost self now just slightly adapted to meet new conditions. All of this was recognized when – sensationally – *Last Tango in Paris* went forth into the world. Whatever its intrinsic values, the picture was blessed with high good fortune in its release. For it was a consummation devoutly wished for by the cell leaders of the Sexual Revolution. Fueled by the not entirely correct belief that The Pill liberated humankind from the practical consequences of promiscuity, and by pent-up resentment against the goody goody blandness with which Fifties popular culture had treated human sexuality, it also derived some energy from the posturings of the decade's self-proclaimed political revolutionaries. What its leaders had been missing was a popular cultural object (in particular, a film) that openly, graphically portrayed heterosexual coupling in an unmistakably artful context.

Whatever failures Brando had endured, and would endure, in finding metaphors through which to assert his political radicalism, *Last Tango in Paris* gave him the opportunity to assert, at last, his sexual radicalism. And that, I think, reflects a general truth. Most of us did not find a way of surfacing our unspoken political radicalism, that contempt for the superficiality and irrelevance of American political life, during the short-lived and vulgarly stated 'revolution' of this time. But many of us did ultimately find ways of bringing our sexual radicalism to the surface, and many lives were indeed changed, for better or for worse, by that process.

I make no large claims for *Last Tango* in this regard. It is, at best, an artifact of an interesting passage in our lives. But in terms of its public life, that is to say in the sub-critical discussion it engendered among people who never saw it or saw it only superficially it became a phenomenon. For it did undeniably contain the pornographic device we have already observed (the isolated room, where the world and its moral conventions cannot intrude) and, in its early passages, it had an undeniable pornographic structure, with each new sexual encounter more outrageous than the last. And these were redeemed (or at least rendered defensible) by the obvious

seriousness with which *Last Tango* developed the issues its sexual encounters so vividly introduced. Sight unseen, this was a movie to be cherished by everyone harboring the belief that a good society was one that confronted sexuality openly, freely and by all of us who loathed the paltering censorship that had for so many decades been imposed on the movies.

As the picture prepared to open, *Last Tango* was more or less simultaneously banned in Italy and booked as the closing night attraction at the New York Film Festival in 1972. Italian law forbade the movie's export until its case was fully adjudicated, but after well publicized negotiations, the picture was allowed out of the country – under armed guard – for its single festival showing. The screening became the hottest ticket in town. And then Kael got the *New Yorker* to break with custom and permit her to review the film, even though it would be months before it could possibly play the theaters.

Her wildly enthusiastic notice increased the anticipatory buzz about the movie, and after it had been freed for export by the Italians the X rating given to it by the Motion Picture Association's code administrators guaranteed a pre-release media frenzy. More importantly, when the picture finally opened in early 1973 it assured that everyone who was anyone (or aspired to be) would make the pilgrimage to the handful of theaters where it was playing. And that assured its profitability. As for Brando, he had now enjoyed, within months, a personal triumph in the largest commercial success and the largest *succès d'estime* anyone could remember. His comeback was as remarkable as his failure had been and, before that, his annunciation had been. He was, of course, nominated for the Academy Award for his performance in *The Godfather*, and he quickly became both the betting and the sentimental favorite to win. Inside the industry and beyond there was a desire to commemorate his achievement, and Hollywood also wanted to send him a signal: 'Come back, all is forgiven.'

On March 27, no one, except producer Howard Koch and some other awards ceremony personnel, expected anything like what happened when his name was read out as winner of the Oscar

Right With Jack Nicholson in *The Missouri Breaks* (1976), an eccentrically unplanned and playful western in which Brando's character adopts some weird disguises to considerable comic effect.

for best actor. They were aware that Brando was not in his seat when show-time arrived, and they noticed his stand-in, a young woman calling herself Sasheen Littlefeather (real name, Maria Cruz), arriving late for the show (she had been delayed as Brando drafted and re-drafted his statement). You could hardly miss her: she was dressed in full tribal regalia. Catching her in the lobby, Koch inquired after her intentions. She showed him Brando's 400-word screed. Too long, said Koch. I'll give you two minutes, and if you're not done you'll be escorted from the stage.

In the event, she actually performed well, considering the boos and cat-calls that occasionally interrupted her. Off-stage, in the press room, she read Brando's entire statement, which concluded: 'I, as a member in this profession, do not feel that I can as a citizen of the United States accept an award here tonight. I think awards in this country at this time are inappropriate to be received or given until the condition of the American Indian is drastically altered. If we are not our brother's keeper, at least let us not be his executioner.'

Most of those who immediately commented expressed outrage, though Michael Caine took the cooly reasonable view that if a man feels he has to speak his piece he ought to have nerve enough to do it himself. Presenting the best picture prize, an equally cool Clint Eastwood wondered if perhaps he should dedicate it to 'all the cowboys shot in John Ford westerns over the years'.

Since Brando was a founder and heavy financial backer of the new and militant American Indian Movement (AIM), no one questioned the authenticity of his feelings on this matter. And there was precedent for rejecting an Oscar: George C. Scott had done the same thing the year before. But he had done so for what most people judged to be a better reason – he didn't believe in competition between artists, particularly elective competition. No such logical connection between belief and action could be attributed to Brando, and a search for deeper motives was immediately launched.

At the time the standard Hollywood wisdom held that he was getting his own back at everyone who had ignored or patronized or rejected him over these many difficult years. But in the light of his subsequent history, one has to think there was more to the matter than that. One cannot escape this thought: having proved, if not beyond doubt, then to his own satisfaction, that his mature skills – and nerve – were the equal of his youthful ones, he was, in effect, announcing his retirement as – shall we say? – 'a contender'. But not as an occasionally working actor.

He stayed away from movies for three years after winning his Oscar, and this period was the height of his dedication to AIM. Perhaps as a result of his recent professional success, perhaps because of the economic security it provided him, perhaps because he felt a need to justify his Oscar night gesture, he took positions that were much more overtly radical than they had been in the past. He was present when participants in the violence at Wounded Knee were brought to trial, and at the Menominee Uprising, where protest also turned to violence. He subsequently went bail for AIM leaders charged with violent crimes, and tried to help others to avoid arrest. He was moved to tears when invited to participate in tribal ceremonies, and moved to another kind of sorrow when some Indians dismissed him as a publicity-seeking actor.

Eventually (and roughly coincident with his first reappearance on the screen) his public activism on behalf of this cause dwindled, though he has never ceased trying to interest Hollywood in a movie about American Indian history. The vehicle of his return to the screen had about it a certain promise both for him (above and beyond his million dollar salary) and for audiences, since his co-star and his director on *The Missouri Breaks* represented the kind of company everyone thought he should be keeping.

This western united him with his Mulholland Drive neighbor, Jack Nicholson, who was an admirer ('He gave us our freedom,' he once said, speaking as an actor, of course), and it reunited him with Arthur Penn, who believed in giving performers the liberty to improvise as a matter of principle. Moreover, the script, by Thomas McGuane, seemed to offer not just possibilities for this kind of playfulness, but to demand them. For McGuane had to leave the country to work on another project before he could do any extended revisions on his first draft

Superman (1978) was the first of a sequence of late-career films in which Brando was essentially just a guest star. Here he plays Superman's father.

1978

(which both stars and the director had individually rejected; it was the idea of working together that finally secured all their commitments). But then, suddenly, the start day was upon them all and no one had done any hard work on the script. As Penn put it, 'We were out there tap dancing for our lives . . . making up the movie as we went along.'

McGuane's story contained a very nice ironic reversal. A band of horse rustlers (led by Nicholson) takes a little spread in Montana to serve as a base for their operations, and the local cattle baron brings in a 'regulator' to drive them out. But as he settles down on the land, and falls in love with the rancher's daughter (nicely played by Kathleen Lloyd) Nicholson reverts to his boyhood identity as a peaceable farmer. On the other hand, Brando's lawman is a schizophrenic growing madder and more murderous by the moment. Movies with less interesting premises than that have been welcomed critically. So have many movies with less interesting performances than this one.

Brando thought it was 'a steal. For the first twenty pages of the script, I'm the character everyone's talking about – he's coming, he's coming. On page 21, I arrive. I can do anything, move like an eel dipped in vaseline. I'm here, I'm there, I'm all over the place. . . . Poor Jack Nicholson, he's right in there at the center, cranking the whole thing out.' As far as it goes, that's a fair summary of the role. But there's more to it. He and Penn agreed that the character, as originally written, had no psychological spine. 'I don't know who this guy is,' Brando complained. 'So in our discussion,' Penn would later recall, 'we decided, "Well, wait a minute – let's turn this apparent deficit into an asset."'

Which is why Brando enters the film hanging upside down from his saddle, wearing white fringed buckskin and talking in an Irish accent. Later he dresses as a preacher talking in a fluting English manner. And still later he turns up in dress and poke bonnet, acting like your basic Middle-western granny. The last, in particular,

1979

As Kurtz, who is found at the end of of Francis Ford Coppola's *Apocalypse Now* (1979) in a jungle hell of his own creation, Brando was almost unrecognizable.

is one of those on-set brainstorms that works – not least because the star improvised a hilarious monologue involving his horse and his mule and their impolite contention for a carrot. Truth to tell, it's Brando's best comic performance, and, inspired by him, Nicholson gets in some good licks, too.

Penn recalled one little nothing of a scene, in which Brando menaces Nicholson as he hoes his garden. 'Once they got going, I couldn't leave the scene. I just stayed there and let them play off one another . . . and I thought, "I don't care what the content of the scene is, you gotta watch these people do it." And that was the pleasure of that movie. Now, admittedly, if you want a simple, clear, coherent narrative, *Missouri Breaks* ain't it.'

Apparently people did. The outrage of disappointed expectations greeted it. Serious reviewers often couched their disapproval on near-to-moral grounds: they just couldn't believe these three heavyweights had 'indulged' themselves in such a loosy-goosy way. But what really got to the critics was that this playfulness violated the sober generic conventions of the western form. Actually, it went further than that, joyously and unselfconsciously converting itself into another genre entirely.

But however much fun Brando had making the film – and he actually stayed beyond his contractually stipulated time, for no extra fee, to finish the job properly – the reception accorded it was all too familiar. It was, like his Sixties films, a commercial failure, and one that raised all the old, boring clichés about how he was wasting himself. It would be too much to say that its reception disappointed him – receptions interested him less than ever, if that is possible. But the fact is that after this film he never acted again. Not really. Not in the sense that *The Godfather* and *Last Tango* had seemed to promise.

From the release of *The Missouri Breaks* in 1976, through *The Freshman* fourteen years later, he would work in a total of just five movies and one television program. In only two – possibly three – of them was his role central to the narrative; in none of them was it long or in any way taxing. Apart from *The Freshman*, these are appearances, guest shots, not performances. They engage neither the actor's emotions, nor the audience's.

Confronting them, this phrase occurs: 'left over life to kill'. And in fact, one would rather not confront them, would have preferred to fade out on *Last Tango in Paris*. The main group of these films was made between 1978 and 1980. For the record they are:

Superman (1978). Brando played Jor-El, the father of the eponymous hero in the film's prologue. On the planet Krypton, populated by an advanced civilization, he's the wisest of its many wise men, and has snow-white hair as befits his status. When the planet starts to blow up he rockets his son into space, aiming him in the general direction of Earth. It is the sort of job Orson Welles was always doing in those days for a lot less money.

Roots: The New Generation (1979). Apparently impressed with the moral seriousness of the phenomenally successful original mini-series, he volunteered for this sequel. 'I'm no snob about television,' he said. 'I think more important things should be done with TV, since it reaches a mass audience.' Indeed, Brando proposed that it should become the serious medium, and leave 'frivolity' to the movie houses. His cameo was as George Lincoln Rockwell, founder of the American Neo-Nazi party. He won an Emmy for it.

Apocalypse Now (1979). He was back working for Coppola, in a movie that was everything *The Godfather* was not: narratively and thematically muddled, inefficiently produced, crazily over-budget. In this resetting of Conrad's *Heart of Darkness* in Vietnam, Brando played Kurtz, the chap who has gone native somewhere up-river. Dressed in black, with his head shaved, he is photographed only in heavy shadow, apparently to disguise his girth. He and Coppola, with whom he 'collaborated' on the script for his scenes, turn an enigmatic figure into an incomprehensible one.

The Formula (1980). This time he is only semi-bald, but he wears a hearing aid (actually it is a radio receiver, picking up his lines as broadcast to him by an assistant director), and talks in a good-ole-boy accent. He is a powerful industrialist, managing a murderous conspiracy designed to keep a chemical substitute for oil from coming to market. His interpretation of this figure is as a foxy old gent, and that robs him – and the film – of menace. His co-star, playing the detective on his trail, is the only other man to reject an Academy Award, which turned out to be about the only thing Brando and George C. Scott had in common.

A pattern is evident here: Brando would idle professionally until he needed some money, then take whatever job seemed to offer the best pay for the least amount of work and, afterward, withdraw again. It would be pleasant to see it as an embrace of the dispassionate professionalism he had once described – not stealing, but entertaining. Yet the work did not measure up even to that modest standard. For it was edged by contempt for both his craft and his public.

Now even the pretense of memorizing lines was abandoned, and so was the pretense of keeping up appearances. For *Last Tango* he had achieved the look of a noble ruin; in his subsequent films he appears in what became his permanent make-up, his final disguise, which is that of a hugely fat man. He also made sure the public knew what he was making – sometimes as much as $2 million for a few days' work. Occasionally he tried to turn that into a form of social criticism: 'What kind of society overpays its actors and neglects its underprivileged?' But what it read as was detestation for self and others. It was not until 1980 that he more or less owned up to what he was doing. 'I'm not an actor and haven't been for years,' he finally admitted. 'I'm a human being – hopefully a concerned and somewhat intelligent one – who occasionally acts.'

By that time, Gary Carey, one of his biographers, estimated that in his last four appearances, totaling well under an hour of screen time, he had made $10 million. And now, for almost a decade, he could afford to disappear from the screen, from public life, entirely. No one knows how he passed his time, and he resented it when people inquired.

The truth is that he didn't do anything consequential. He was like an old gentleman retired from corporate life, filling his direction-less days as best he could. He added to his family (counting adoptees, he eventually had nine children). He read a lot, and never lightly. The easily impressionable said that he was continuing to search for the meaning of life. He put it more modestly: 'I've sort of lived a contemplative life, trying to figure out what it is I would like to do. I never really knew.' He also said he wrote a bit. He traveled a bit, too, mostly back and forth to his island, where he puttered inconclusively with various visionary schemes for tropical agriculture. He called his friends all over the world, at all hours of the day and night. And he ate. People found him curled up in bed with full gallons of ice cream. Thinking about him in his mansion, one began to think of Norma Desmond in hers.

In the late summer of 1989 a trailer for *The Dry White Season*, his first film in eight years, was shown in a crowded theater. One of his close-ups flashed on the screen. A gasp went up, so shocking was his appearance – grotesquely wrinkled and flabby. The little performance, as an idealist-cynical lawyer with pip-pip Oxbridge accent fighting apartheid laws in South Africa, was fine – he had two nice scenes. But he went on Connie Chung's television show to denounce the producers for failing, he said, to make the contributions they had promised to various organizations opposing the South African regime. Ever hopeful of his favor, ever guilty about its own bad behavior in the past, Hollywood gave him another Academy Award nomination.

The following summer there was *The Freshman*. It was a sweet little farce, about an innocent college boy (Matthew Broderick) who falls in with the Mafia. Broderick and the rest of the young cast found him avuncular and supportive and anxious that his reputation not overwhelm them. Brando is reprising Don Corleone – same accent, but funny. People keep mentioning this uncanny resemblance, and when he overhears this he glares at them. It is a good running gag. And this is a good running performance, his first since *The Missouri Breaks*. He has a lovely moment when he visits the boy in his dorm room and awkwardly tries to articulate his affection for him. It is another of his singular, treasurable moments – pure behavioral magic. That moment is so truthful, and so startling in its casual context, that it makes you mist up, for it reminds you that when we came in Brando was the young man sitting on the other side of that line, asking for understanding and not

1989

A Dry White Season (1989), his first film in eight years, allowed Brando to make a telling contribution to a worthwhile, liberal-minded project about the fight against South African apartheid.

quite receiving it. To put it simply, it is richer in resonances than its creator could possibly know.

Eileen Heckart, a thoughtful and serious actress of Brando's generation, once said that 'anyone' could become a technically proficient actor, but added, 'The difference between anyone and a great actor is made up of those moments . . . in which they kindle a spark – something that makes a moment so real that what they are doing becomes great acting.'

She, of course, chose Brando to exemplify her meaning. Most actors do. Anne Jackson called him 'the daddy of them all. He dares and defies, and I love him for it.' A character man named Paul Benedict, who contributed a marvelous comic turn to *The Freshman* (he's the pompous and mean-spirited teacher of film theory), put it yet more simply: 'To those of us who came up in the Fifties, he's the man. He's the god.' Not long after he spoke, *Life*

magazine devoted a special issue to the hundred most influential Americans of the century. Brando was the only actor who appeared in it, precisely because everyone its editors and reporters talked to, everyone who knows anything at all about acting, insisted that, evade though he will responsibility for a talent he cannot take credit for, he cannot evade history.

Alas, he could not evade tragedy, either. For on the night of May 16, 1990, his son Christian shot and killed a young man named Dag Drollet, lover of Cheyenne, another Brando child and a deeply troubled 20-year-old, who, it was alleged, had put Christian up to the crime with her tales of repeated beatings at the hands of Drollet.

What the full truth about this crime was, no one will ever know, for Cheyenne fled for Brando's South Seas retreat, from which there was no hope of extraditing her. There were reports of suicide attempts, one of which, a few years later, after the girl had been in and out of

Christian Brando (left) at his trial. He was sentenced
to a ten-year term for voluntary manslaughter, but
served only five.

mental hospitals, was successful. Precisely because
Cheyenne was the only witness to the crime, the first-
degree murder charge against Christian was reduced to
voluntary manslaughter, to which he entered a guilty
plea, and for which he was sentenced to a ten-year term,
of which he served about five years.

The story was, of course, a tabloid sensation. It fitted
so neatly the pre-existent mega-narrative of the
dysfunctional celebrity family, with the children
alternately indulged and ignored by their famous father.
In this narrative Christian was portrayed as addicted at
various times to drugs and alcohol. An incapacity for
stable relationships, a chequered academic career,
dashed hopes as an actor, a work life consisting solely of

odd, menial jobs (at the time of the crime he was
identified as 'a free-lance welder') were outlined in the
report of one social worker. Cheyenne was, of course,
portrayed as highly erratic in her behavior, very
manipulative of her family, with a particularly strong hold
over Christian, who, according to the same social work
report, may have, as a result of his addictions, suffered a
reduced mental capacity.

This is all-too-familiar stuff. The supermarket tabloids,
not to mention several generations of ghosted
autobiographies by the children of the rich and famous,
have taught us not to be surprised by their miserable and
melodramatic doings. In this milieu, *un*happy families
seem to be all alike. One also notices in the journalism

about them a certain grim and unworthy satisfaction with their troubles – an implication that a well-deserved comeuppance has been achieved.

But that's all psychobabble posing as social and moral comment; it's unworthy of extended comment here. What is worth noting is Marlon Brando's response to his son's crime. When the police were summoned to Brando's Mulholland Drive home, one of the investigating detectives found himself in an eerily ingratiating conversation with Brando, in which he was subjected to questions about his own children, his own beliefs. In the course of their talk the actor spoke of his difficulties in providing moral instruction for his kids, implying, as well, that if he had it to do over again he would conduct his life differently than he had. The detective described Brando as humble, meek, a tired and beaten man who seemed older than his years.

As Christian's legal drama played out over the next year, this proved to be an attitude Brando often struck. He (justifiably) attacked the circus aspects of the affair, observing that had Christian been the scion of any anonymously rich man the case would have been handled in much quieter fashion. That aside, however, he reversed course and gave the press what it had for so long wanted from him – access – patiently responding to their most inane and invasive questions. His idea was to take the heat off his son and absorb it himself.

More remarkable was his testimony at his son's pre-sentencing hearing, which was televised in full. His appearance seemed particularly grossed-out, but despite the formality of the courtroom, his attempt was to establish a sort of rueful intimacy with the audience. He was like a father discussing 'the kids' with other veterans of the generational battles late at night as the Cognac went around. He took full responsibility for his errors of commission and the omission; he took pride in Christian's good qualities – his honesty, his struggles to escape addiction and to make a life for himself free of his father's fame; he was frank about his tumultuous relationship with the boy's mother, Anna Kashfi, and the damage that might have done him. His most moving moment came, perhaps, when he asked the investigating officers to unzip the body

bag in which they had placed Dag Drollet so that Brando could kiss him goodbye.

It was a very effective performance – if, indeed, it was a performance. The victim's father, Jacques, thought it was: 'Brando is an actor and even in his private life he is always acting. He can cry and lie like a horse can run.' He added, 'I think he is making the whole case his own case.' This, of course, was precisely so. And no one can doubt that the strategy worked. Brando had always despised the workings of the celebrity system, and his opposition to it – often so outrageously stated – had done him considerable harm in the past. How much happier he might have been had he suffered these intrusive fools more gladly, as most of his starry peers had learned to do. Now, though, things were reversed. The media needed to be won over, and with them public opinion and the legal system, too. This he accomplished with his pieties, his remorse, his eagerness to take more than his share of responsibility for the crime. Many a parent, reading of his version of his travails, could identify with him. There but for the grace of God...

That there was an element of performance in what he did is beyond doubt. The only (unanswerable) question is how much of it was based on authentic emotion. My own guess is that it was an exquisite mixture of artifice and authentic regret for things undone. For my part I would rather have seen him play *Lear* on stage – or even on screen – rather than spew a version of it in bits and pieces in these tawdry circumstances. Yet 'the work' was fascinating – and, of course as unpremeditated as it was unwelcome to the actor. One felt one's heart going out to him – reluctantly, knowing it was being manipulated.

As the court proceedings wound their way to a conclusion, Brando let it be known that he intended, at last, to write his autobiography, for which he was paid an advance that surely covered his huge, unexpected legal fees. When it came out in September 1994, it proved to be a genial and unrevealing work. It did, however, contain this passage: '*Last Tango in Paris* required a lot of emotional arm wrestling with myself, and when it was finished, I decided that I wasn't ever again going to destroy myself to make a movie. I felt I had violated my innermost self and didn't want to suffer like that anymore'. Thereafter I decided to make my living in a way that was less devastating emotionally. In subsequent pictures I stopped trying to experience the emotions of my characters as I had always done before, and simply to play the part in a technical way.'

He had not been able entirely to play his courtroom role purely technically. The mixture of the real and the artificial was too exquisite to discern the true from the false. But in the three formal roles he has since essayed, Brando's acting has, in all honesty, not been up to the mark even in terms of pure technique. He was working the fringes now – out there in pick-up land, where people were willing to take a chance that his presence might spark their variously dim and risible projects, interest a major studio in distributing it, should the great man actually show up in a mood to do a bit of acting. The unlovely Salkind family, who had overpaid him for his *Superman* stint, were back, offering him $5 million (for five days) in *Christopher Columbus – The Discovery*. He would later claim that he protested its ludicrous script, even provided some rewrites that were rejected by these international freebooters of the cinema. If, as rumour had it, these included a moment where naked Jewish girls were seen boiling in oil as Brando's character, Torquemada, stalked the torture chambers of the Inquisition, one can see why even the Salkinds balked at his notions. In the event, he never gave a more spiritless performance, refusing to color his work with so much as a smirk or a snarl, scarcely varying his prevailing monotone. If we are to take anything from this dismal portrayal of a character apparently utterly untouched by an inner life, it is that, we are watching a man – Brando – broken by unhappiness going through the motions to pay his bills.

He was a little more himself in *Don Juan De Marco*, as a psychiatrist with a difficult case (beautifully played by Johnny Depp) on his hands. The kid is some sort of schizophrenic, but utterly irresistible to women, with the attentions he lavishes on them – are they fantasies or reality? – having nothing but a therapeutic effect on them. The movie has a sort of wacky romanticism about it, not to mention a high degree of originality. Unfortunately it

keeps stumbling on – Brando. He, at times, visibly can't, or won't, remember his lines. Worse, his sheer bulk prevents him from acting. He is too large, now, for the kind of twinkle-toeing that worked so well for him in *The Freshman*. And his attempts to mime healthy passion for his wife (the still lithesome Faye Dunaway) are grotesque. He and Depp, a wonderful actor who has put more than one critic in mind of the young Brando, bonded on the film and there is talk of their working together sometime in the future. But the truth is that though he is more committed to his character here than he was in the Columbus film, he is not fully committed to it. Almost always when he's on screen our attention is focused on him in the wrong way. We find ourselves thinking about Brando the troubled man, not Brando, the smart, stable, even rather jolly character – he's supposed to represent the reality principle – that he is trying to play.

Yet, there were far worse depths still to be tested, namely *The Island of Dr Moreau*, the third screen incarnation of H. G. Wells's novel about the eponymous scientist determined to create men from animals. Here Brando was challenging Charles Laughton's definitive portrayal of Moreau in *Island of Lost Souls*, in which, some 65 years earlier, the great English actor played the mad scientist as an almost clubbable English eccentric – until the truth of his craziness began to dawn on the shipwrecked explorer who had penetrated his remote lair, and his failed experiments – half-men, half-beasts – rise in rebellion against their torments.

In Brando's update he does a plummy English accent, and first appears to us borne along on a primitive version of a Popemobile, wearing something like vestments and blessing the crowd of grotesques who worship him as father and lawgiver. They all have an electronic implant which, when he touches the transmitter he carries, sends shock waves through them. Oh, yes, Brando appears in this first sequence wearing dead white make-up (to protect him from the unbearable sun) and carmine lipstick (no explanation given). But there is nothing frightening about this Moreau, who unlike the previous ones (Burt Lancaster also had a go at the role) is here said to be trying to create a perfect human being, freed

1995

In *Don Juan De Marco* (1995), in which he played a psychiatrist, Brando bonded well with Johnny Depp but was handicapped by his own bulk and by an inability to learn his lines.

apparently of original sin, instead of just fooling around with the idea of making men out of beasts. In any event, not much is made of this aspect of his experiments in genetic engineering and Brando's character appears to have wandered dottily in from a P.G. Wodehouse adaptation, Laughton, too, had his funny side, but there was iron in the man. And scary obsession. His control over his creatures was absolute; when he raged, they cringed in authentic terror. Brando never rages. He tries to calm them by playing a little Gershwin on the piano and explaining the difference between tonal and atonal music. His playing, by the way, appears to be unfaked – another unsuspected accomplishment – and when they murder him he scarcely mutters a protest, let alone a

command, then disappears from the picture, his contractual time expired. The film has yet another inconsequential half-hour to run, as the rebellion is put down and David Thewlis, who is third billed, but the film's actual lead – Val Kilmer is also present as Moreau's demented assistant, but also disappears abruptly – finally escapes with his life.

This is a movie that is, in the end, more about desperate deal memos than it is about actual narrative, a picture on which the leading actors ganged up on the original director, who was replaced on short notice, with obviously inadequate preparation, by the gifted John Frankenheimer, himself back from some years of wandering the wilderness of made-for-TV movies. It is also a picture so bad, so dramatically undeveloped, that one's attention finally fastens on the makeup effects, which strike one, at last, as little more interesting than they were in the Laughton original, despite the many recent advances in latex technology. As for Brando, he strikes one now as completely undirectable, self-amused by his accent, by his little behavioral quirks, which he never stitches together into a character. Indeed, his performance offers no evidence that he has thought Moreau through in any meaningful way.

We are, in work like this, well past 'technical' acting. We are in realms of amateurishness scarcely seen in public outside high school theatricals, work that would get any other actor fired for incompetence. It is not funny. It is not interesting, except perhaps as an exercise in loathing of self, audience, fellow players that is without parallel – at least in my experience – in screen performance. We have had actors who cannot act, but all of them, down to the humblest B picture performers of the kind Brando and his ilk drove from the screen, were at least trying. Brando, fluting and piping in *Dr Moreau*, is not.

Acting of this kind is inhuman. That is to say, we cannot find any connection between what we're seeing and anything we recognize as authentic human behavior. And what Brando is doing is completing an arc that is without precedent in the history of performance. For an actor to have touched both the heights of the sublime and these depths of the ridiculous in the course of a career is simply, thunderously, amazing.

And yet, still, one cannot entirely evade the crazy hope that this is, despite Brando's advanced age, just one more phase in a career of phases, there that is yet time for him to find the players, the director, the property, the patient, non-exploitative producers who will inspire him to one last gathering of forces, one final performance that will glow with the mastery of maturity. Fat chance, one says, even as one types those words. But such is his hold on us – those of his first audience who still linger in the nearly empty auditorium – that one lets them stand, evidence of vain hope's triumph over despairing experience.

One wonders: does it drive him crazy, this determined refusal of others to accept him on his own discounted

terms? One thinks of two other actors, each in his way Brando's peer. The first is John Barrymore, he whose name was so frequently evoked when Brando was coming up. The parallels between their late lives seem more vivid than whatever parallels may have existed between their early lives – the self-parodies their audiences witnessed, the pervasive sense of waste that their supporters feel in contemplating their overall records. Two or three things Edmund Wilson wrote about Barrymore seem apposite to Brando: 'He tried hard to find some role in life itself that he could count on and that would express him' and 'whenever, through exercise of will, he had achieved a high point of intensity by imposing on life his personal dream the role always failed and let him down with a crash'. Wilson speculated that Barrymore, as well as his brother Lionel and his sister Ethel, failed of fulfillment because 'they never had the actor's vocation'. Wilson adds: 'You see it very clearly if you compare them with their uncle, John Drew, who, glass of fashion and mold of form though he was, took the theater with professional seriousness, and even in his later years, at his blindest and most arthritic, kept his cast and himself up to scratch with the rigor of an old general at maneuvers.'

It is saving, this sense of vocation, and the professionalism that derives from it. It is where, at last, 'meaning' is to be found, if by that word we signify something modest – in the case of actors the search for truthful behavior, authentic emotion, and the means of vividly imparting them to an audience, assuring them that they are not alone in their feelings, that what they experience in their privacy is shared by others. By making these matters public, art comforts (and sometimes discomfits), but above all makes connections, assuages our loneliness – and perhaps the artist's as well. It is not nothing to have a gift for such work, and it is not nothing to exercise it with care and sobriety. And to look upon it as a calling and respond to that calling with passion. It is a completely honorable way to fill one's days – and one's thoughts.

Lacking a calling, all the Barrymores drifted into addiction. Lacking a calling, Brando drifted into self-absorption. And then into the self-contempt that analogizes so well with John Barrymore's. Curious, is it not, that two actors who are among the greatest members of their profession that America has produced in this century were accidental actors, men for whom acting was not a cherished dream they could not help but embrace, but merely a way of escaping inconsequence, something to do until they could discover what they really wanted to do. Which, in turn, became a bad dream in which the dreamer desperately twists and turns trying to elude the demon of his own talent and the demon of (to him) false acclaim.

Here another acting name intrudes on one's thoughts. Paul Newman is almost exactly Brando's age, and he is everything Brando is not. He is fit and attractive. He has endured personal tragedy with dignity and courage. He continues to find serious work that engages and challenges him. He has also found causes that elicit his concern, and he is practical-minded and effective on their behalf. He has, as well, found a way to remain present in the world, and at the same time to maintain his privacy. To put it simply, he has been a responsible artist and a responsible man, and so far as a stranger can tell, he leads a life of contentment and coherence, befitting a man who has worked seriously to develop the character he lives and the characters he plays.

It may be true that there are fewer 'moments' in his career, fewer of those seismic shocks of recognition where the actor brings us face to face with some truth we all acknowledge and share, but have not previously seen represented on the screen or stage. But the kind of epiphanies we are talking about are not created out of moral imperatives – hard work and a good life have nothing to do with their making. They are, as Brando's frantic desire to dismiss praise of them acknowledges, accidents of a sort – the products, perhaps, of genes and instincts and opportunity interacting unpredictably; the products, possibly, of that thing people like to call genius, for which, as Laurence Olivier once remarked, the theater has no room, because it is too troubling.

Troubling especially to those who possess and are possessed by it. How do you base a life on something that strikes you out of nowhere, is summoned up, usually,

without conscious effort on your part? By putting yourself in places where the lightning seems most likely to strike. But how hard that is to do, especially when you think of that gift as not valuable or consequential in a world that appears to be lost in desperate agony; especially when you were taught long ago to consider yourself unworthy of special praise, and a highly unlikely receptacle for special endowments. One thinks – only half comically – that here is one final point of reference between Marlon Brando and the rest of us. One thinks that perhaps, in his sleepless early morning hours, he, too, wishes he were Paul Newman. Wishes, that is to say, that he did not have to waste the gains he considers ill-gotten on a stunned and reclusive search for coherence.

Of that, we cannot speak. Indeed, all we can confidently speak of in contemplating this life are our own memories of it. We may treasure, as he does not, the moments he gave us, at the same time speculating about the ones he didn't give us, out of spite or goofiness or whatever has moved him to not move us. Looking at him now, one can't help recalling the illimitable promise of his youth and perhaps of our own, and the inevitable confusions and compromises life imposes on us, the inevitable follies we impose on ourselves. Of the many illusions celebrity foists upon us, the illusion of coherence, the sense that there are privileged people in the world who somehow know what they are doing in ways that we do not, is the largest, and possibly the most dangerous. But Marlon Brando has kept faith with incoherence. Whatever he has done and not done, no actor in his life and his work has more consistently kept us in touch with the erratic – that which is unpredictable and dangerous in ourselves and in the world. We continue to wish him well, some of us, for in so doing, we wish ourselves well, too. Wish ourselves, that is, that most elusive of miracles, the miracle of self-understanding.

FILMOGRAPHY

THE MEN
Director: Fred Zinnemann
Screenplay: Carl Foreman
Photography: Robert de Grasse
Cast: Marlon Brando, Teresa Wright, Everett Sloane, Jack Webb, Howard St John
Running time: 85 mins
Released: 1950
Produced by Stanley Kramer

A STREETCAR NAMED DESIRE
Director: Elia Kazan
Screenplay: Tennessee Williams, from his play
Photography: Harry Stradling
Cast: Vivien Leigh, Marlon Brando, Kim Hunter, Karl Malden
Running time: 122 mins
Released: 1951
Produced by Charles K Feldman/Elia Kazan

VIVA ZAPATA
Director: Elia Kazan
Screenplay: John Steinback
Photography: Joe MacDonald
Cast: Marlon Brando, Jean Peters, Joseph Wiseman, Anthony Quinn, Arnold Moss, Margo, Frank Silvera
Running time: 113 mins
Released: 1952
Produced by 20th Century Fox

JULIUS CAESAR
Director: Joseph L Mankiewicz
Screenplay: Joseph L Mankiewicz, from the play by William Shakespeare
Photography: Joseph Ruttenberg
Cast: John Gielgud, James Mason, Marlon Brando, Greer Garson, Deborah Kerr, Louis Calhern, Edmond O'Brien, George Macready, Michael Pate, John Hoyt, Alan Napier
Running time: 121 mins
Released: 1953
Produced by MGM

THE WILD ONE
Director: Laslo Benedek
Screenplay: John Paxton, from the story 'The Cyclist's Raid' by Frank Rooney
Photography: Hal Mohr
Cast: Marlon Brando, Lee Marvin, Mary Murphy, Robert Keith, Jay C Flippen
Running time: 79 mins
Released: 1954
Produced by Columbia/Stanley Kramer

ON THE WATERFRONT
Director: Elia Kazan
Screenplay: Budd Schulberg
Photography: Boris Kaufman
Cast: Marlon Brando, Eva Marie Saint, Lee J Cobb, Rod Steiger, Karl Malden, Pat Henning, Leif Erickson, James Westerfield, John Hamilton
Running time: 108 mins
Released: 1954
Produced by Columbia/Sam Spiegel

DESIREE
Director: Henry Koster
Screenplay: Daniel Taradash, from the novel by Annemarie Selinko
Photography: Milton Krasner
Cast: Jean Simmons, Marlon Brando, Merle Oberon, Michael Rennie, Cameron Mitchell, Elizabeth Sellars, Cathleen Nesbitt, Isobel Elsom
Running time: 110 mins
Released: 1954
Produced by 20th Century Fox

GUYS AND DOLLS
Director: Joseph L Mankiewicz
Screenplay: Joseph L Mankiewicz, from the musical by Jo Swerling and Abe Burrows
Photography: Oliver Smith
Cast: Frank Sinatra, Marlon Brando, Jean Simmons, Vivian Blaine, Stubby Kaye, B S Pully, Robert Keith, Sheldon Leonard, George E Stone
Running time: 149 mins
Released: 1955
Produced by Samuel Goldwyn

THE TEAHOUSE OF THE AUGUST MOON
Director: Daniel Mann
Screenplay: John Patrick, from his play
Photography: John Alton
Cast: Marlon Brando, Glenn Ford, Eddie Albert, Paul Ford, Michiko Kyo, Henry Morgan
Running time: 123 mins
Released: 1956
Produced by MGM

SAYONARA
Director: Joshua Logan
Screenplay: Paul Osborn, from the novel by James A Michener
Photography: Ellsworth Fredericks
Cast: Marlon Brando, Miyoshi Umeki, Miiko Taka, Red Buttons, Ricardo Montalban, Patricia Owens, Kent Smith, Martha Scott, James Garner
Running time: 147 mins
Released: 1957
Produced by Goetz Pictures-Pennebaker

THE YOUNG LIONS
Director: Edward Dmytryk
Screenplay: Edward Anhalt, from the novel by Irwin Shaw
Photography: Joe MacDonald
Cast: Marlon Brando, Montgomery Clift, Dean Martin, Hope Lange, Barbara Rush, May Britt, Maximilian Schell, Lee Van Cleef
Running time: 167 mins
Released: 1958
Produced by 20th Century Fox

THE FUGITIVE KIND
Director: Sidney Lumet
Screenplay: Tennessee Williams and Meade Roberts, from the play by Tennessee Williams
Photography: Boris Kaufman
Cast: Marlon Brando, Anna Magnani
Running time: 119 mins
Released: 1960
Produced by United Artists/Martin Jurow/Richard A Shepherd/Pennebaker

ONE EYED JACKS
Director: Marlon Brando
Screenplay: Guy Trooper and Calder Willingham, from the novel 'The Authentic Death of Hendry Jones' by Charles Neider
Photography: Charles Lang
Cast: Marlon Brando, Karl Malden, Pina Pellicier, Katy Jurado, Slim Pickens, Ben Johnson, Timothy Carey, Elisha Cook Jnr
Running time: 141 mins
Released: 1961
Produced by Paramount/Pennebaker

MUTINY ON THE BOUNTY
Director: Lewis Milestone
Screenplay: Charles Lederer

Photography: Robert Surtees
Cast: Trevor Howard, Marlon Brando, Richard Harris, Hugh Griffith, Tarita, Richard Haydn, Percy Herbert, Duncan Lamont, Gordon Jackson, Chips Rafferty, Noel Purcell
Running time: 185 mins
Released: 1962
Produced by MGM/Arcola

THE UGLY AMERICAN

Director: George Englund
Screenplay: Stewart Stern, from the novel by William J Lederer and Eugene Burdick
Photography: Clifford Stine
Cast: Marlon Brando, Eiji Okada, Sandra Church, Pat Hingle, Arthur Hill, Jocelyn Brando, Kukrit Pramoj
Running time: 120 mins
Released: 1963
Produced by Universal International/George Englund

BEDTIME STORY

Director: Ralph Levy
Screenplay: Stanley Shapiro and Paul Henning
Photography: Clifford Stine
Cast: David Niven, Marlon Brando, Shirley Jones, Dody Goodman, Aram Stephen, Marie Windsor
Running time: 99 mins
Released: 1964
Produced by Universal-International/Lankershim/Pennebaker

THE SABOTEUR, CODE NAME 'MORITURI'

Director: Bernhard Wicki
Screenplay: Daniel Taradash, from the novel by Werner Jeorg Kosa
Photography: Conrad Hall
Cast: Yul Brynner, Marlon Brando, Trevor Howard, Jane Maslin
Running time: 122 mins
Released: 1965
Produced by 20th Century Fox/Arcola/Colony

THE CHASE

Director: Arthur Penn
Screenplay: Lillian Hellman, from the novel by Horton Foote
Photography: Joseph La Shelle
Cast: Marlon Brando, Jane Fonda, Robert Redford, Angie Dickinson, Janice Rule, James Fox, Robert Duvall, E G Marshall, Miriam Hopkins, Henry Hull
Running time: 135 mins
Released: 1966
Produced by Columbia/Sam Spiegel

THE APPALOOSA (aka SOUTHWEST TO SONORA)

Director: Sidney J Furie
Screenplay: James Bridges and Roland Kibbee, from the novel by Robert MacLeod
Photography: Russell Melly
Cast: Marlon Brando, Anjanette Comer, John Saxon, Rafael Campos, Frank Silvera
Running time: 99 mins
Released: 1966
Produced by Universal

A COUNTESS FROM HONG KONG

Director: Charles Chaplin
Screenplay: Charles Chaplin
Photography: Arthur Ibbetson
Cast: Marlon Brando, Sophia Loren, Patrick Cargill, Margaret Rutherford, Charles Chaplin, Sydney Chaplin, Oliver Johnston, John Paul
Running time: 120 mins
Released: 1967
Produced by Universal

REFLECTIONS IN A GOLDEN EYE

Director: John Huston
Screenplay: Chapman Mortimer and Gladys Hill, from the novel by Carson McCullers
Photography: Aldo Tonti
Cast: Marlon Brando, Elizabeth Taylor, Brian Keith, Julie Harris, Robert Forster, Zorro David
Running time: 108 mins
Released: 1967
Produced by Warner Seven Arts

CANDY

Director: Christian Marquand
Screenplay: Buck Henry, from the novel by Terry Southern
Photography: Giuseppe Rotunno
Cast: Ewa Aulin, Richard Burton, Marlon Brando, James Coburn, Walter Matthau, Charles Aznavour, John Huston, Elsa Martinelli, Ringo Starr, John Astin
Running time: 124 mins
Released: 1968
Produced by Selmur/Dear/Corona

QUEIMADA (aka BURN!)

Director: Gillo Pontecorvo
Screenplay: Franco Solinas and Giorgio Arlorio
Photography: Marcello Gatti
Cast: Marlon Brando, Renato Salvatori, Norman Hill, Evaristo Marquez
Running time: 132 mins
Released: 1968
Produced by PEA/PPA

THE NIGHT OF THE FOLLOWING DAY

Director: Hubert Cornfield
Screenplay: Hubert Cornfield and Robert Phippeny, from the novel 'The Snatchers' by Lionel White
Photography: Willy Kurant
Cast: Marlon Brando, Richard Boone, Rita Moreno, Pamela Franklin, Jess Hahn
Running time: 100 mins
Released: 1969
Produced by Universal/Gina

THE NIGHTCOMERS

Director: Michael Winner
Screenplay: Michael Hastings
Photography: Robert Paynter
Cast: Marlon Brando, Stephanie Beacham, Thora Hird, Harry Andrews, Verna Harvey, Christopher Ellis, Anna Palk
Running time: 96 mins
Released: 1971
Produced by Scimitar/Kastner-Kanter-Ladd

THE GODFATHER

Director: Francis Ford Coppola
Screenplay: Francis Ford Coppola and Mario Puzo, from the novel by Mario Puzo
Photography: Gordon Willis
Cast: Marlon Brando, Al Pacino, Robert Duvall, James Caan, Richard Castellano, Diane Keaton, Talia Shire, Richard Conte, John Marley, Sterling Hayden, John Cazale
Running time: 175 mins
Released: 1971
Produced by Paramount/Alfran

LAST TANGO IN PARIS

Director: Bernardo Bertolucci
Screenplay: Bernardo Bertolucci and Franco Arcalli
Photography: Vittorio Storaro
Cast: Marlon Brando, Maria Schneider, Jean-Pierre Léaud
Running time: 129 mins
Released: 1972
Produced by Lews Artistes Associés/PEA/United Artists

THE MISSOURI BREAKS

Director: Arthur Penn
Screenplay: Thomas McGuane
Photography: Michael Butler
Cast: Marlon Brando, Jack Nicholson, Randy Quaid, Kathleen Lloyd, Frederick Forrest, Harry Dean Stanton, John McLian, John P Ryan, Richard Bradford
Running time: 126 mins
Released: 1976
Produced by United Artists/Elliott Kastner

SUPERMAN

Director: Richard Donner
Screenplay: Mario Puzo, David Newman, Robert Benton and Leslie Newman
Photography: Geoffrey Unsworth
Cast: Christopher Reeve, Marlon Brando, Margot Kidder, Jackie Cooper, Glenn Ford, Phyllis Thaxter, Trevor Howard, Gene Hackman, Ned Beatty, Susannah York, Valerie Perrine
Running time: 142 mins
Released: 1978
Produced by Warner/Alexander Salkind

ROOTS: THE NEW GENERATIONS*

Director: John Erman, Charles S Dubin, George Stanford Brown and Lloyd Richards
Screenplay: Ernest Kinoy, Sidney A Glass, Thad Mumford, Daniel Wilcox, John McGreevey
Photography: Joseph M Wilcots
Cast: James Earl Jones, George Stanford, Olivia de Havilland, Henry Fonda, Greg Morris, Richard Thomas, Dorian Harewood, Ruby Dee, Ossie Davis, George Voskovec, John Rubinstein, Pam Crier, Percy Rodrigues, Beah Richards, Robert Culp, Paul Winfield, Dina Merrill, Brock Peters, Andy Griffith, Marlon Brando, Michael Constantine, Damon Evans, Avon Long, Fay Hauser
Running time: 6x96 mins
Released: 1979
Produced by ABC/David Wolper

APOCALYPSE NOW

Director: Francis Coppola
Screenplay: John Milius and Francis Coppola
Photography: Vittorio Storaro
Cast: Martin Sheen, Robert Duvall, Frederic Forrest, Marlon Brando, Sam Bottoms, Denis Hopper, Harrison Ford, Albert Hall, Larry Fishburne, Scott Glenn
Running time: 153 mins
Released: 1979
Produced by Omni/Zoetrope

THE FORMULA

Director: John G Avildsen
Screenplay: Steven Shagan, from his novel
Photography: James Crabe
Cast: George C Scott, Marlon Brando, Marthe Keller, John Gielgud, Beatrice Straight, Richard Lynch
Running time: 117 mins
Released: 1980
Produced by MGM/CIP

A DRY WHITE SEASON

Director: Euzhan Palcy
Screenplay: Colin Welland and Euzhan Palcy, from the novel by André Brink
Photography: Kevin Pike and Pierre-William Glenn
Cast: Donald Sutherland, Janet Suzman, Zakes Mokae, Jürgen Prochnow, Susan Sarandon, Marlon Brando, Winston Ntshona, Thoko Ntshinga
Running time: 107 mins
Released: 1989
Produced by MGM

THE FRESHMAN

Director: Andrew Bergman
Screenplay: Andrew Bergman
Photography: William A Fraker
Cast: Marlon Brando, Matthew Broderick, Bruno Kirby, Penelope Ann Miller, Frank Whaley, Jon Polito, Paul Benedict, Maximilian Schell
Running time: 102 mins
Released: 1990
Produced by Tri-Star/Lobell-Bergman

CHRISTOPHER COLUMBUS – THE DISCOVERY

Director: John Glen
Screenplay: John Briley, Mario Puzo
Photography: Alec Mills
Cast: Marlon Brando, Tom Selleck, Rachel Ward, Robert Davis, Benicio Del Toro
Running time: 120 mins
Released: 1992
Produced by: Ilya Salkind

DON JUAN DE MARCO

Director: Jeremy Leven
Screenplay: Jeremy Laven
Photography: Ralf Bode
Cast: Marlon Brando, Johnny Depp, Faye Dunaway
Running time: 92 mins
Released: 1995
Produced by: Francis Ford Coppola, Fred Fuchs, Patrick Palmer

THE ISLAND OF DR MOREAU

Director: John Frankenheimer
Screenplay: Ron Hutchinson, Richard Stanley
Photography: William A Fraker
Cast: Marlon Brando, Val Kilmer
Running time: 95 mins
Released: 1996
Produced by: Edward R Pressman

THE BRAVE

Director: Johnny Depp
Screenplay: Johnny Depp, Paul McCudden
Photography: Vilko Filac
Cast: Marlon Brando, Marshall Bell, Johnny Depp
Running time: 123 mins
Released: 1997
Produced by Charles Jr Evans

*Made for television

PLAYS

I REMEMBER MAMA (1944)

Writer: John Van Druten, from the novel "Mama's Bank Account" by Kathryn Forbes
Director: John Van Druten
Cast: Joan Tetzel, Mady Christians, Richard Bishop, Carolyn Hummel, Frances Heflin, Oswald Marshall, Marlon Brando

TRUCKLINE CAFE (1946)

Writer: Maxwell Anderson
Director: Harold Clurman
Cast: Frank Overton, Ralph Theadore, John Sweet, Kevin McCarthy, June Walker, Karl Malden, Ann Shepherd, Marlon Brando

CANDIDA (1946)

Writer: George Bernard Shaw
Director: Guthrie McClintic
Cast: Mildred Natwick, Wesley Addy, Olivier Cliff, Cedric Hardwicke, Katharine Cornell, Marlon Brando

A FLAG IS BORN (1946)

Writer: Ben Hecht
Director: Luther Adler
Cast: Quentin Reynolds, Paul Muni, Celia Adler, Marlon Brando, Mario Berini, George David Baxter

THE EAGLE HAS TWO HEADS (1946)

Writer: Jean Cocteau
Cast: Tallulah Bankhead, Marlon Brando (fired after first night)

A STREETCAR NAMED DESIRE (1947)

Writer: Tennessee Williams
Director: Elia Kazan
Cast: Jessica Tandy, Marlon Brando, Kim Hunter, Karl Malden

ACKNOWLEDGEMENTS

The publisher would like to thank the following for supplying images for this book. Every effort has been made to acknowledge all copyright holders. However, should any photographs not be correctly attributed, the publisher will undertake any appropriate changes in future editions of the book. The images listed below are protected by copyright.

Alpha: 11

Aquarius: 6, 9, 10, 14, 17, 19, 20, 26, 33, 38, 39, 43, 46, 49, 66, 67, 69, 72b, 73, 74, 76, 78, 79, 80, 81, 83, 88, 89, 92, 93, 94, 95, 107, 108, 111, 114, 117, 118, 124, 129, 130b, 132, 134l, 135, 137, 138, 140, 147, 155, 163, 165, 169, 173, 175, 179

Camera Press: 2, 122

Kobal Collection/Performing Arts Research Center: 21, 25, 27
Kobal Collection: 24, 34, 35, 40, 44, 47, 57, 58, 61, 62, 63, 65, 68, 70, 71, 75, 77, 84, 90, 91, 96, 100, 102, 104, 109, 119, 126, 130t, 131, 133, 134r, 136, 139, 142, 143, 144, 149, 150, 153, 153, 159, 161, 167, 176, 183

Magnum: 7, 55

INDEX